DESCENDING STORIES

SHOWA
GENROKU
RAKUGO
SHINJU

Haruko Kumota

THE STORY SO FAR

YOTARO'S ODYSSEY

Yotaro falls in love with Yakumo Yurakutei's *rakugo* when he hears it in prison. Once free, he becomes Yakumo's apprentice and is soon made a *zenza*. As his appreciation for *rakugo* grows, the incredible *rakugo* of the late Sukeroku takes hold of him and he commits an unthinkable faux pas at a solo recital by his teacher. Facing expulsion, Yotaro begs forgiveness. Yakumo relents, but extracts three promises from his student. Then he begins to tell the tale of his own promise with Sukeroku...

YAKUMO AND SUKEROKU

Yakumo Yurakutei VII takes two apprentices on the same day: Kikuhiko and Hatsutaro. Promoted to *shin'uchi* together, the two are soon popular *rakugo* artists, with Hatsutaro adopting the name "Sukeroku," and Kikuhiko finding his own style at last.

But after arguing with their shisho, Sukeroku is expelled from the lineage, and disappears with Kikuhiko's former lover Miyokichi. After their shisho's death, Kikuhiko goes in search of Sukeroku at a hot springs town in the countryside, in order to make him inherit the Yakumo name. However, in a terrible accident, Sukeroku and Miyokichi are killed. Taking in their child Konatsu in memory of the two, Kikuhiko inherits the Yakumo name himself, in order to put an end to the story...

CAST OF CHARACTERS

Yakumo and Sukeroku

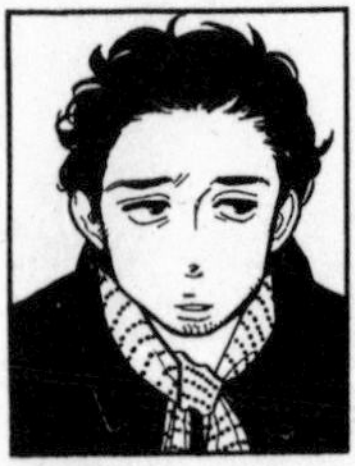

Sukeroku
Apprentice of Yakumo VII, making him a brother apprentice to Kikuhiko, until his expulsion.

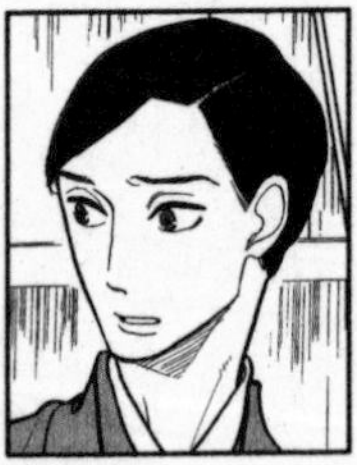

Kikuhiko
Yakumo Yurakutei VIII as a young *zenza*. The same age as Sukeroku.

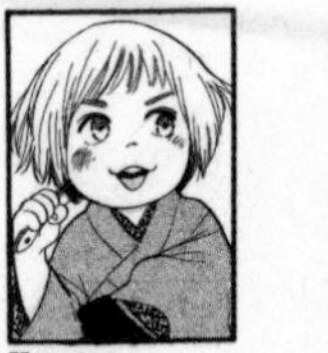

Konatsu
Konatsu in her youth. Daughter of Sukeroku and Miyokichi.

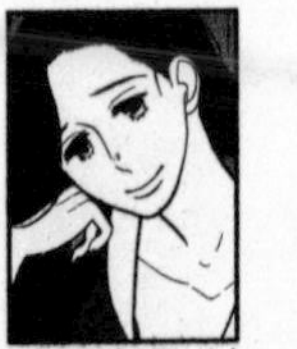

Miyokichi (Yurie)
Konatsu's mother. Dies falling from a window with Sukeroku.

Yotaro's Odyssey

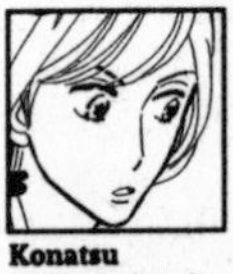

Konatsu
Sukeroku's only daughter, taken in by Yakumo.

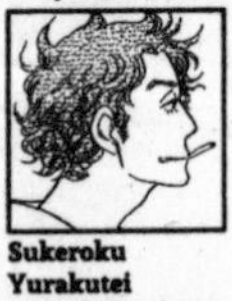

Sukeroku Yurakutei
Legendary *rakugo* artist hailed as a genius before his untimely death.

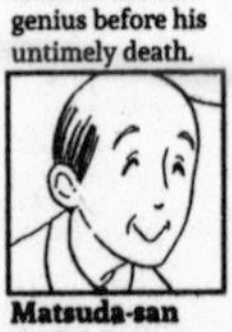

Matsuda-san
Faithful servant and driver of Yakumo VIII, and Yakumo VII before him.

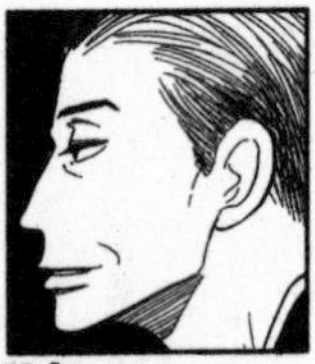

Yakumo Yurakutei VIII
Renowned as the Showa period's last great master of *rakugo*.

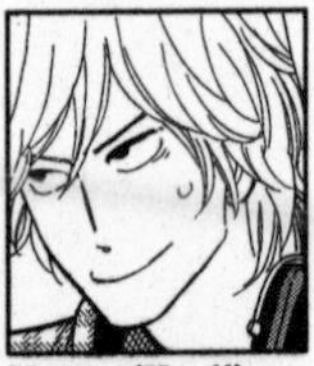

Yotaro (Kyoji)
Reformed street tough who became Yakumo's apprentice.

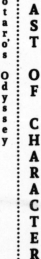

SUKEROKU AGAIN

Taking the promises he made to Yakumo to heart, Yotaro diligently polishes his craft. With the *rakugo* world fading and only one *yose* left in Tokyo, he is finally promoted to *shin'uchi*—adopting the name "Sukeroku III." Meanwhile, Konatsu reveals that she is pregnant. Yotaro marries her, becoming father to her child.

Seeing his apprentice struggle to find his own *rakugo*, Yakumo sets him a challenge: to perform the story "*Inokori*" at their father-and-son recital. At the recital, though, Yakumo collapses onstage and is rushed to the hospital. Upon his recovery, he stubbornly announces his intention to retire from *rakugo*.

Realizing that the day of his shisho's retirement is not far off, Yotaro visits the Kameya Inn in a far-off hot springs town to view rare live footage of Yakumo and Sukeroku. There he sees Yakumo and Sukeroku in their youth, cheerfully performing their *rakugo*. He also learns a dark secret from Yakumo and Konatsu's past.

Yotaro resolves to protect Yakumo, the last light of Showa *rakugo*, even as despair at his aging body pushes Yakumo towards retirement.

Will Yakumo-shisho ever take the stage again?

Cast of Characters

Sukeroku Again

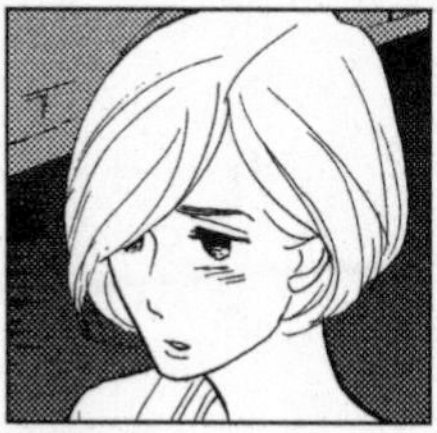

Konatsu
Only daughter of the late Sukeroku II, taken in by Yakumo. Had a child without revealing the father. Now married to Yotaro.

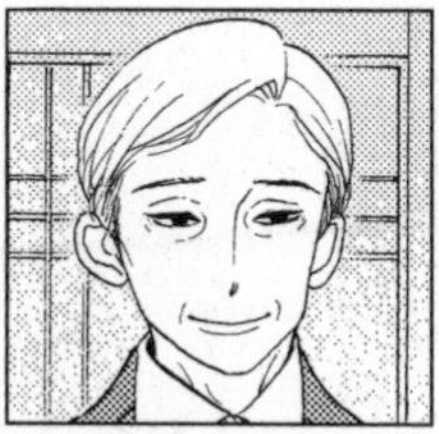

Yakumo Yurakutei VIII
Now the most powerful figure in the world of *rakugo* and president of the *Rakugo* Association. Accepted no apprentices except Yotaro, leaving nobody to inherit the Yakumo name.

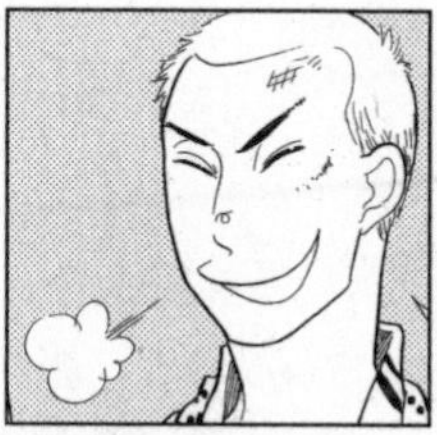

Sukeroku Yurakutei III (a.k.a. Yotaro)
Promoted to *shin'uchi*, Yotaro inherits the Sukeroku name and marries Konatsu to form a family. Loves *rakugo* with all his heart.

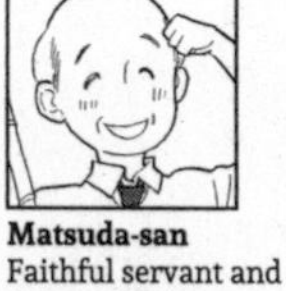

Matsuda-san
Faithful servant and driver of Yakumo VIII. Part of the Yurakutei family in all but name.

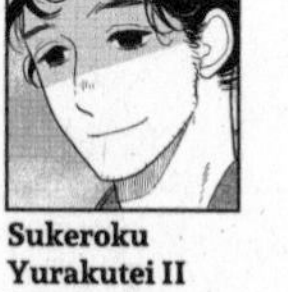

Sukeroku Yurakutei II
Konatsu's deceased father, whose *rakugo* remains legendary.

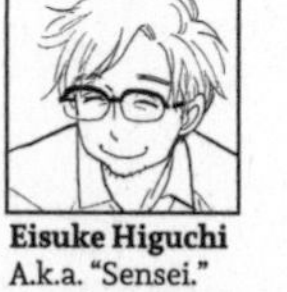

Eisuke Higuchi
A.k.a. "Sensei." Popular writer and fan of Yotaro.

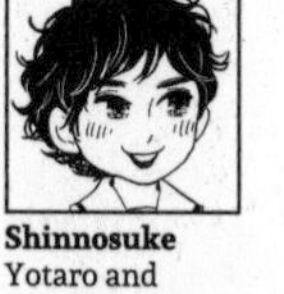

Shinnosuke
Yotaro and Konatsu's son, whose real father remains a secret.

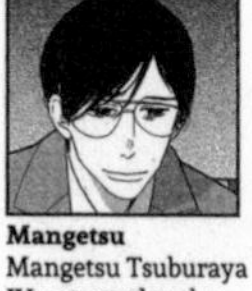

Mangetsu
Mangetsu Tsuburaya IV, returned to the stage after 10 years away. A devoted admirer of Yakumo.

DESCENDING STORIES

SHOWA GENROKU RAKUGO SHINJU

Contents

Sukeroku Again

XII..5
XIII..53
XIV..101

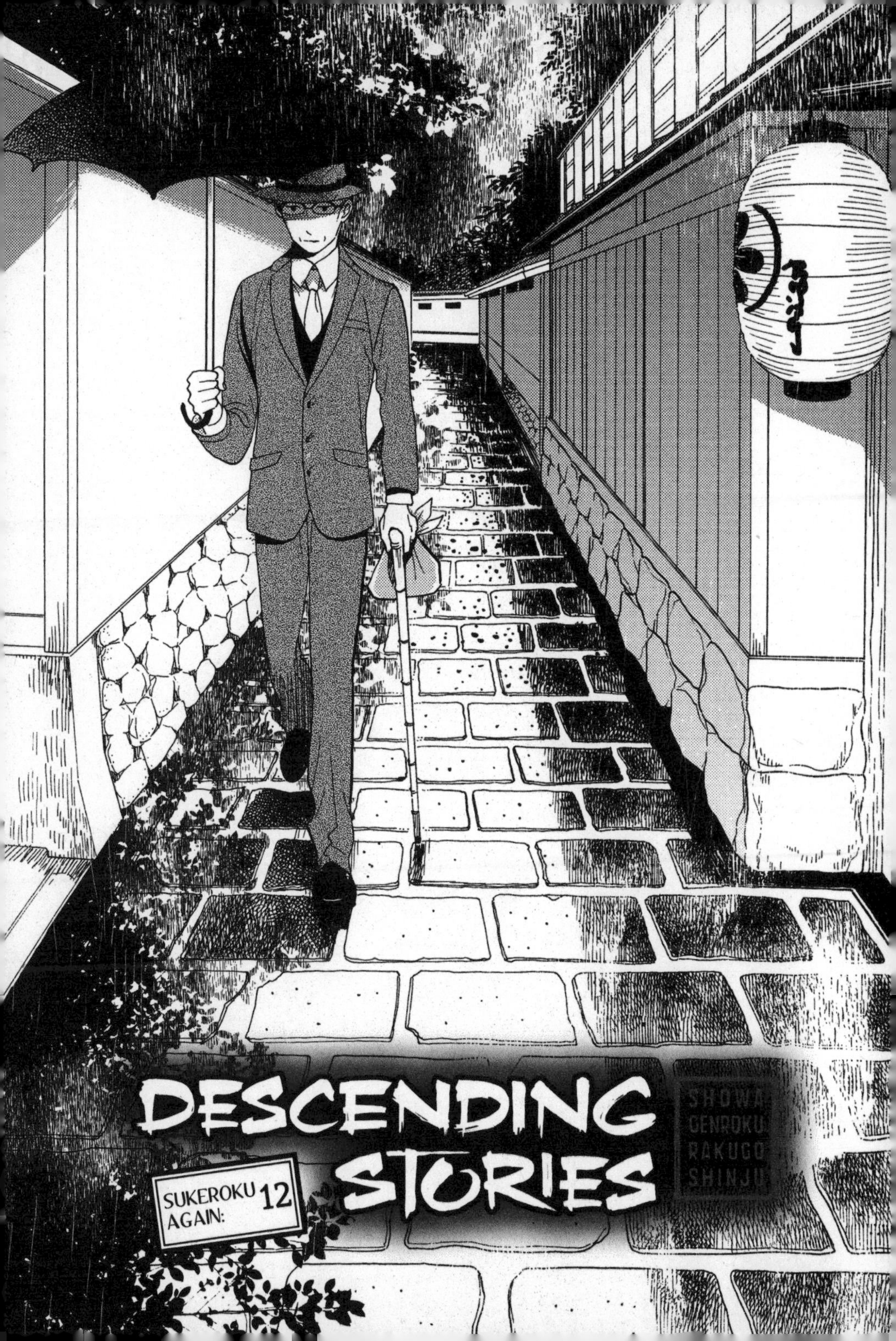
DESCENDING STORIES
SHOWA GENROKU RAKUGO SHINJU
SUKEROKU AGAIN: 12

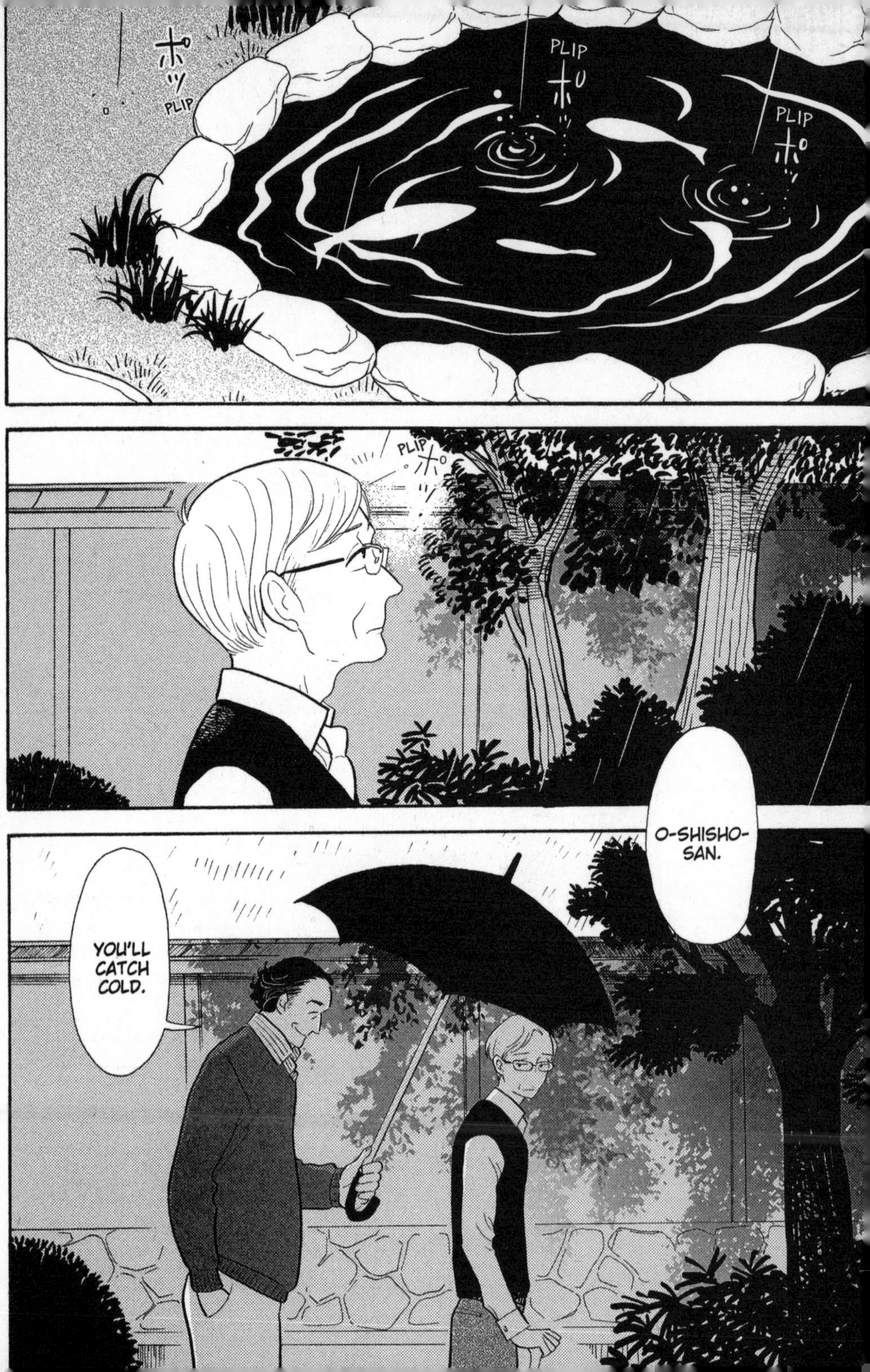
PLIP
PLIP
ポツ
PLIP
PLIP
O-SHISHO-SAN.
YOU'LL CATCH COLD.

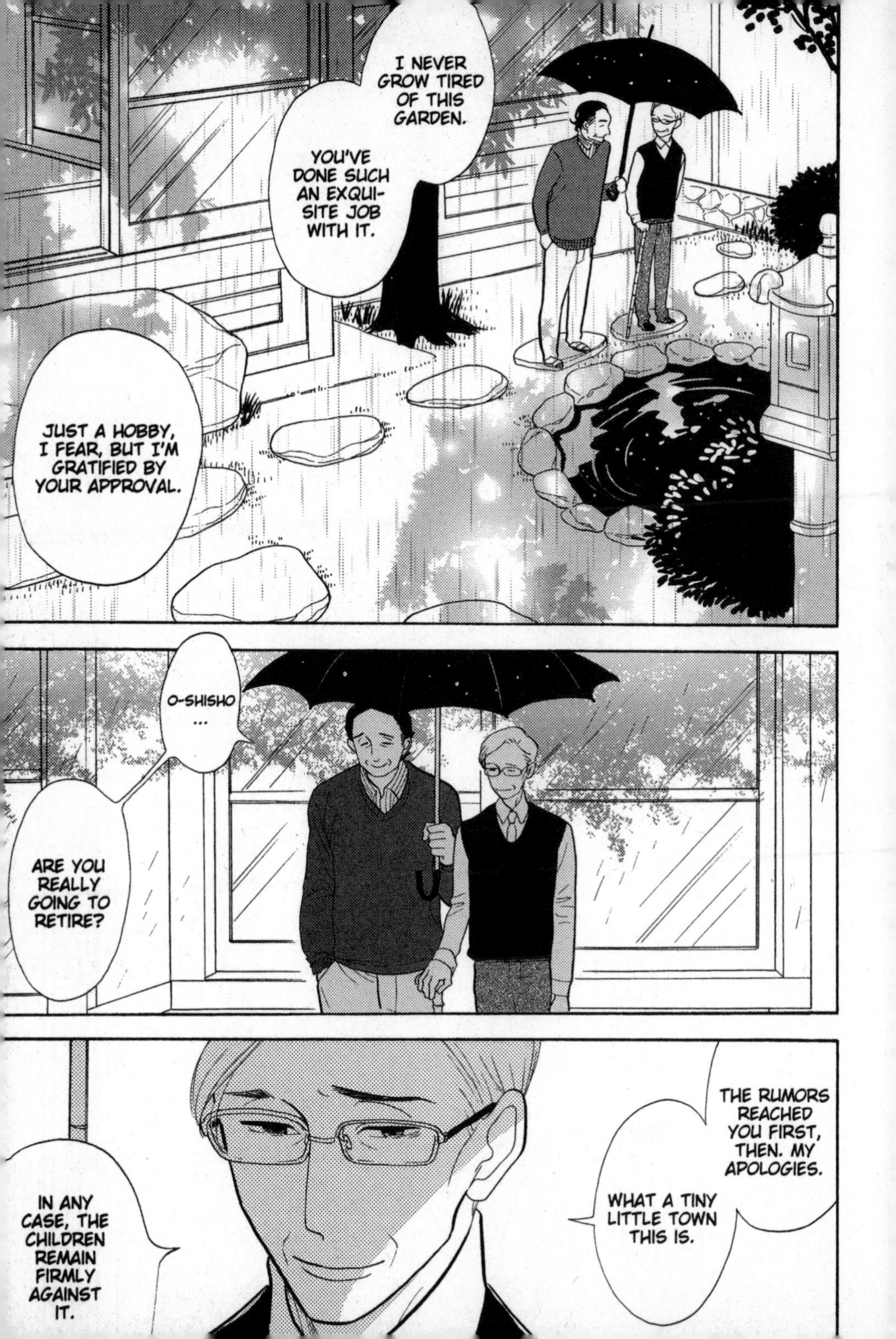
I NEVER GROW TIRED OF THIS GARDEN.
YOU'VE DONE SUCH AN EXQUISITE JOB WITH IT.
JUST A HOBBY, I FEAR, BUT I'M GRATIFIED BY YOUR APPROVAL.
O-SHISHO ...
ARE YOU REALLY GOING TO RETIRE?
THE RUMORS REACHED YOU FIRST, THEN. MY APOLOGIES.
WHAT A TINY LITTLE TOWN THIS IS.
IN ANY CASE, THE CHILDREN REMAIN FIRMLY AGAINST IT.

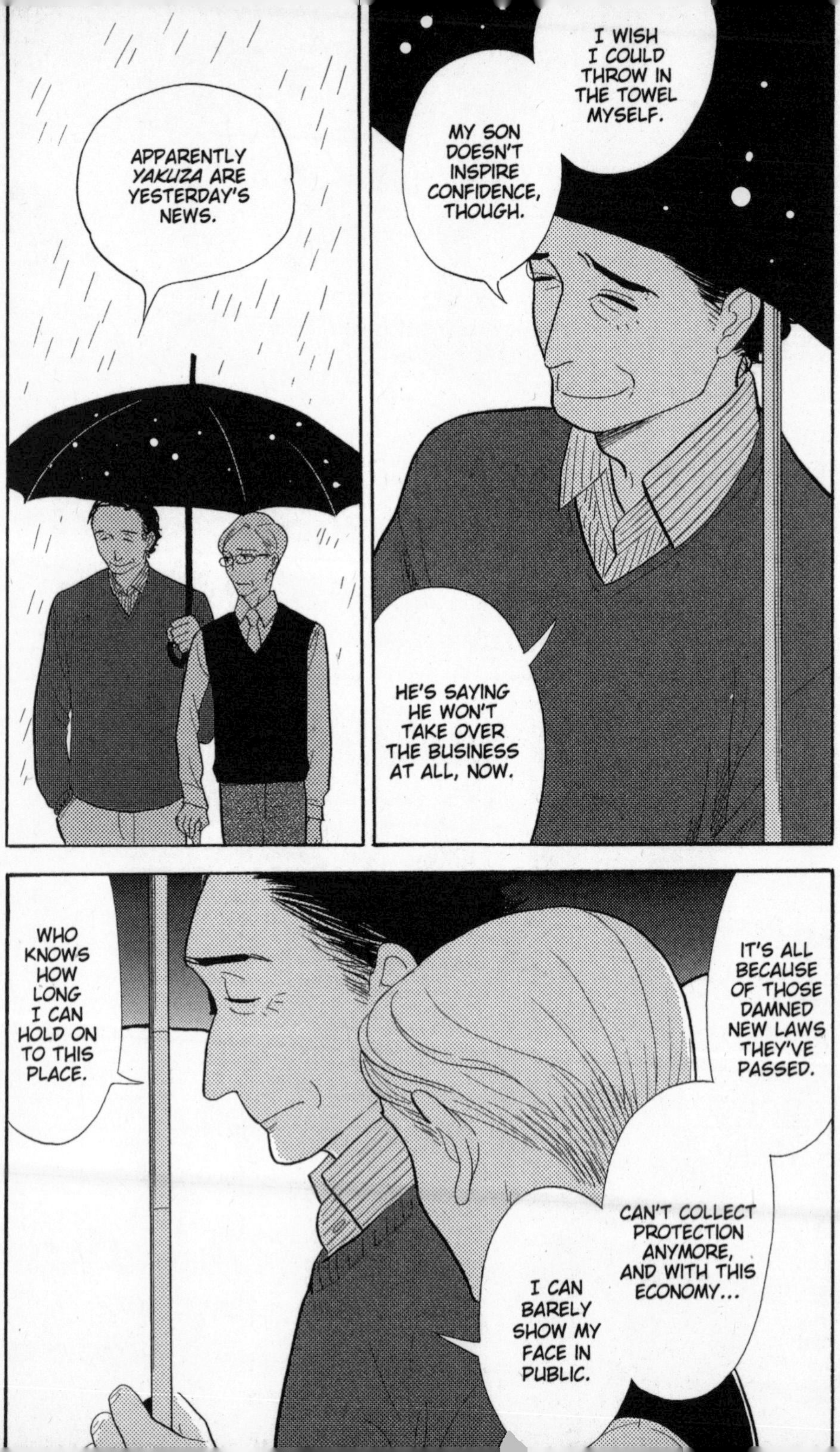
I WISH I COULD THROW IN THE TOWEL MYSELF.
MY SON DOESN'T INSPIRE CONFIDENCE, THOUGH.
HE'S SAYING HE WON'T TAKE OVER THE BUSINESS AT ALL, NOW.
APPARENTLY *YAKUZA* ARE YESTERDAY'S NEWS.
IT'S ALL BECAUSE OF THOSE DAMNED NEW LAWS THEY'VE PASSED.
CAN'T COLLECT PROTECTION ANYMORE, AND WITH THIS ECONOMY...
I CAN BARELY SHOW MY FACE IN PUBLIC.
WHO KNOWS HOW LONG I CAN HOLD ON TO THIS PLACE.

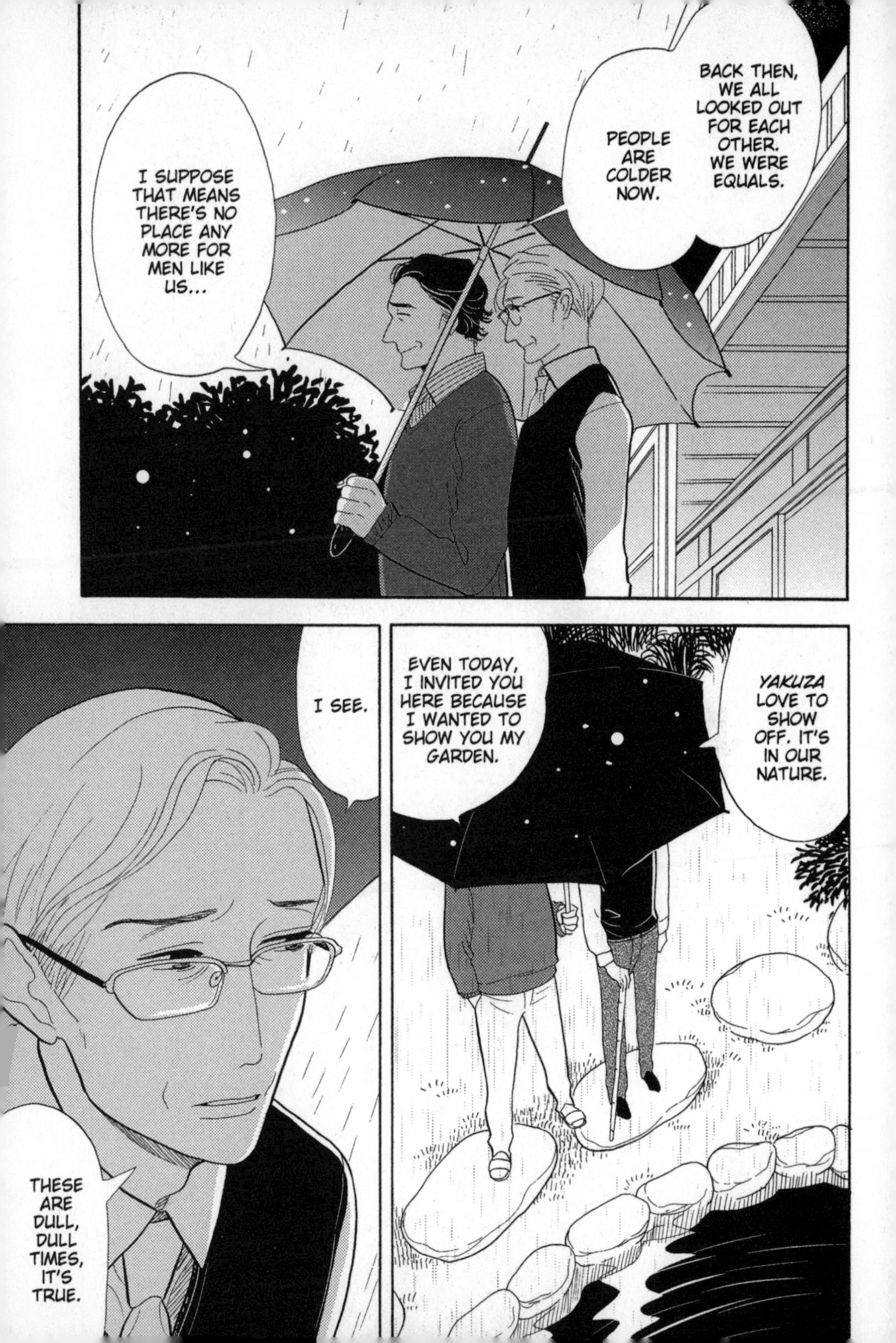
BACK THEN, WE ALL LOOKED OUT FOR EACH OTHER. WE WERE EQUALS.
PEOPLE ARE COLDER NOW.
I SUPPOSE THAT MEANS THERE'S NO PLACE ANY MORE FOR MEN LIKE US...
YAKUZA LOVE TO SHOW OFF. IT'S IN OUR NATURE.
EVEN TODAY, I INVITED YOU HERE BECAUSE I WANTED TO SHOW YOU MY GARDEN.
I SEE.
THESE ARE DULL, DULL TIMES, IT'S TRUE.

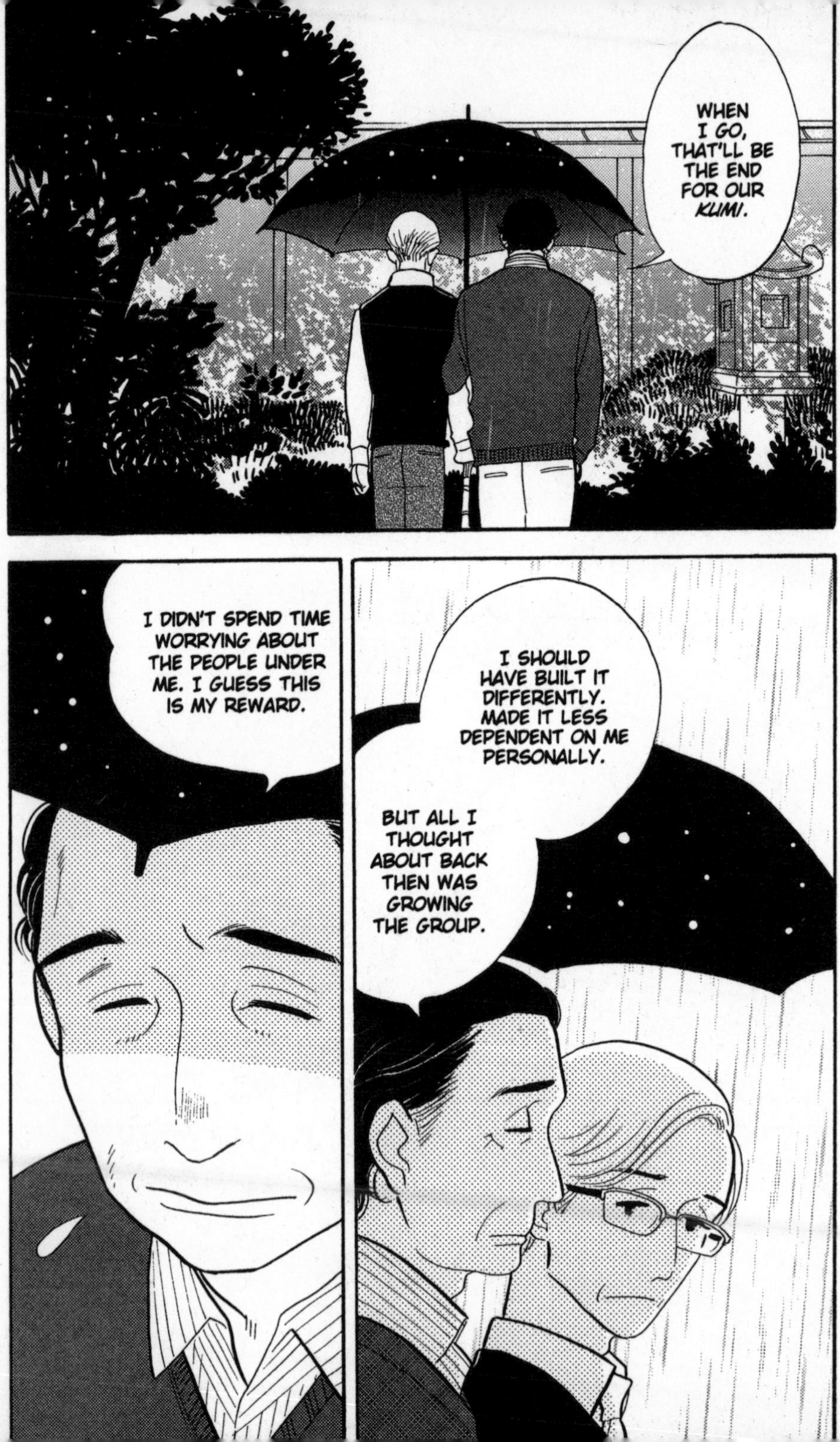
WHEN I GO, THAT'LL BE THE END FOR OUR *KUMI*.
I SHOULD HAVE BUILT IT DIFFERENTLY. MADE IT LESS DEPENDENT ON ME PERSONALLY.
BUT ALL I THOUGHT ABOUT BACK THEN WAS GROWING THE GROUP.
I DIDN'T SPEND TIME WORRYING ABOUT THE PEOPLE UNDER ME. I GUESS THIS IS MY REWARD.

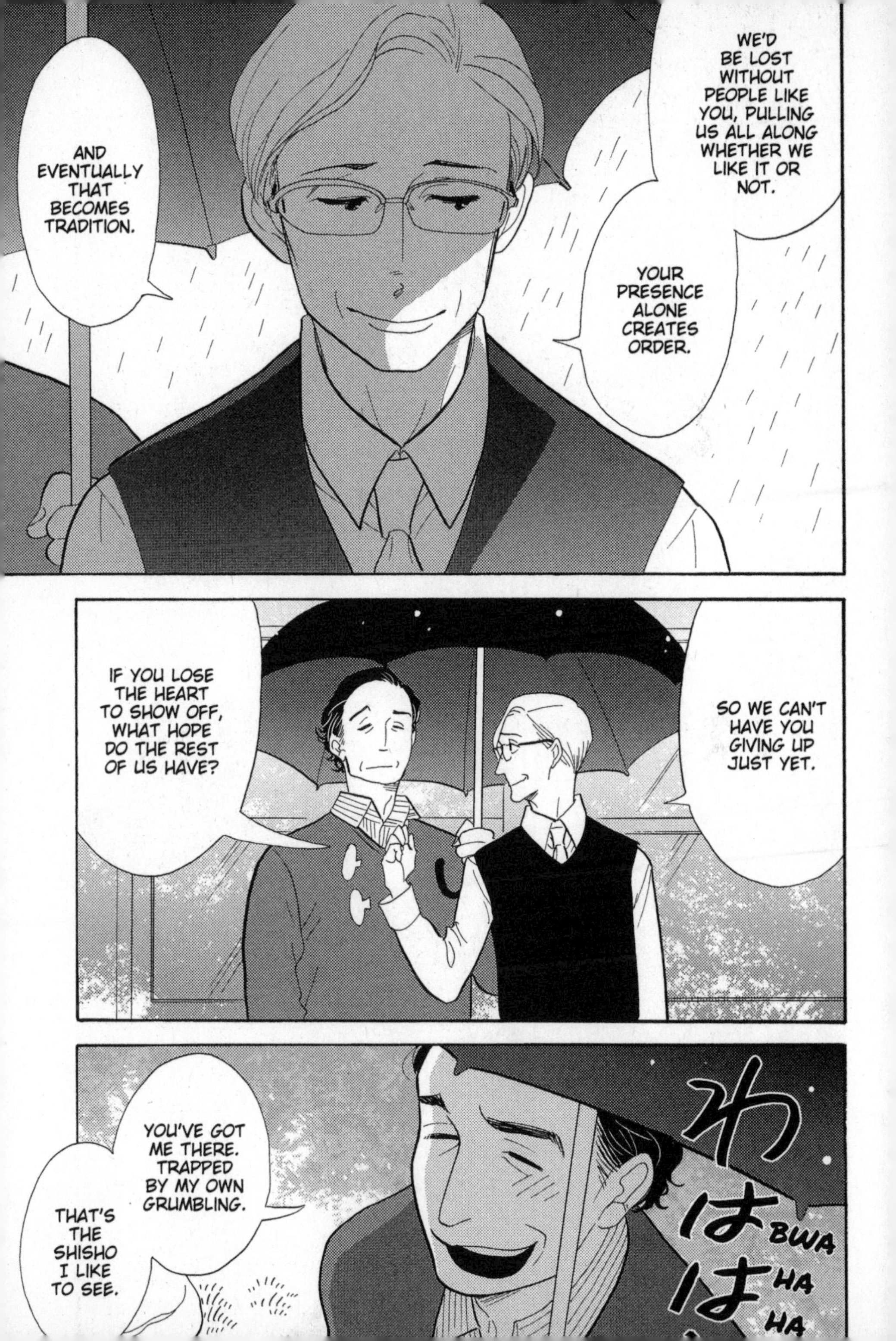
WE'D BE LOST WITHOUT PEOPLE LIKE YOU, PULLING US ALL ALONG WHETHER WE LIKE IT OR NOT.
YOUR PRESENCE ALONE CREATES ORDER.
AND EVENTUALLY THAT BECOMES TRADITION.
SO WE CAN'T HAVE YOU GIVING UP JUST YET.
IF YOU LOSE THE HEART TO SHOW OFF, WHAT HOPE DO THE REST OF US HAVE?
わはは
BWA HA HA
YOU'VE GOT ME THERE. TRAPPED BY MY OWN GRUMBLING.
THAT'S THE SHISHO I LIKE TO SEE.

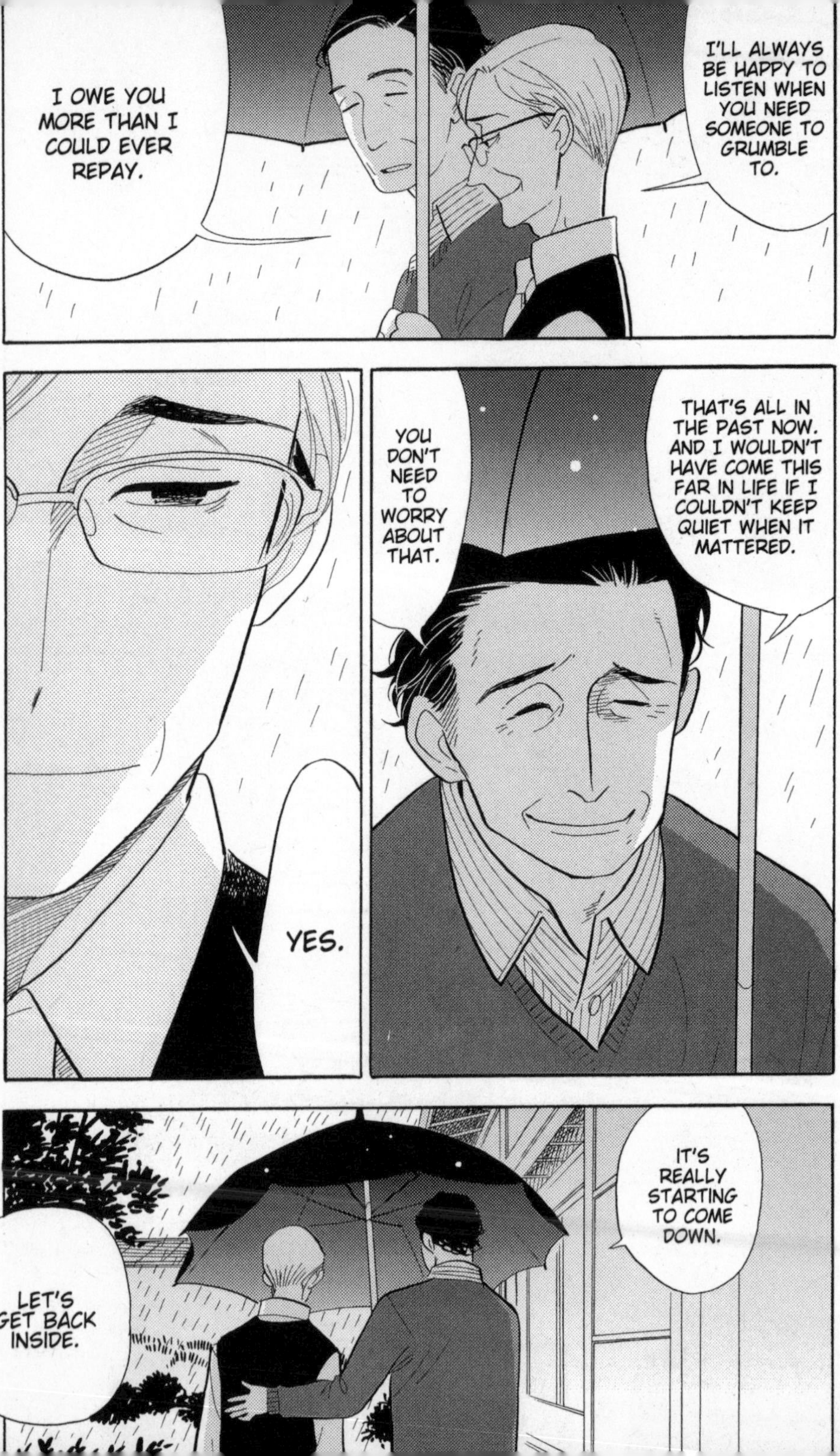
I'LL ALWAYS BE HAPPY TO LISTEN WHEN YOU NEED SOMEONE TO GRUMBLE TO.
I OWE YOU MORE THAN I COULD EVER REPAY.
THAT'S ALL IN THE PAST NOW. AND I WOULDN'T HAVE COME THIS FAR IN LIFE IF I COULDN'T KEEP QUIET WHEN IT MATTERED.
YOU DON'T NEED TO WORRY ABOUT THAT.
YES.
IT'S REALLY STARTING TO COME DOWN.
LET'S GET BACK INSIDE.

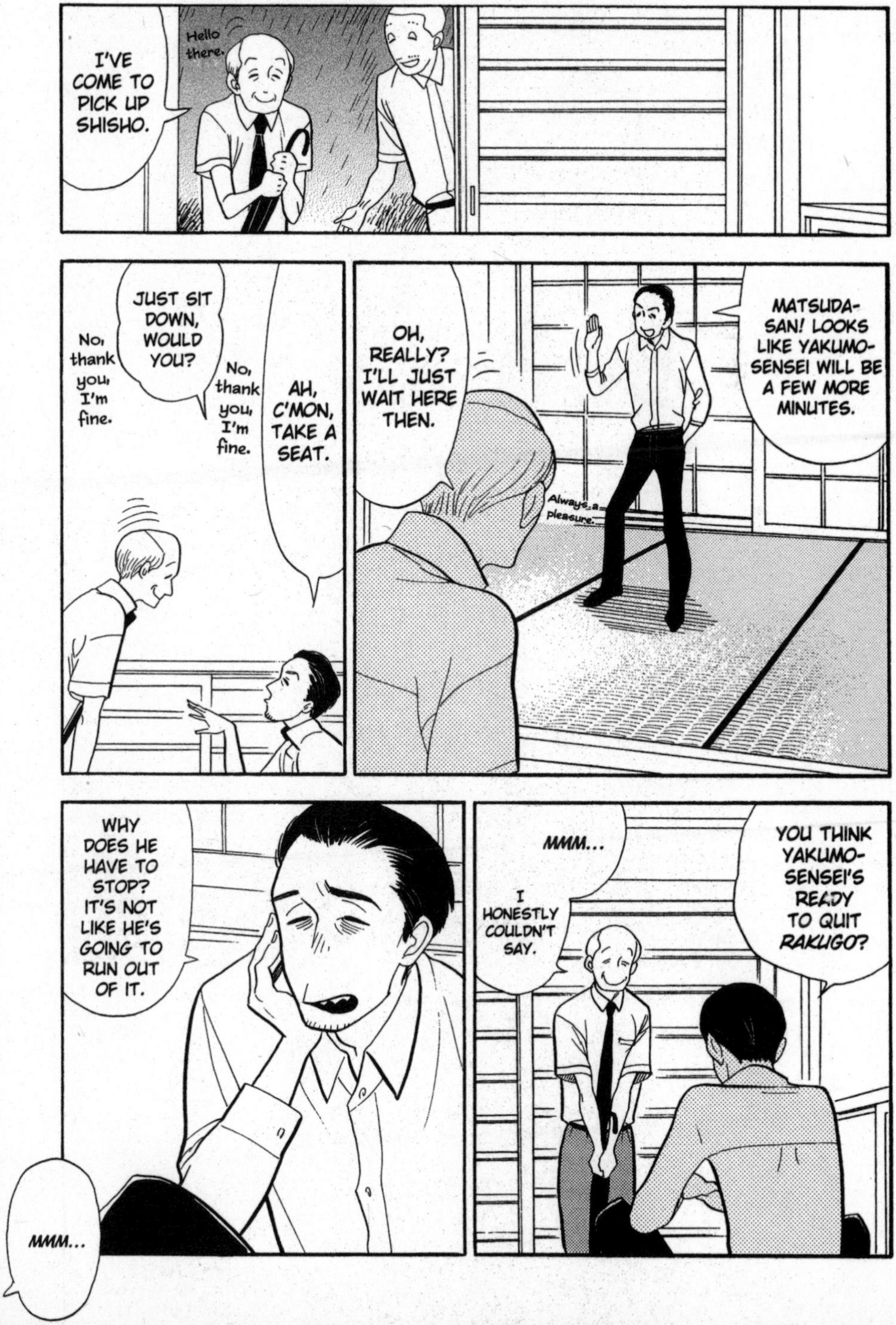
Hello there.
I'VE COME TO PICK UP SHISHO.
MATSUDA-SAN! LOOKS LIKE YAKUMO-SENSEI WILL BE A FEW MORE MINUTES.
OH, REALLY? I'LL JUST WAIT HERE THEN.
Always a pleasure.
AH, C'MON, TAKE A SEAT.
No, thank you, I'm fine.
JUST SIT DOWN, WOULD YOU?
No, thank you, I'm fine.
YOU THINK YAKUMO-SENSEI'S READY TO QUIT *RAKUGO*?
MMM...
I HONESTLY COULDN'T SAY.
WHY DOES HE HAVE TO STOP? IT'S NOT LIKE HE'S GOING TO RUN OUT OF IT.
MMM...

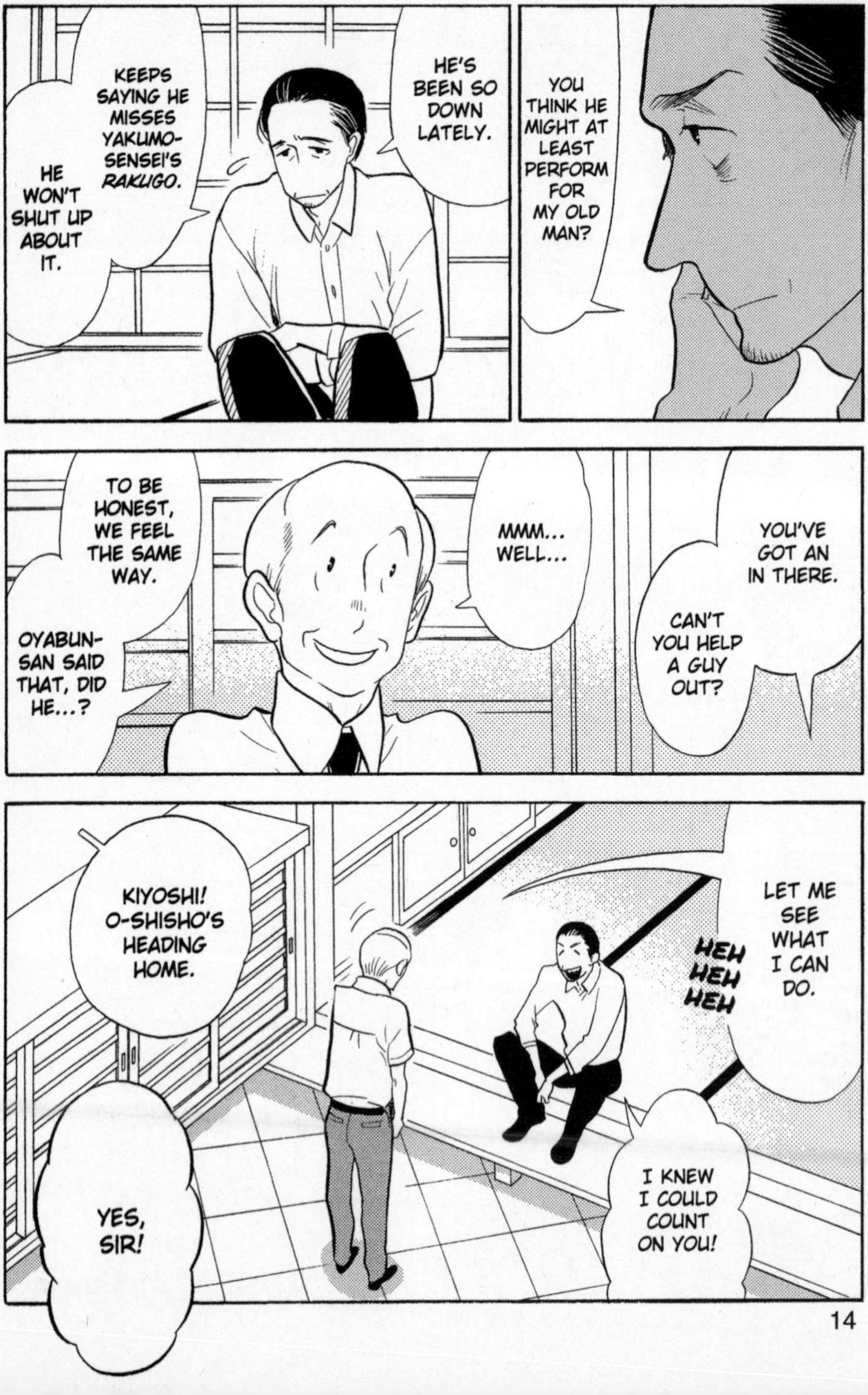

YOU THINK HE MIGHT AT LEAST PERFORM FOR MY OLD MAN?
HE'S BEEN SO DOWN LATELY.
KEEPS SAYING HE MISSES YAKUMO-SENSEI'S *RAKUGO*.
HE WON'T SHUT UP ABOUT IT.
YOU'VE GOT AN IN THERE.
CAN'T YOU HELP A GUY OUT?
MMM... WELL...
TO BE HONEST, WE FEEL THE SAME WAY.
OYABUN-SAN SAID THAT, DID HE...?
LET ME SEE WHAT I CAN DO.
HEH HEH HEH
I KNEW I COULD COUNT ON YOU!
KIYOSHI! O-SHISHO'S HEADING HOME.
YES, SIR!

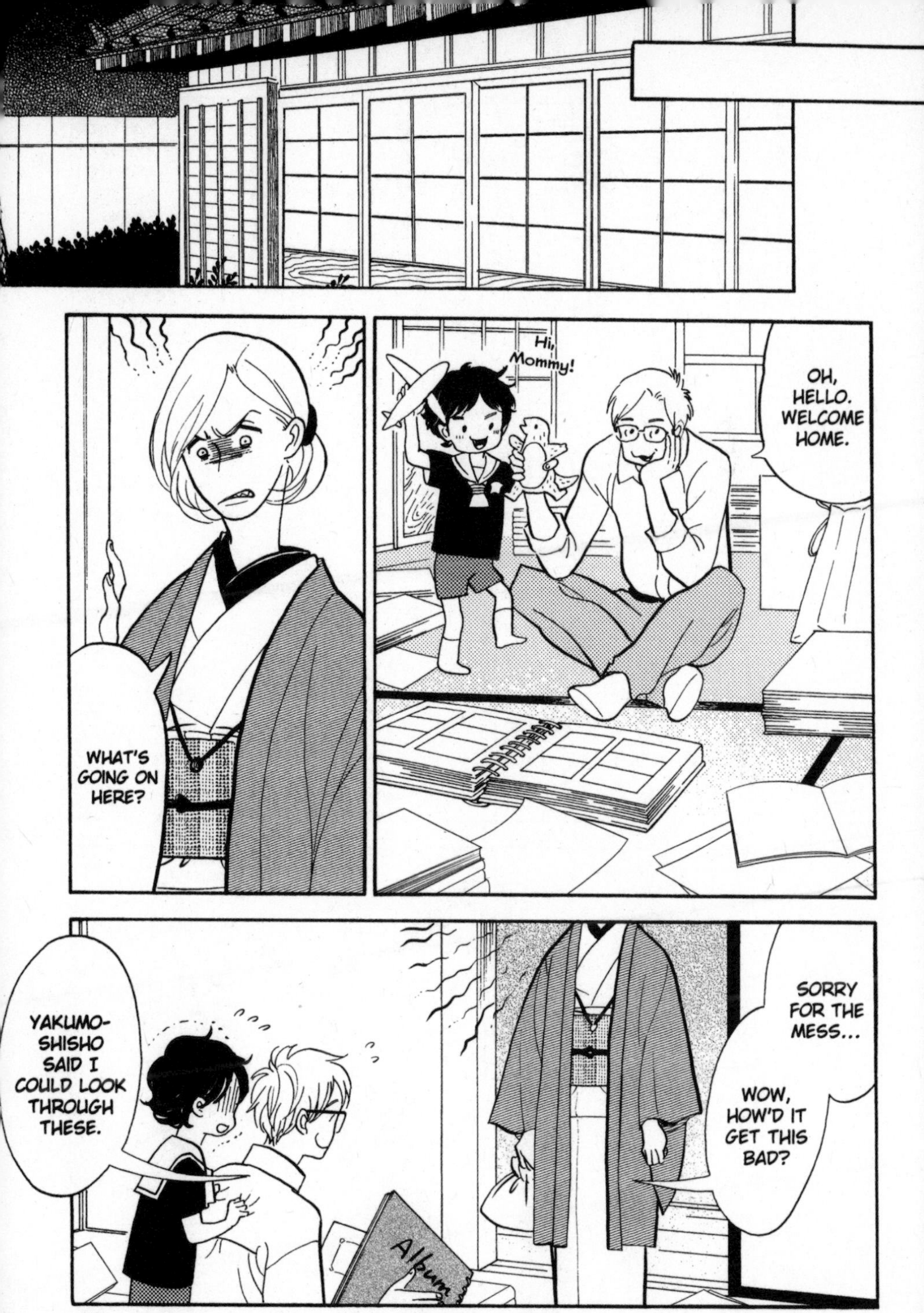
OH, HELLO. WELCOME HOME.
Hi, Mommy!
WHAT'S GOING ON HERE?
SORRY FOR THE MESS...
WOW, HOW'D IT GET THIS BAD?
YAKUMO-SHISHO SAID I COULD LOOK THROUGH THESE.
Album

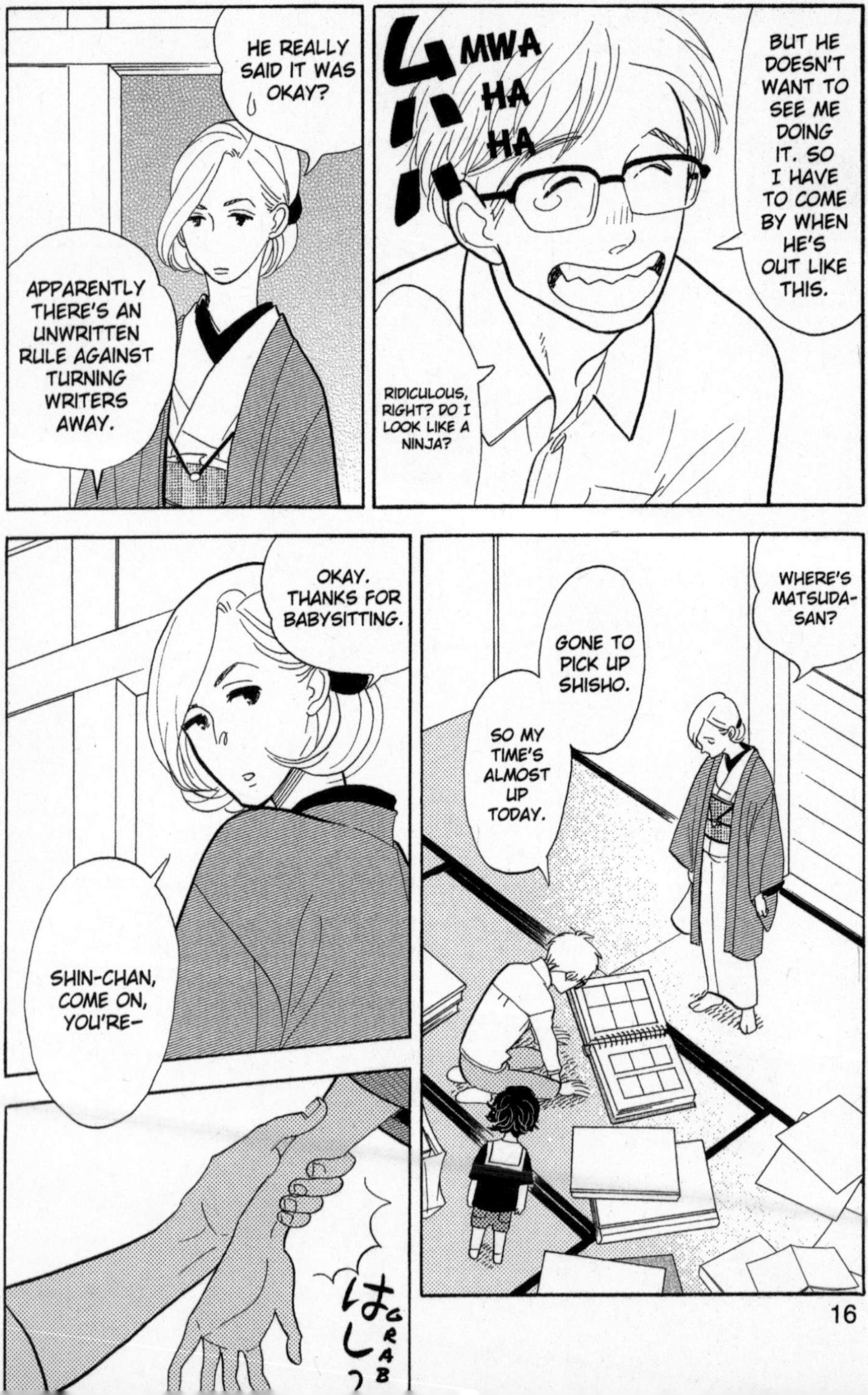
BUT HE DOESN'T WANT TO SEE ME DOING IT. SO I HAVE TO COME BY WHEN HE'S OUT LIKE THIS.
MWA HA HA
RIDICULOUS, RIGHT? DO I LOOK LIKE A NINJA?
HE REALLY SAID IT WAS OKAY?
APPARENTLY THERE'S AN UNWRITTEN RULE AGAINST TURNING WRITERS AWAY.
WHERE'S MATSUDA-SAN?
GONE TO PICK UP SHISHO.
SO MY TIME'S ALMOST UP TODAY.
OKAY. THANKS FOR BABYSITTING.
SHIN-CHAN, COME ON, YOU'RE-
はしっ
GRAB

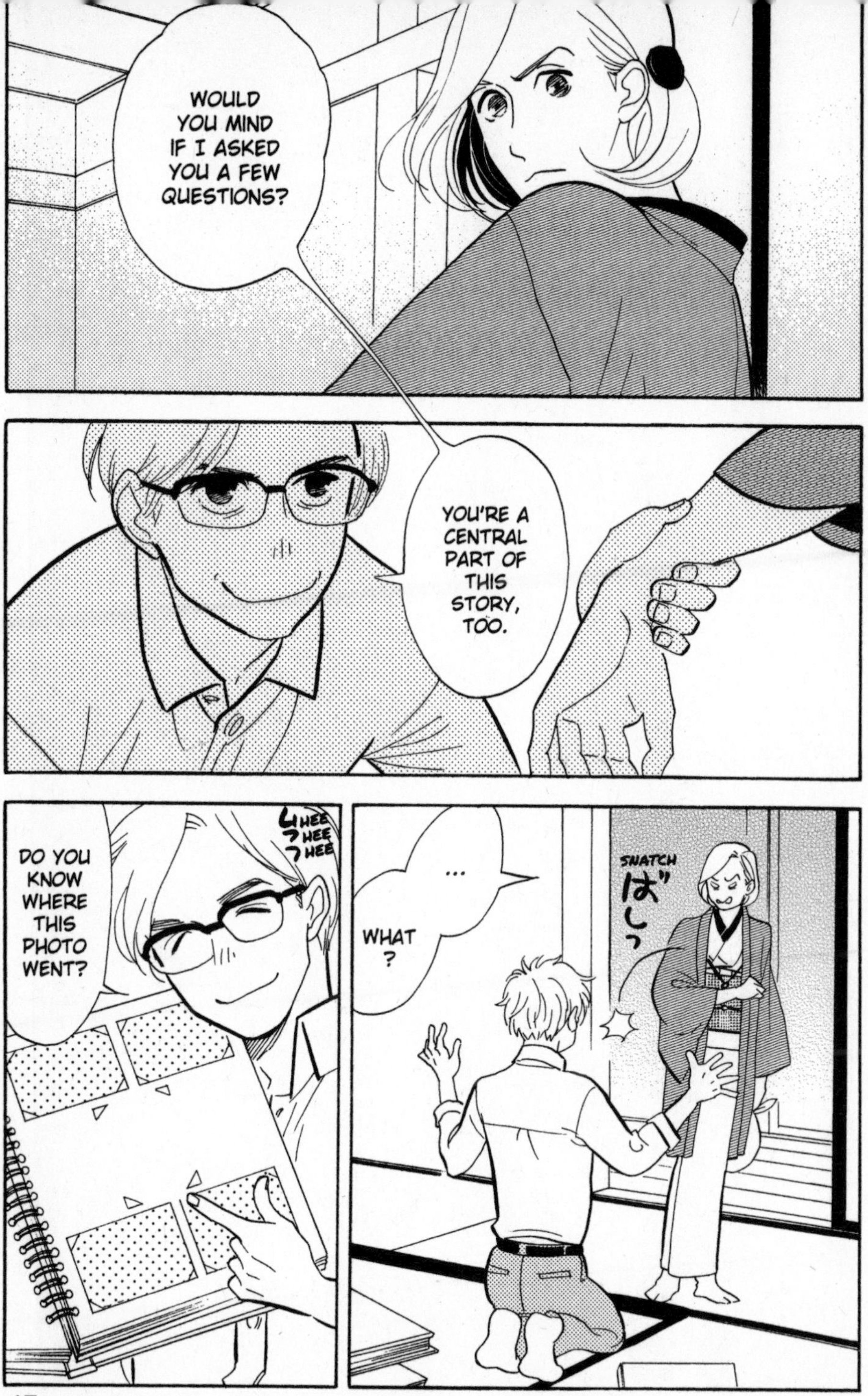
WOULD YOU MIND IF I ASKED YOU A FEW QUESTIONS?
YOU'RE A CENTRAL PART OF THIS STORY, TOO.
SNATCH
ばしっ
...
WHAT ?
HEE HEE HEE
DO YOU KNOW WHERE THIS PHOTO WENT?

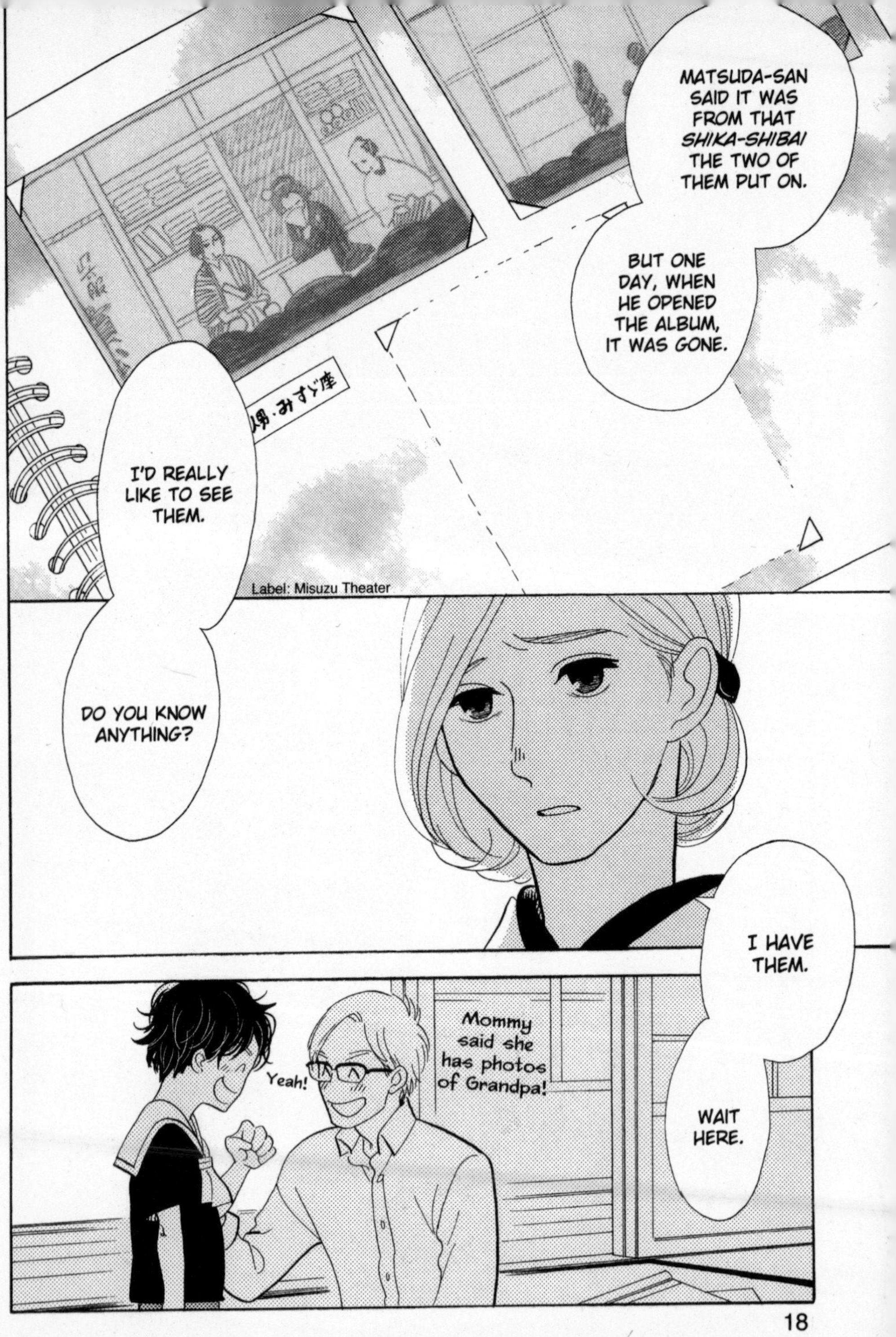
MATSUDA-SAN SAID IT WAS FROM THAT *SHIKA-SHIBAI* THE TWO OF THEM PUT ON.
BUT ONE DAY, WHEN HE OPENED THE ALBUM, IT WAS GONE.
I'D REALLY LIKE TO SEE THEM.
Label: Misuzu Theater
DO YOU KNOW ANYTHING?
I HAVE THEM.
WAIT HERE.
Mommy said she has photos of Grandpa!
Yeah!

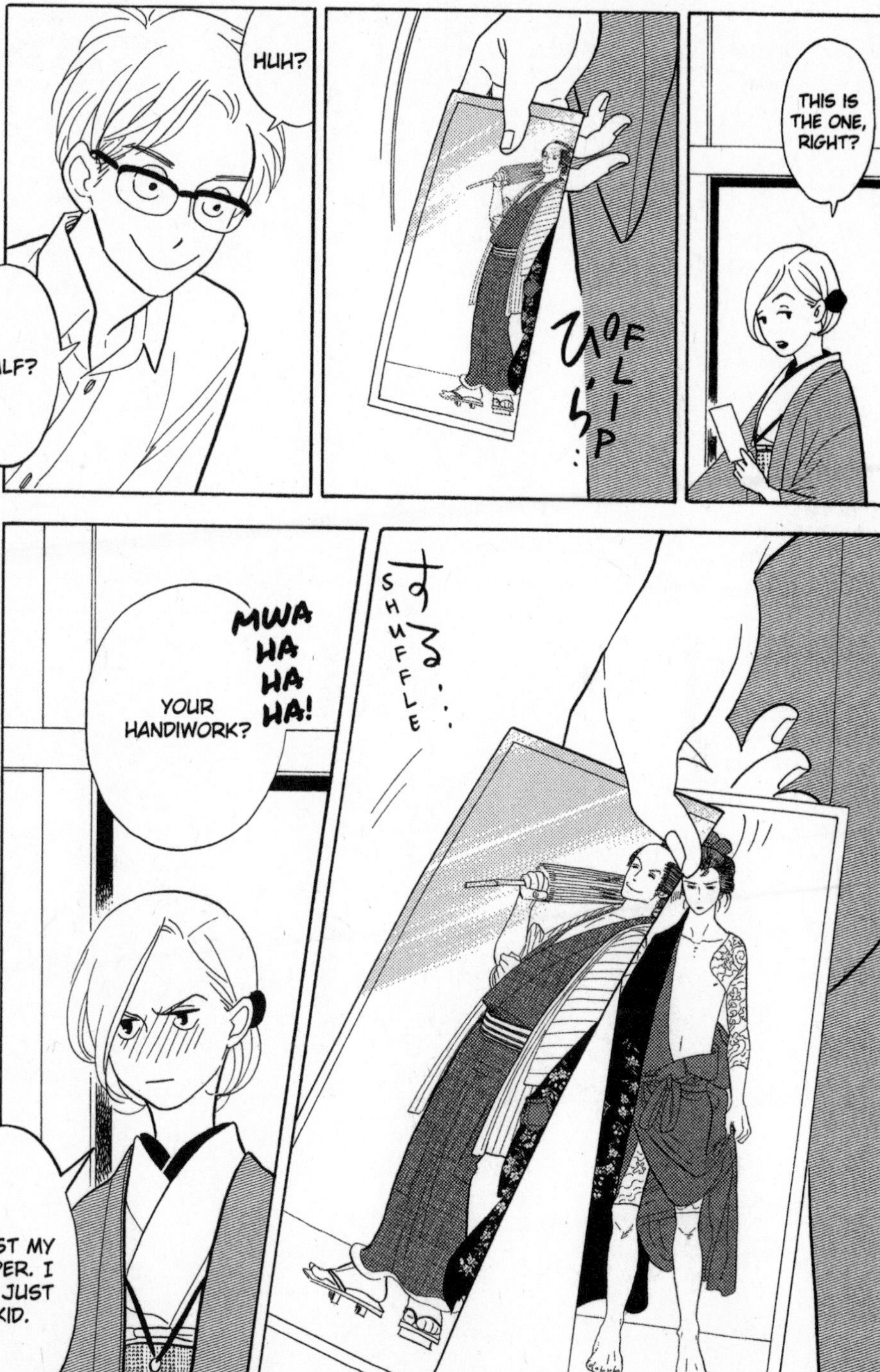
THIS IS THE ONE, RIGHT?
ひら…
FLIP
HUH?
HALF?
する…
SHUFFLE
MWA HA HA HA!
YOUR HANDIWORK?
I LOST MY TEMPER. I WAS JUST A KID.

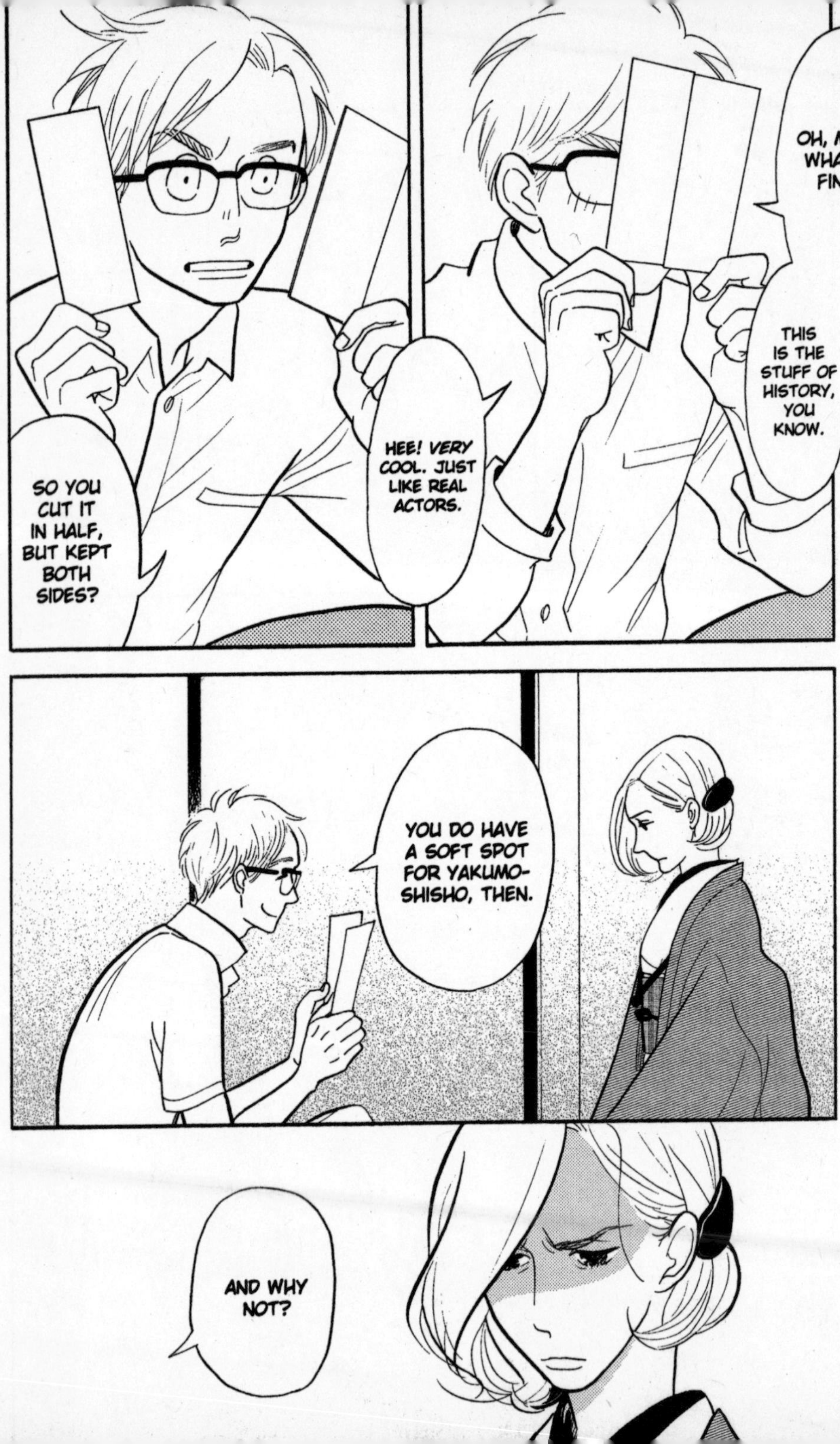
OH, MY... WHAT A FIND.
THIS IS THE STUFF OF HISTORY, YOU KNOW.
HEE! VERY COOL. JUST LIKE REAL ACTORS.
SO YOU CUT IT IN HALF, BUT KEPT BOTH SIDES?
YOU DO HAVE A SOFT SPOT FOR YAKUMO-SHISHO, THEN.
AND WHY NOT?

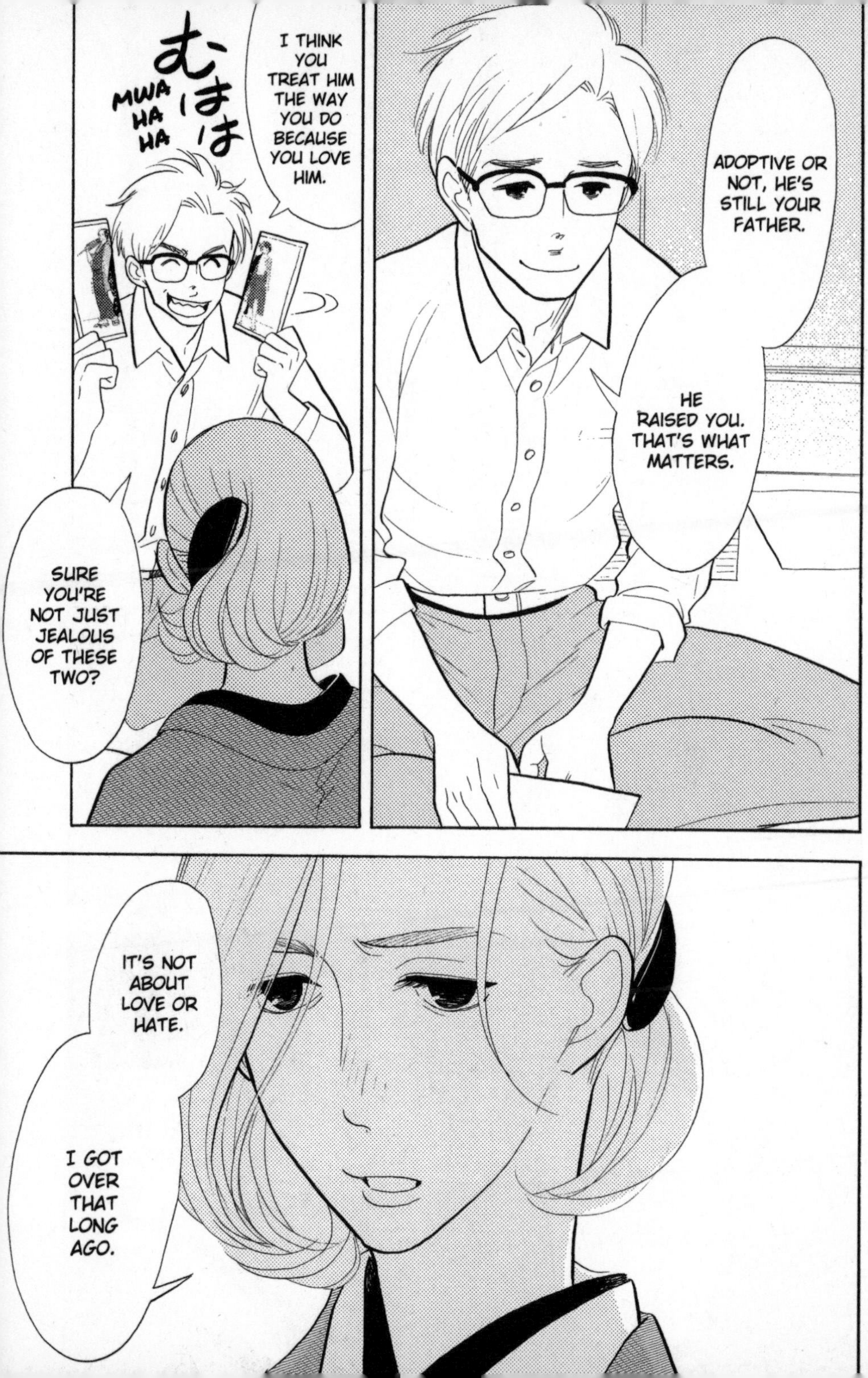
ADOPTIVE OR NOT, HE'S STILL YOUR FATHER.
HE RAISED YOU. THAT'S WHAT MATTERS.
I THINK YOU TREAT HIM THE WAY YOU DO BECAUSE YOU LOVE HIM.
むはは
MWA HA HA
SURE YOU'RE NOT JUST JEALOUS OF THESE TWO?
IT'S NOT ABOUT LOVE OR HATE.
I GOT OVER THAT LONG AGO.

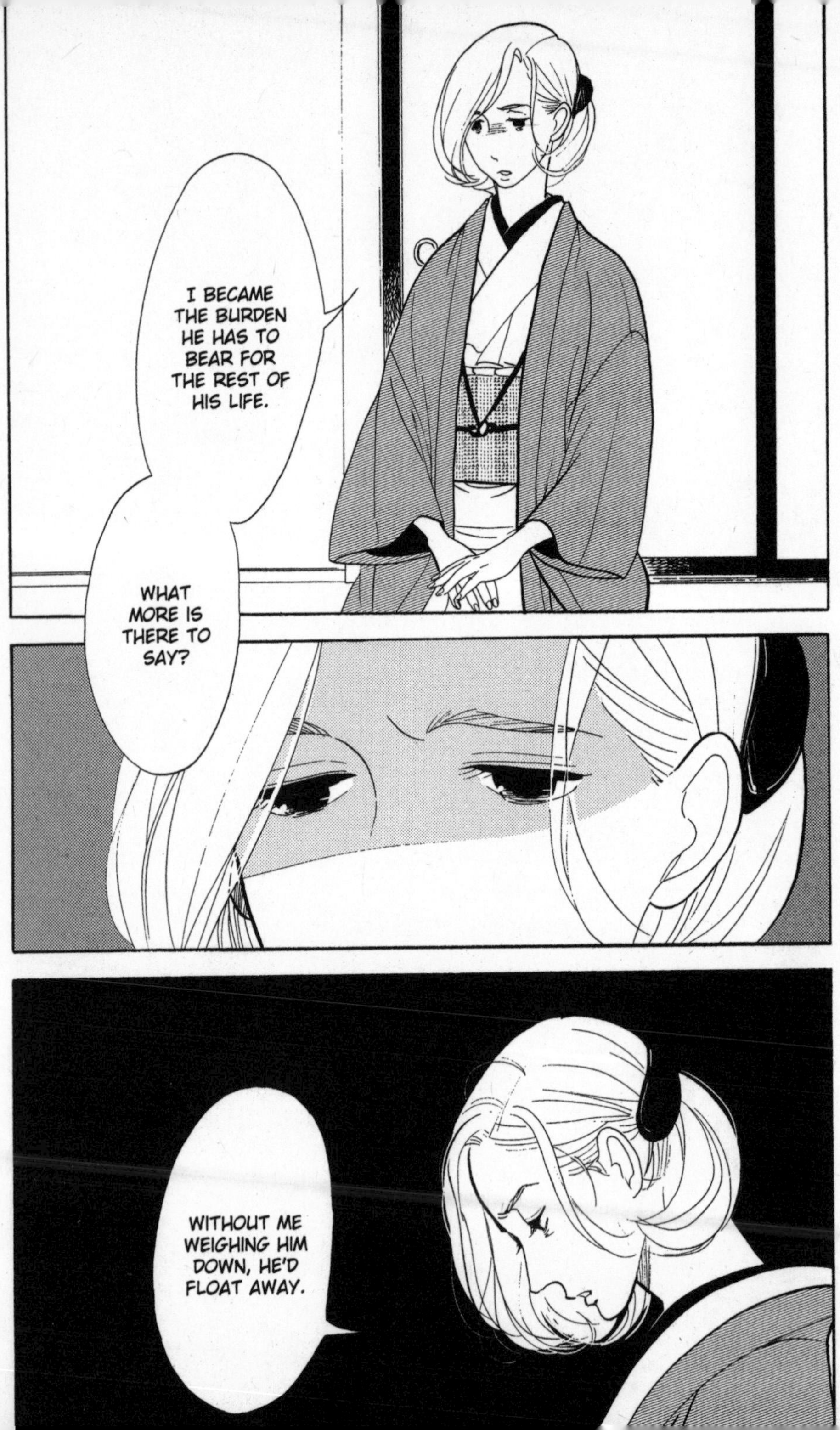
I BECAME THE BURDEN HE HAS TO BEAR FOR THE REST OF HIS LIFE.
WHAT MORE IS THERE TO SAY?
WITHOUT ME WEIGHING HIM DOWN, HE'D FLOAT AWAY.

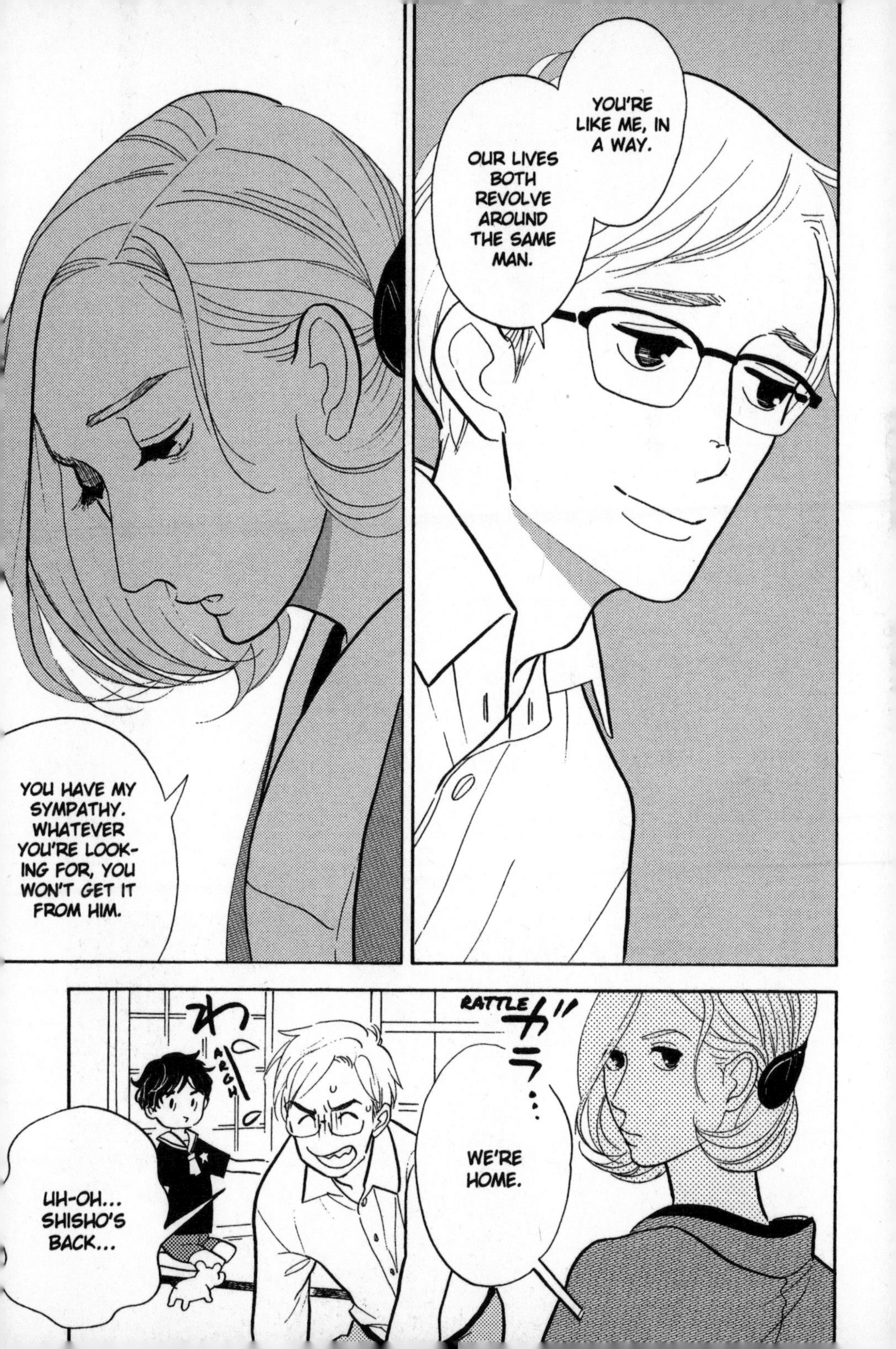
YOU'RE LIKE ME, IN A WAY.
OUR LIVES BOTH REVOLVE AROUND THE SAME MAN.
YOU HAVE MY SYMPATHY. WHATEVER YOU'RE LOOKING FOR, YOU WON'T GET IT FROM HIM.
RATTLE
WE'RE HOME.
ARGH
UH-OH... SHISHO'S BACK...

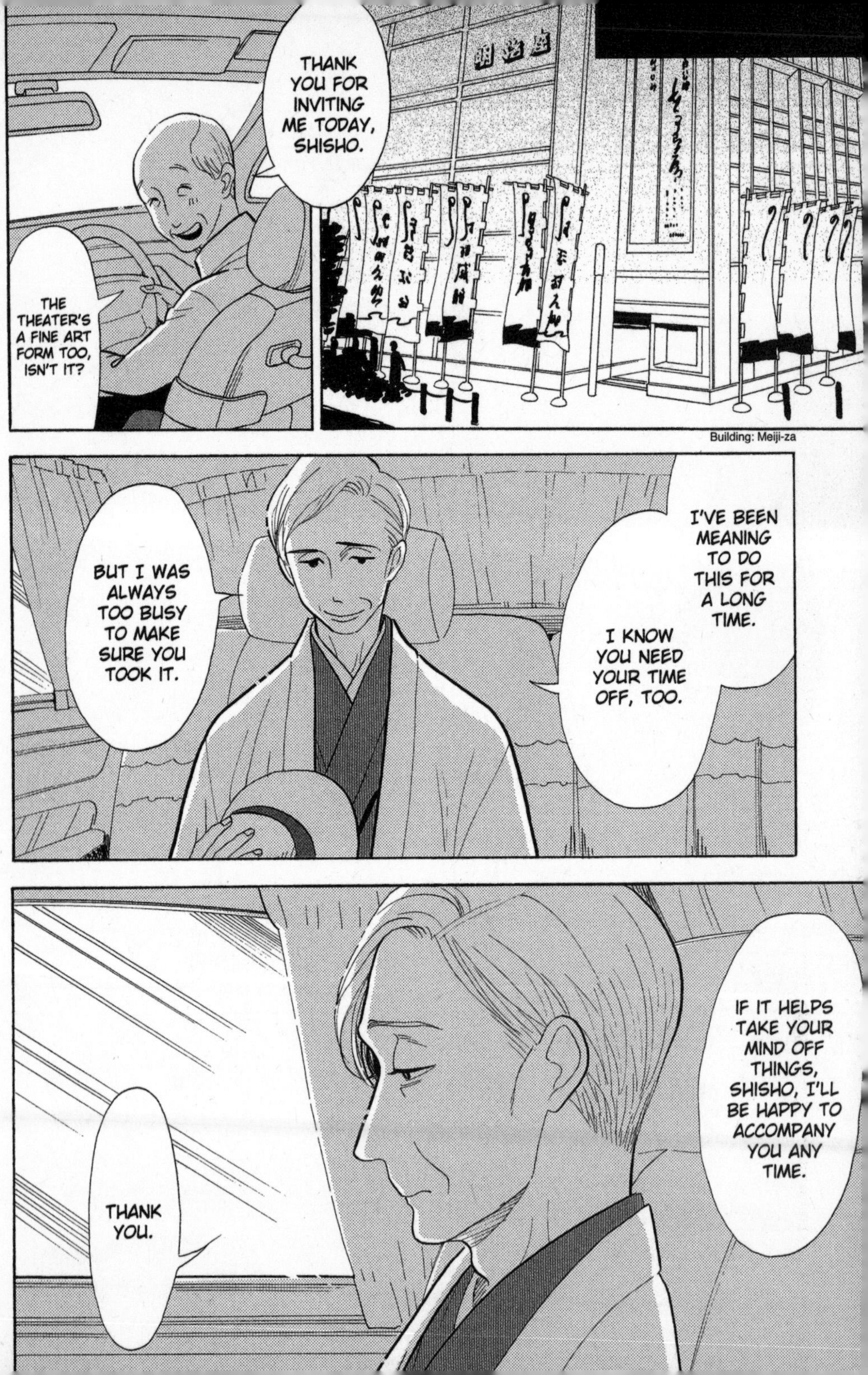
THANK YOU FOR INVITING ME TODAY, SHISHO.
THE THEATER'S A FINE ART FORM TOO, ISN'T IT?
I'VE BEEN MEANING TO DO THIS FOR A LONG TIME.
I KNOW YOU NEED YOUR TIME OFF, TOO.
BUT I WAS ALWAYS TOO BUSY TO MAKE SURE YOU TOOK IT.
IF IT HELPS TAKE YOUR MIND OFF THINGS, SHISHO, I'LL BE HAPPY TO ACCOMPANY YOU ANY TIME.
THANK YOU.

Building: Meiji-za

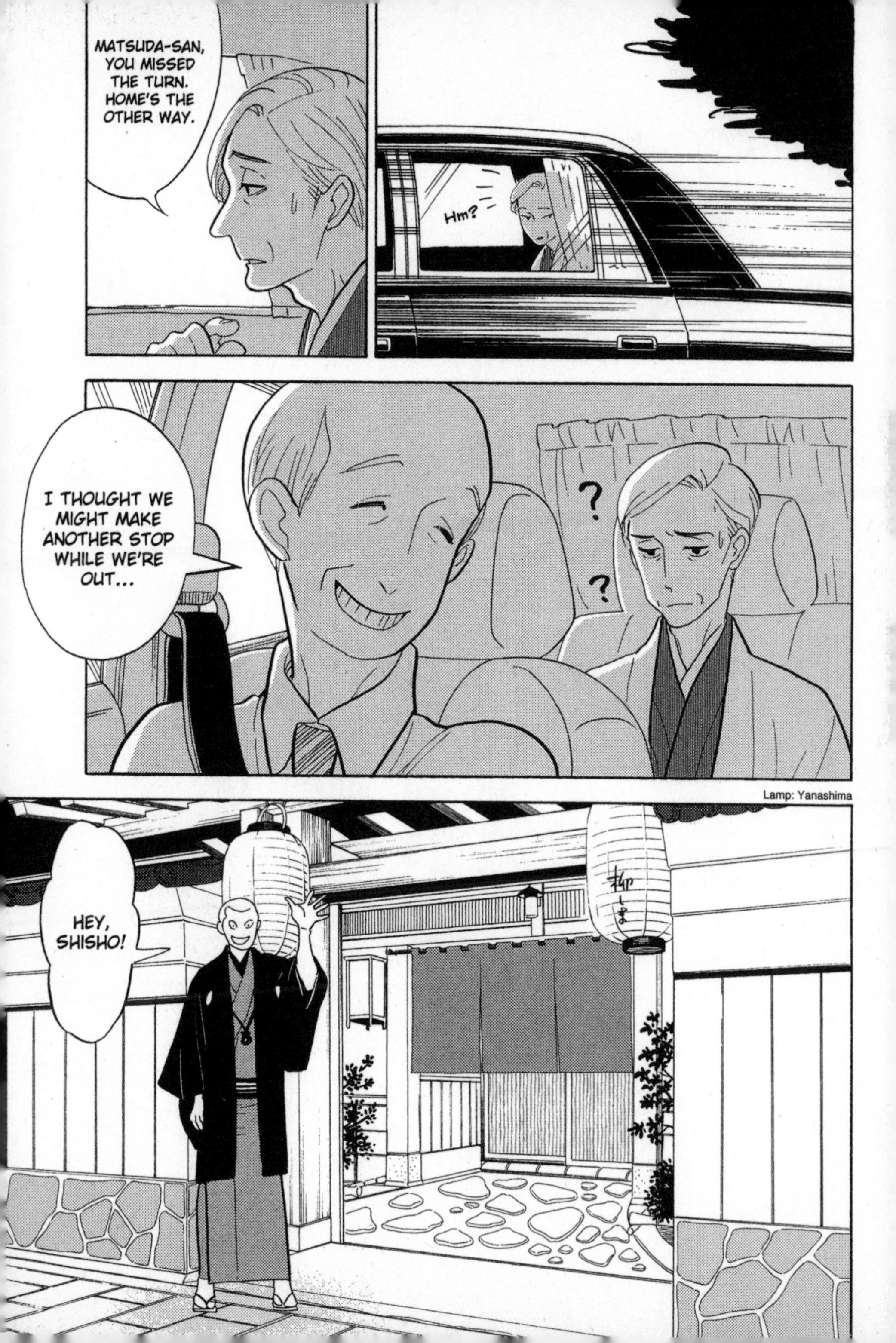
Hm?
MATSUDA-SAN, YOU MISSED THE TURN. HOME'S THE OTHER WAY.
I THOUGHT WE MIGHT MAKE ANOTHER STOP WHILE WE'RE OUT...
Lamp: Yanashima
HEY, SHISHO!

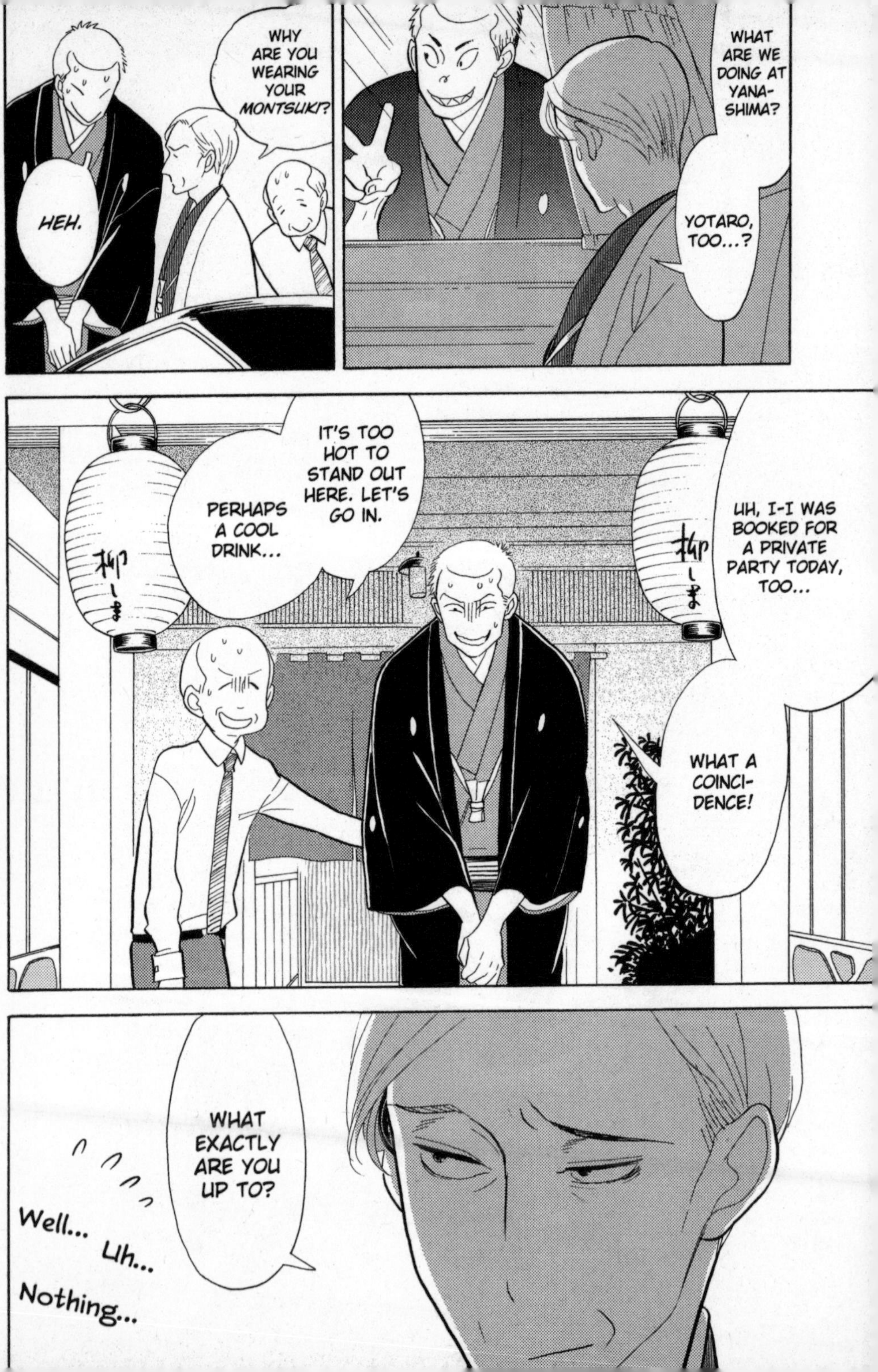
WHAT ARE WE DOING AT YANA-SHIMA?
YOTARO, TOO...?
WHY ARE YOU WEARING YOUR *MONTSUKI*!?
HEH.
UH, I-I WAS BOOKED FOR A PRIVATE PARTY TODAY, TOO...
柳しま
WHAT A COINCIDENCE!
IT'S TOO HOT TO STAND OUT HERE. LET'S GO IN.
PERHAPS A COOL DRINK...
柳しま
WHAT EXACTLY ARE YOU UP TO?
Well... Uh... Nothing...

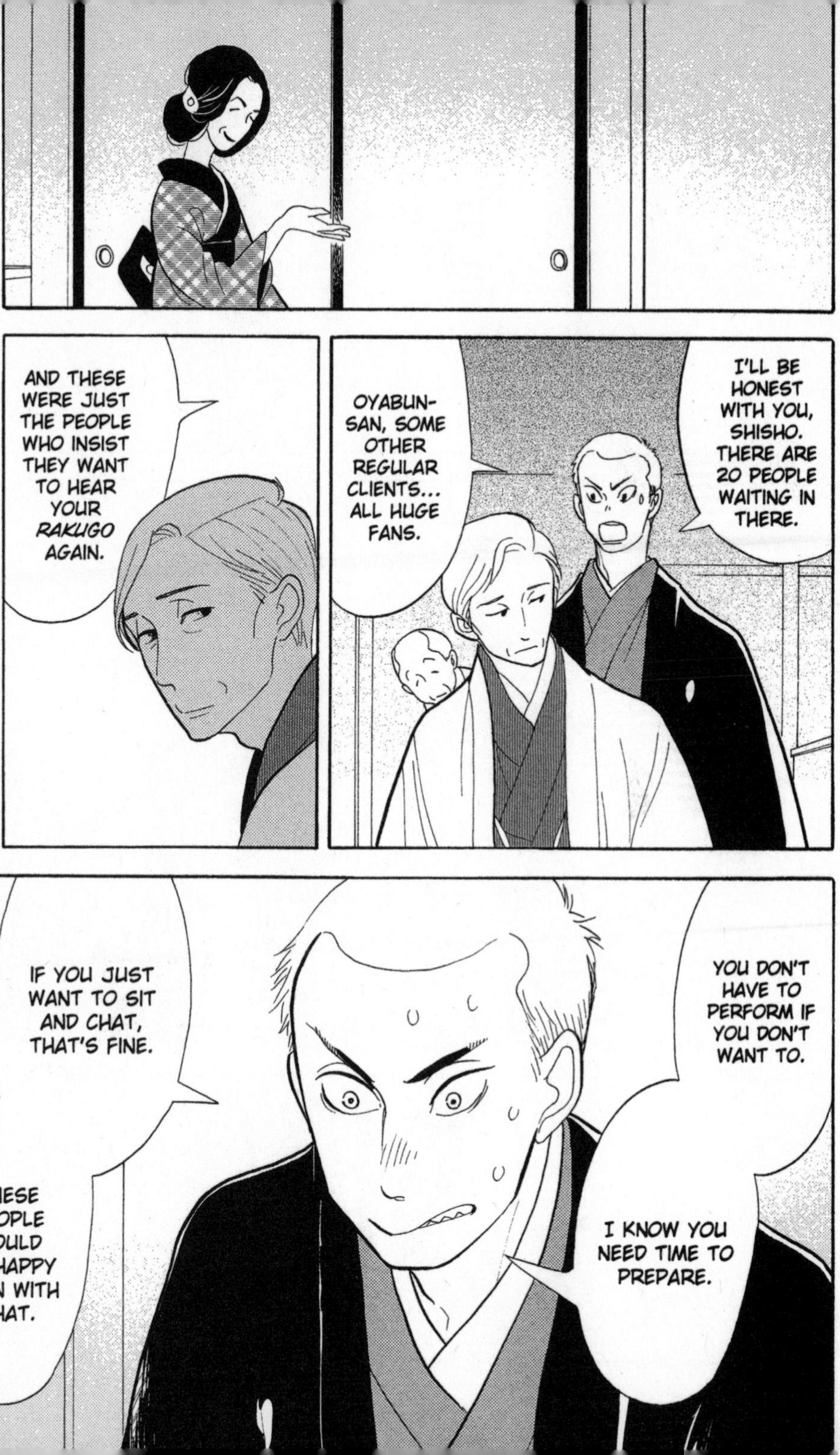
I'LL BE HONEST WITH YOU, SHISHO. THERE ARE 20 PEOPLE WAITING IN THERE.
OYABUN-SAN, SOME OTHER REGULAR CLIENTS... ALL HUGE FANS.
AND THESE WERE JUST THE PEOPLE WHO INSIST THEY WANT TO HEAR YOUR *RAKUGO* AGAIN.
YOU DON'T HAVE TO PERFORM IF YOU DON'T WANT TO.
I KNOW YOU NEED TIME TO PREPARE.
IF YOU JUST WANT TO SIT AND CHAT, THAT'S FINE.
THESE PEOPLE WOULD BE HAPPY EVEN WITH THAT.

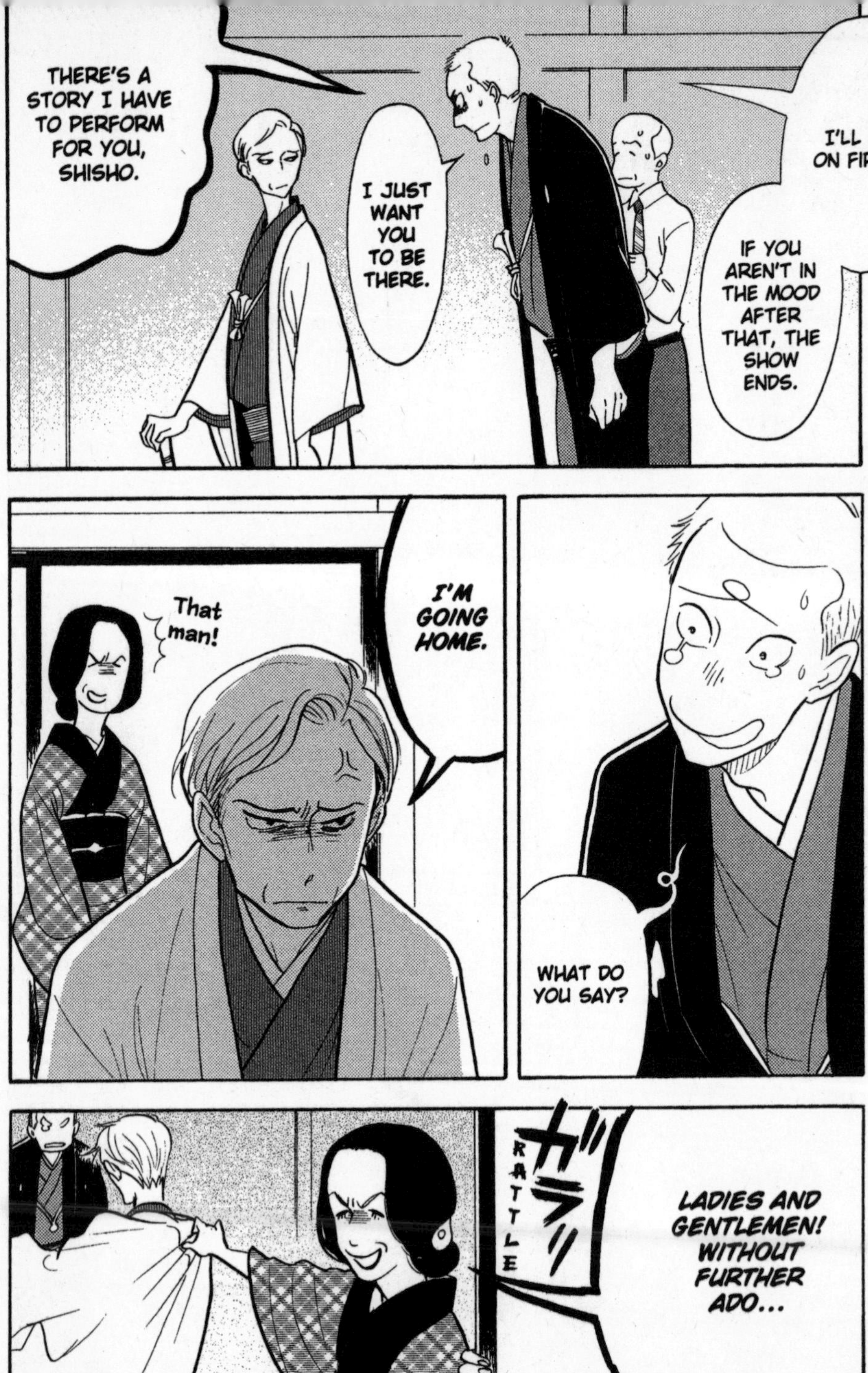
I'LL GO ON FIRST.
IF YOU AREN'T IN THE MOOD AFTER THAT, THE SHOW ENDS.
THERE'S A STORY I HAVE TO PERFORM FOR YOU, SHISHO.
I JUST WANT YOU TO BE THERE.
WHAT DO YOU SAY?
I'M GOING HOME.
That man!
LADIES AND GENTLEMEN! WITHOUT FURTHER ADO...
RATTLE

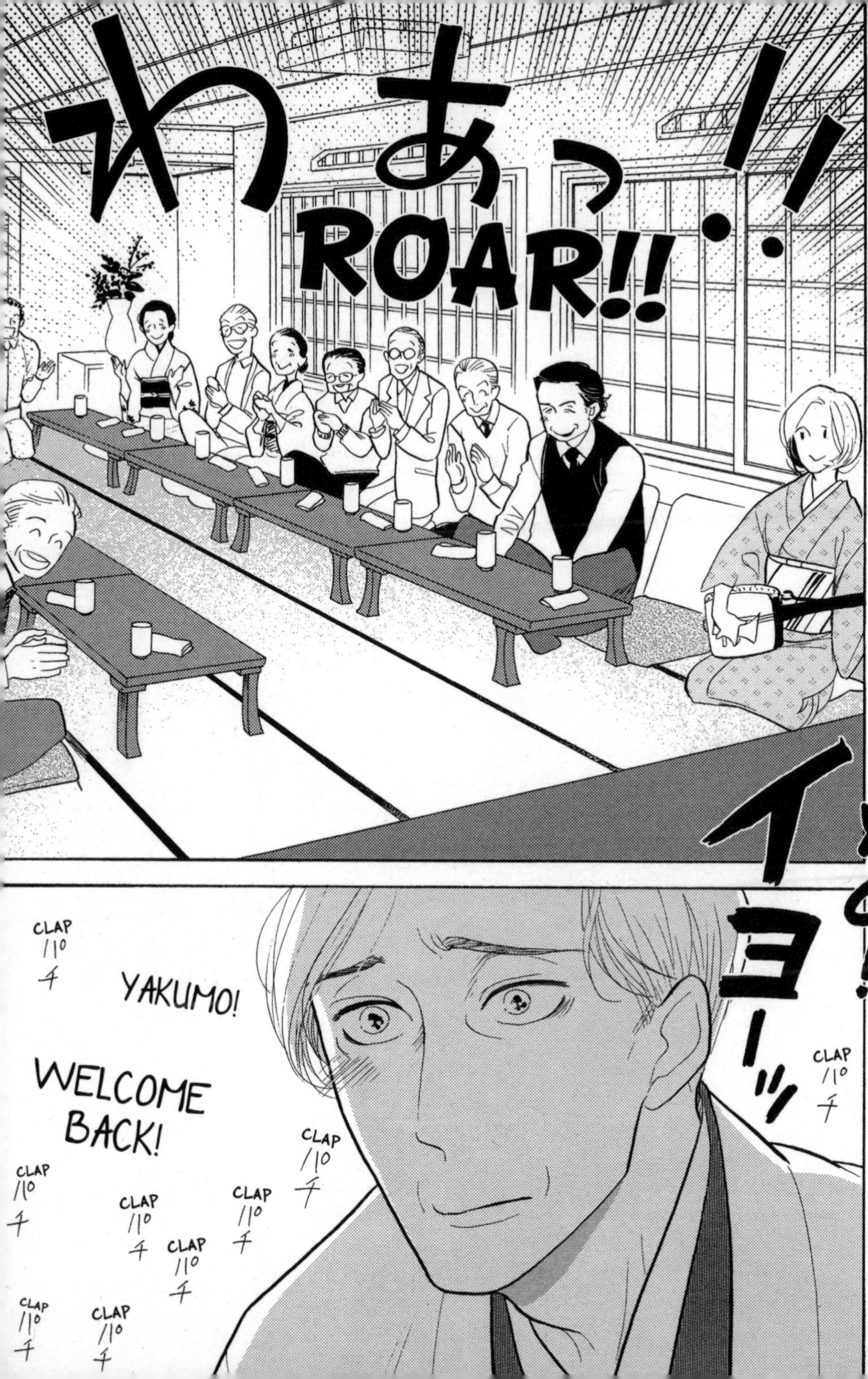
わあっ!!
ROAR!!
イヨーッ
YO!
CLAP パチ
YAKUMO!
WELCOME BACK!
CLAP パチ
CLAP パチ
CLAP パチ
CLAP パチ
CLAP パチ
CLAP パチ
CLAP パチ
CLAP パチ

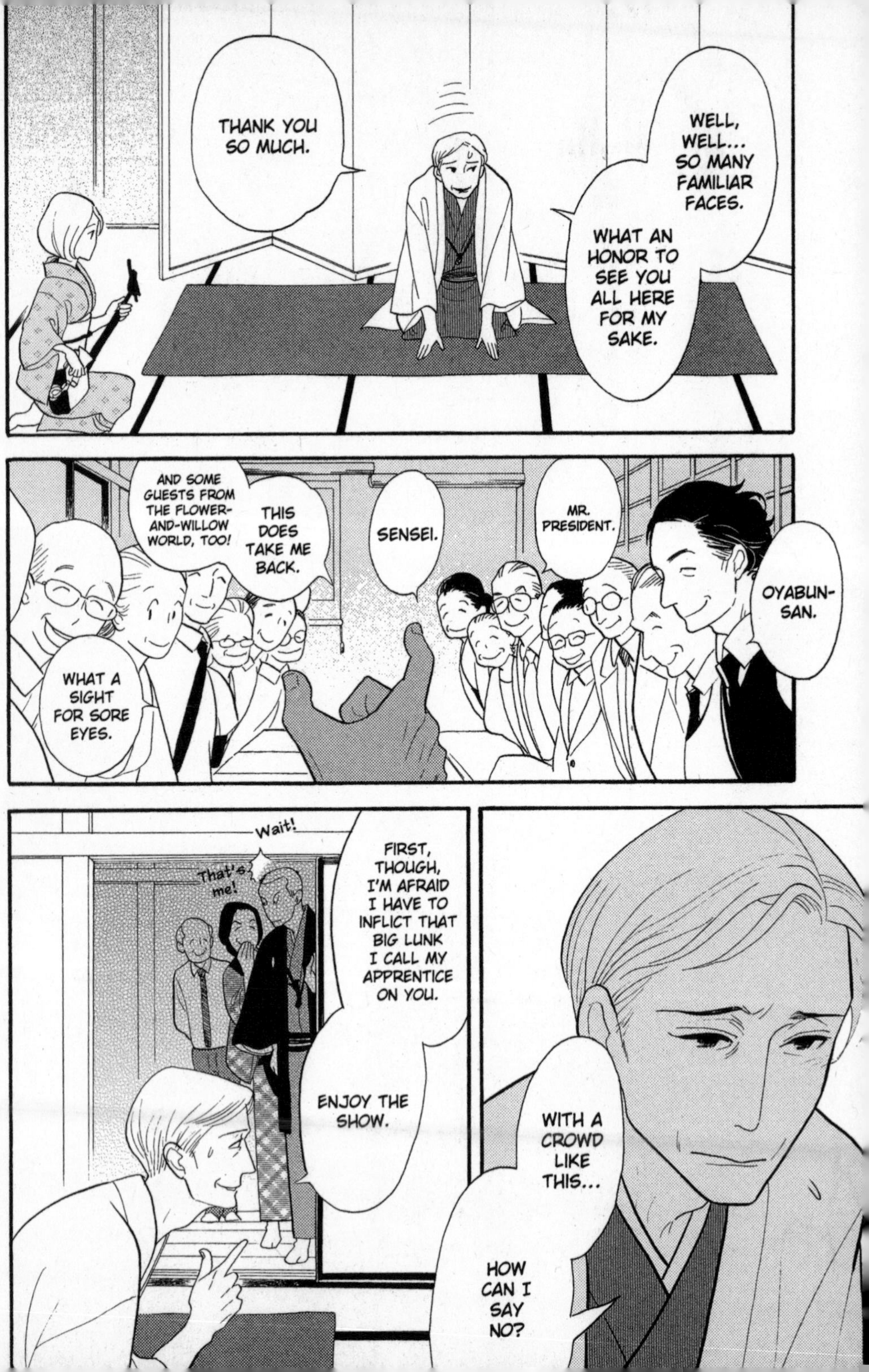
WELL, WELL... SO MANY FAMILIAR FACES.
WHAT AN HONOR TO SEE YOU ALL HERE FOR MY SAKE.
THANK YOU SO MUCH.
OYABUN-SAN.
MR. PRESIDENT.
SENSEI.
THIS DOES TAKE ME BACK.
AND SOME GUESTS FROM THE FLOWER-AND-WILLOW WORLD, TOO!
WHAT A SIGHT FOR SORE EYES.
WITH A CROWD LIKE THIS...
HOW CAN I SAY NO?
FIRST, THOUGH, I'M AFRAID I HAVE TO INFLICT THAT BIG LUNK I CALL MY APPRENTICE ON YOU.
ENJOY THE SHOW.
Wait!
That's me!

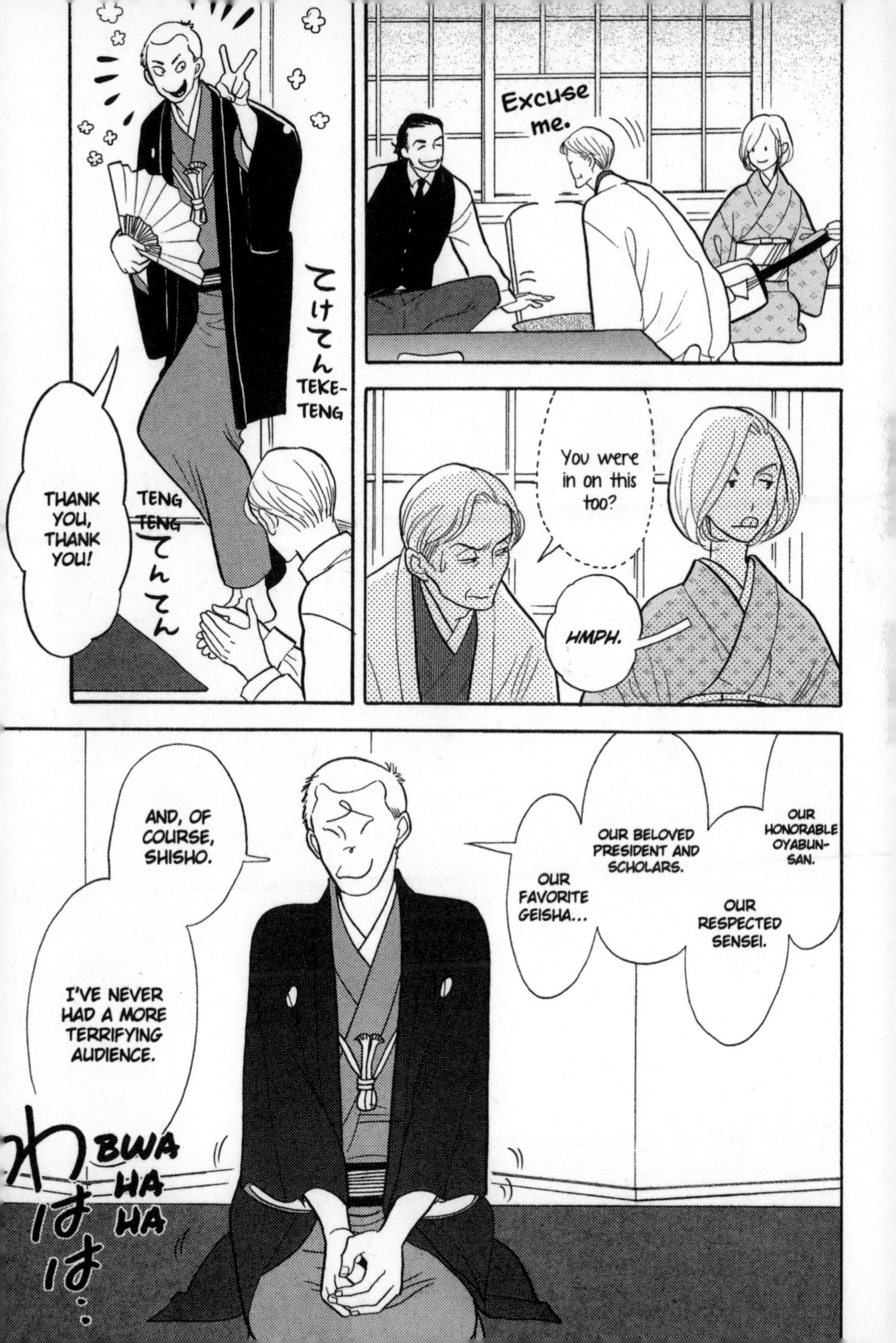
Excuse me.
You were in on this too?
HMPH.
てけてん TEKE-TENG
TENG TENG てんてん
THANK YOU, THANK YOU!
OUR HONORABLE OYABUN-SAN.
OUR RESPECTED SENSEI.
OUR BELOVED PRESIDENT AND SCHOLARS.
OUR FAVORITE GEISHA...
AND, OF COURSE, SHISHO.
I'VE NEVER HAD A MORE TERRIFYING AUDIENCE.
わはは‥ BWA HA HA

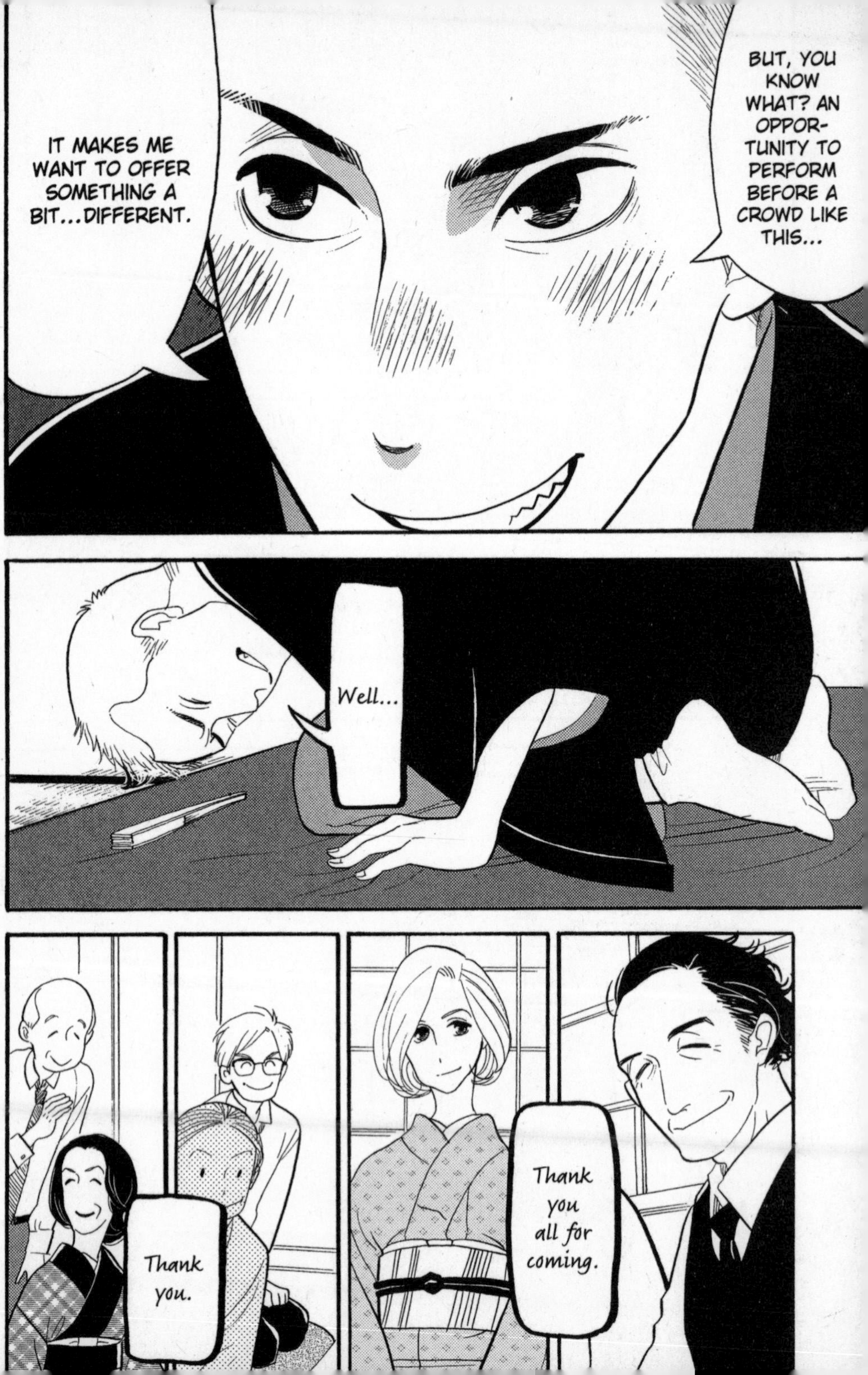
BUT, YOU KNOW WHAT? AN OPPOR-TUNITY TO PERFORM BEFORE A CROWD LIKE THIS...
IT MAKES ME WANT TO OFFER SOMETHING A BIT...DIFFERENT.
Well...
Thank you all for coming.
Thank you.

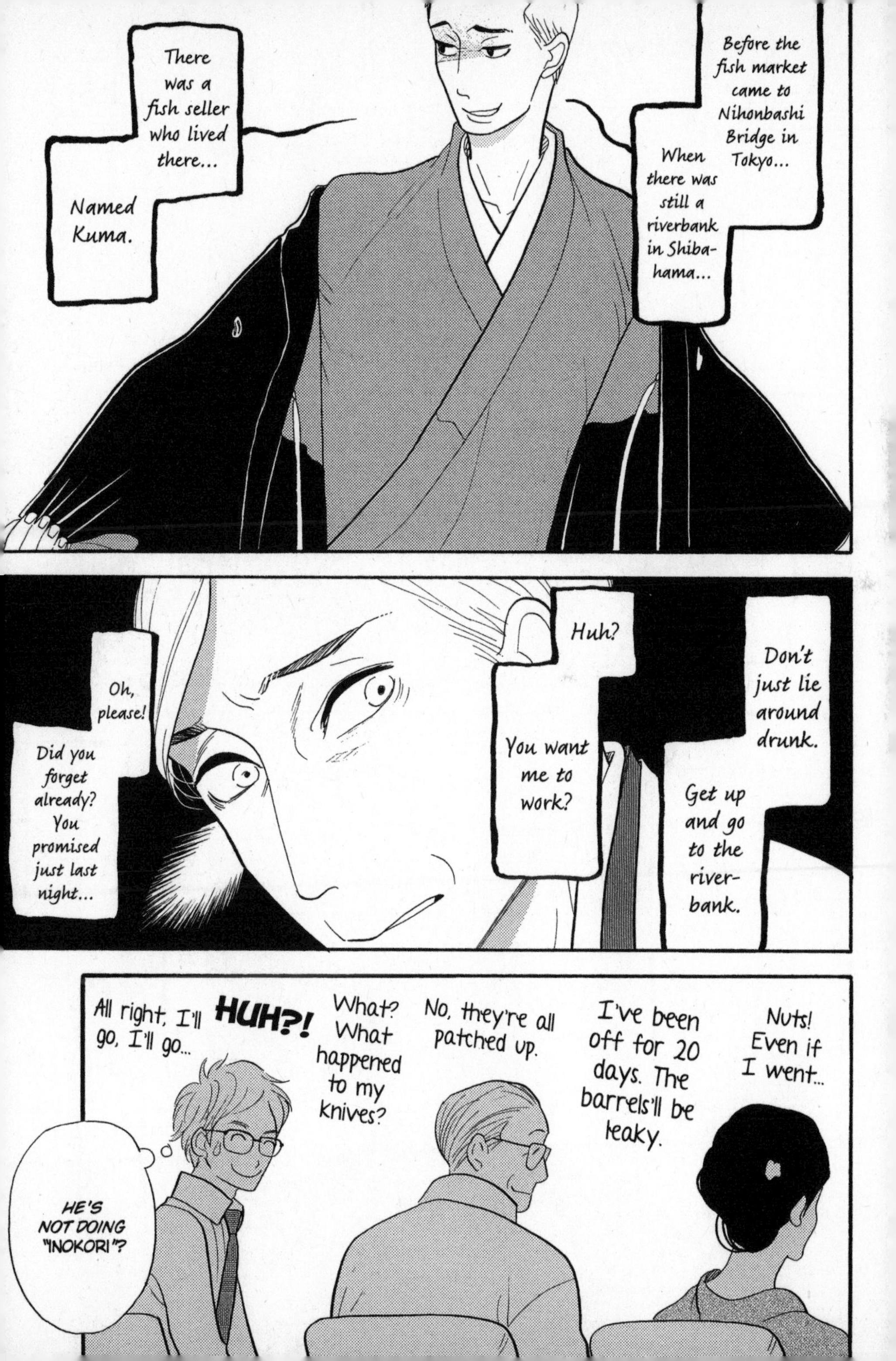
Before the fish market came to Nihonbashi Bridge in Tokyo...
When there was still a riverbank in Shiba-hama...
There was a fish seller who lived there...
Named Kuma.
Don't just lie around drunk.
Get up and go to the river-bank.
Huh?
You want me to work?
Oh, please!
Did you forget already? You promised just last night...
Nuts! Even if I went...
I've been off for 20 days. The barrels'll be leaky.
No, they're all patched up.
What? What happened to my knives?
HUH?!
All right, I'll go, I'll go...
HE'S NOT DOING "INOKORI"?

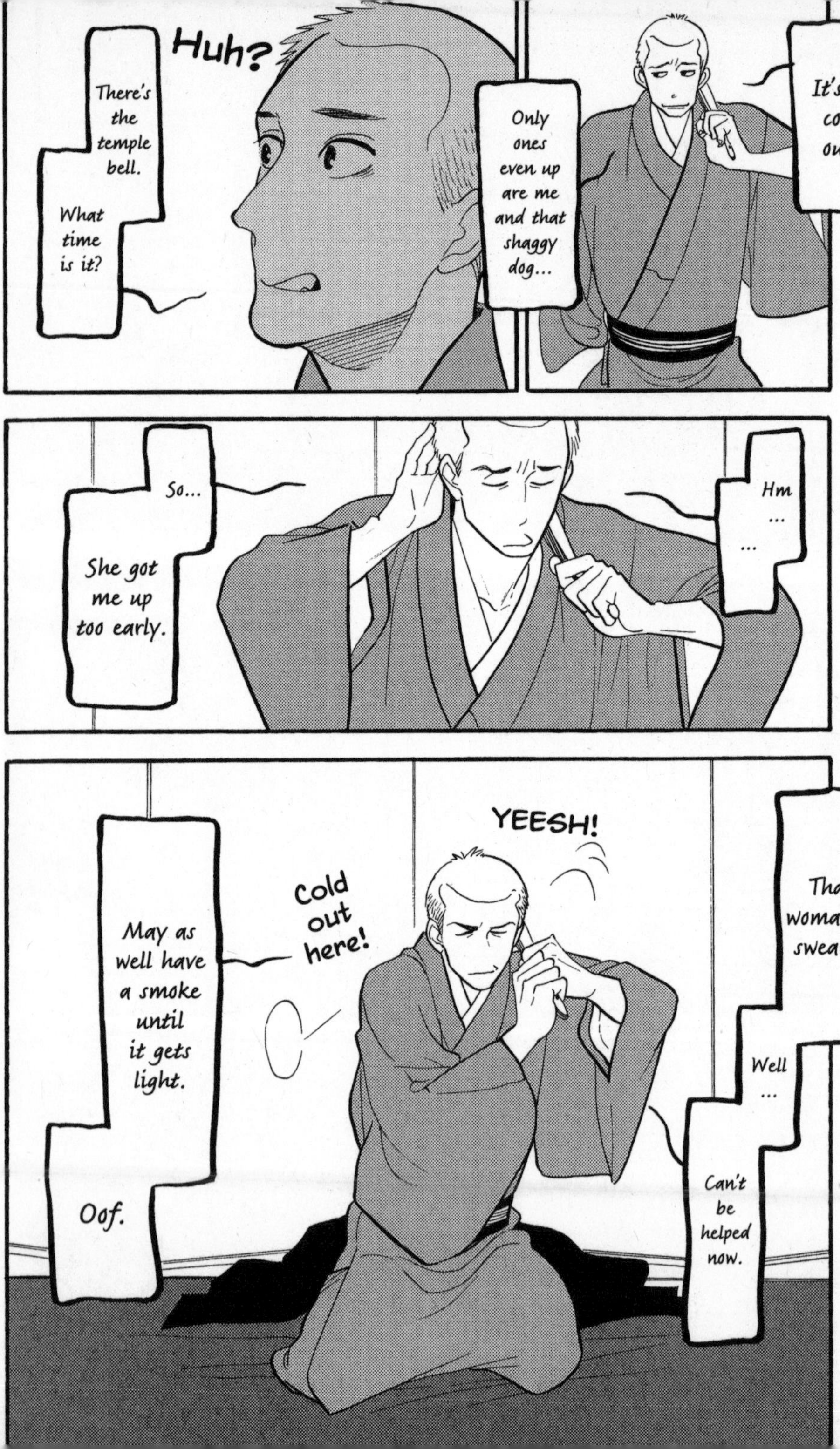

It's so cold out!
Only ones even up are me and that shaggy dog...
Huh?
There's the temple bell. What time is it?
Hm … …
So... She got me up too early.
That woman, I swear... Well... Can't be helped now.
YEESH!
Cold out here!
May as well have a smoke until it gets light. Oof.

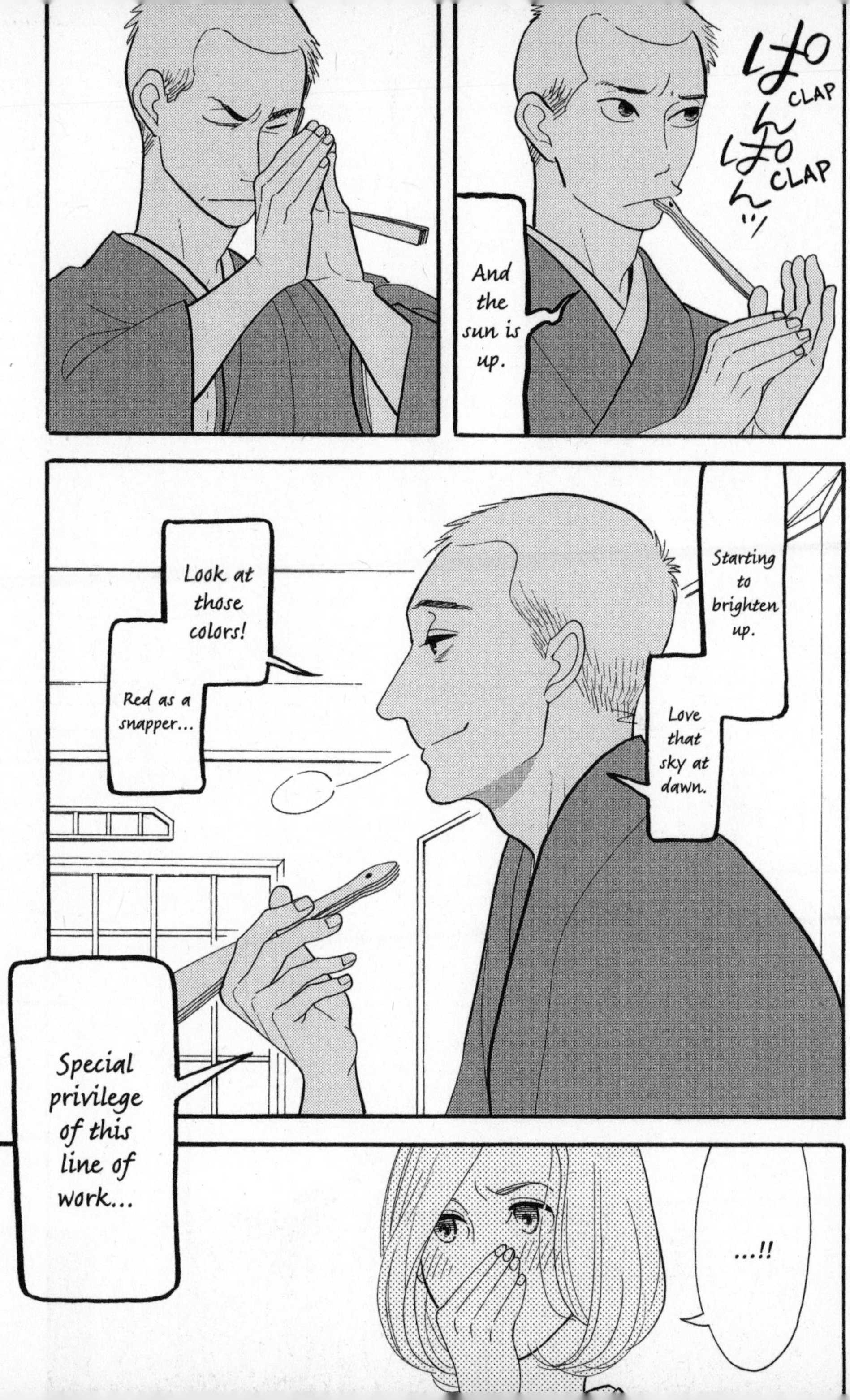
ぱんぱんッ
CLAP
CLAP
And the sun is up.
Starting to brighten up.
Love that sky at dawn.
Look at those colors!
Red as a snapper...
Special privilege of this line of work...
...!!

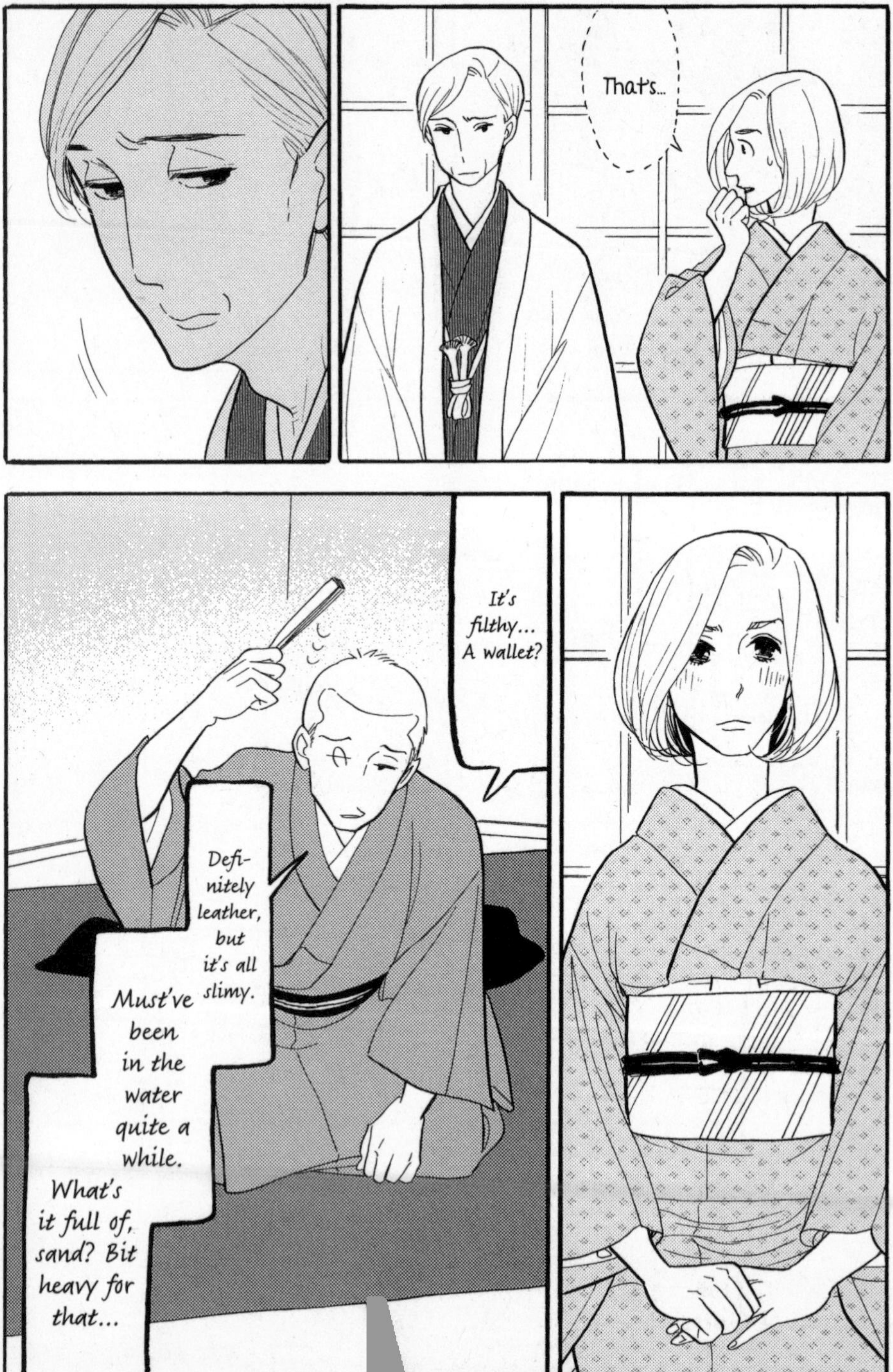
That's...
It's filthy... A wallet?
Defi-nitely leather, but it's all slimy.
Must've been in the water quite a while.
What's it full of, sand? Bit heavy for that...

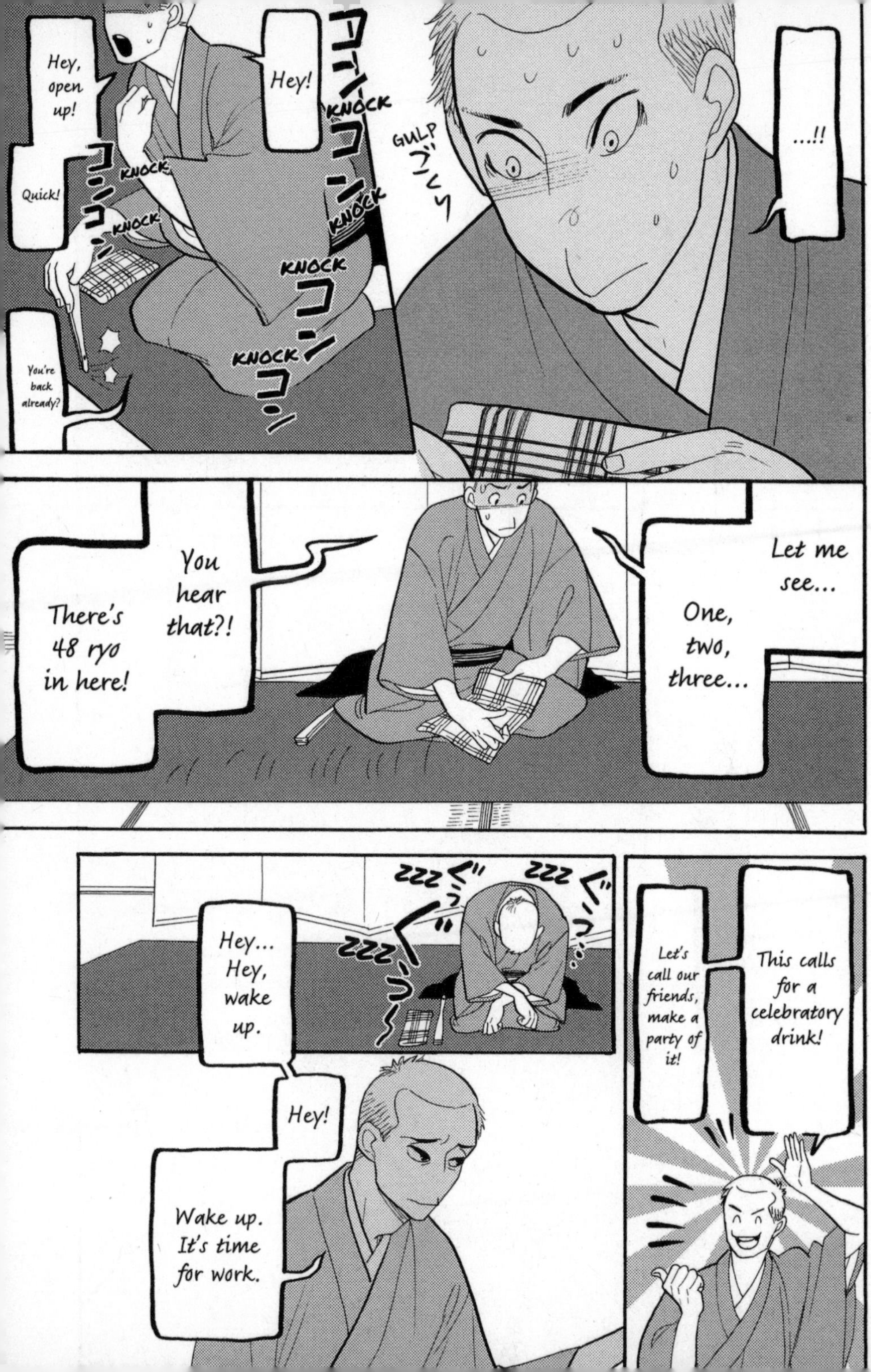
...!!
GULP
Hey!
KNOCK
KNOCK
KNOCK
Hey, open up!
KNOCK
Quick!
KNOCK
You're back already?
Let me see...
One, two, three...
You hear that?!
There's 48 ryo in here!
This calls for a celebratory drink!
Let's call our friends, make a party of it!
ZZZ
ZZZ
ZZZ
Hey... Hey, wake up.
Hey!
Wake up. It's time for work.

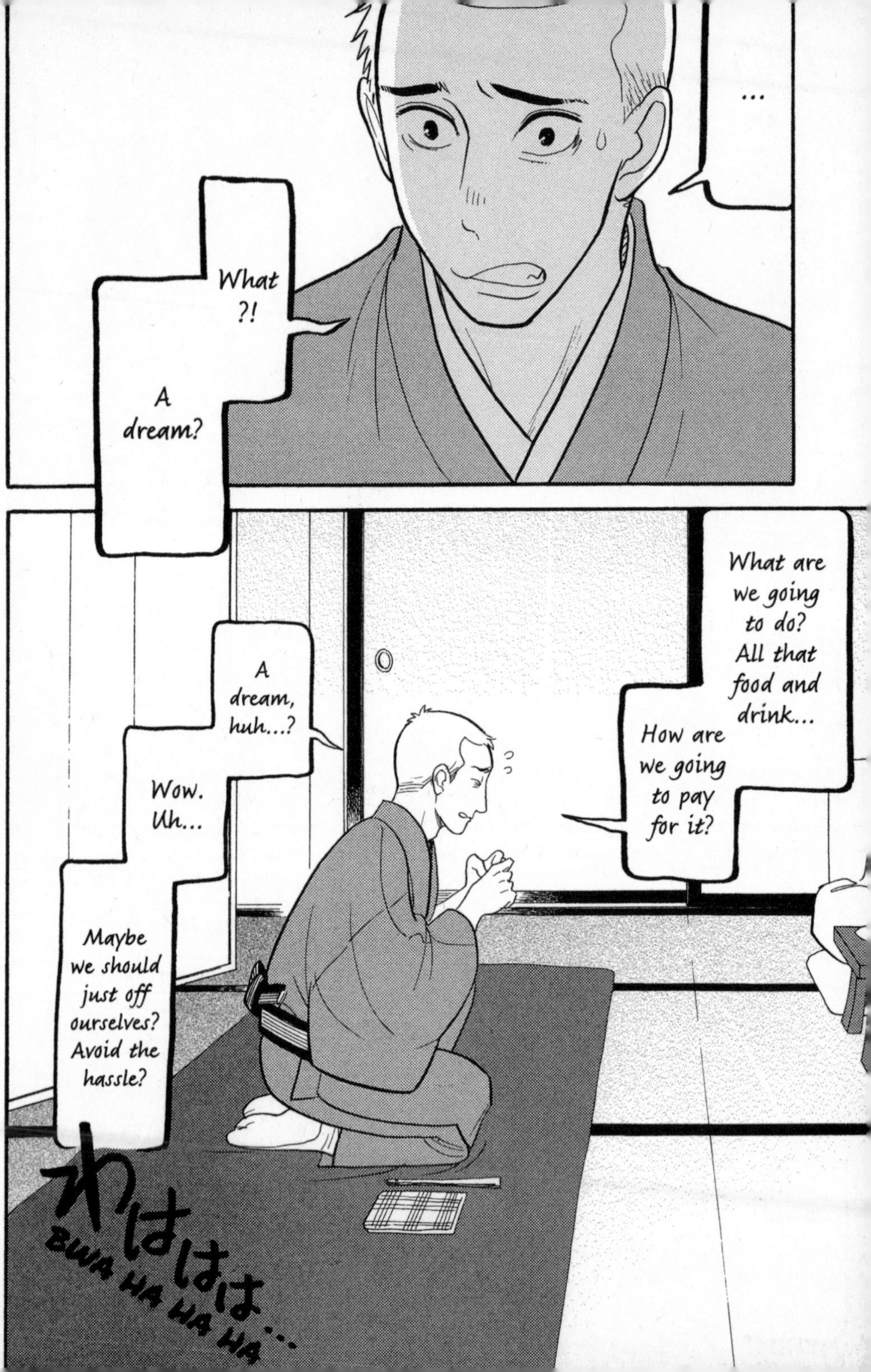
...
What ?! A dream?
What are we going to do? All that food and drink...
How are we going to pay for it?
A dream, huh...?
Wow. Uh...
Maybe we should just off ourselves? Avoid the hassle?
わははは…
BWA HA HA HA

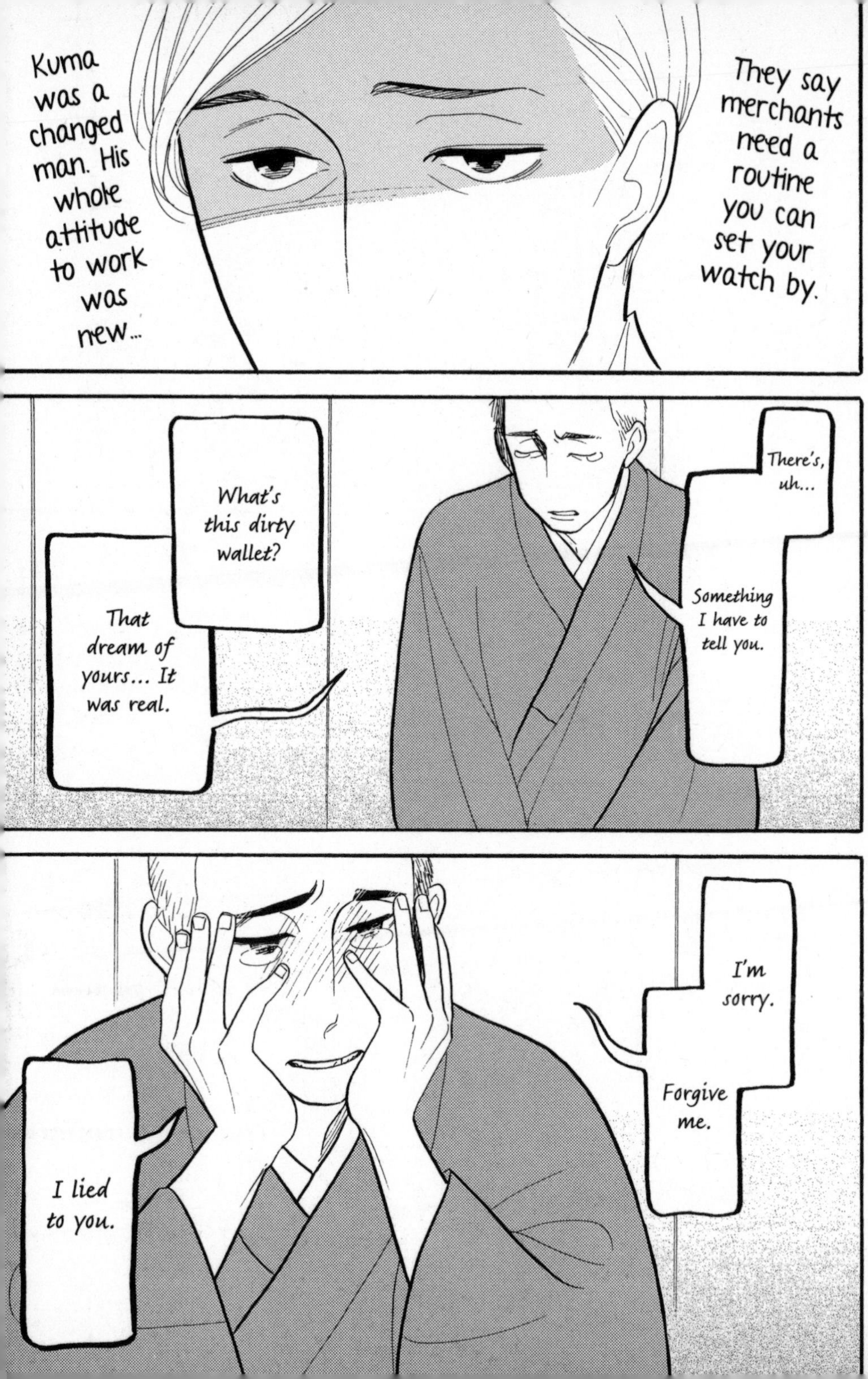
They say merchants need a routine you can set your watch by.
Kuma was a changed man. His whole attitude to work was new...
There's, uh...
Something I have to tell you.
What's this dirty wallet?
That dream of yours... It was real.
I'm sorry.
Forgive me.
I lied to you.

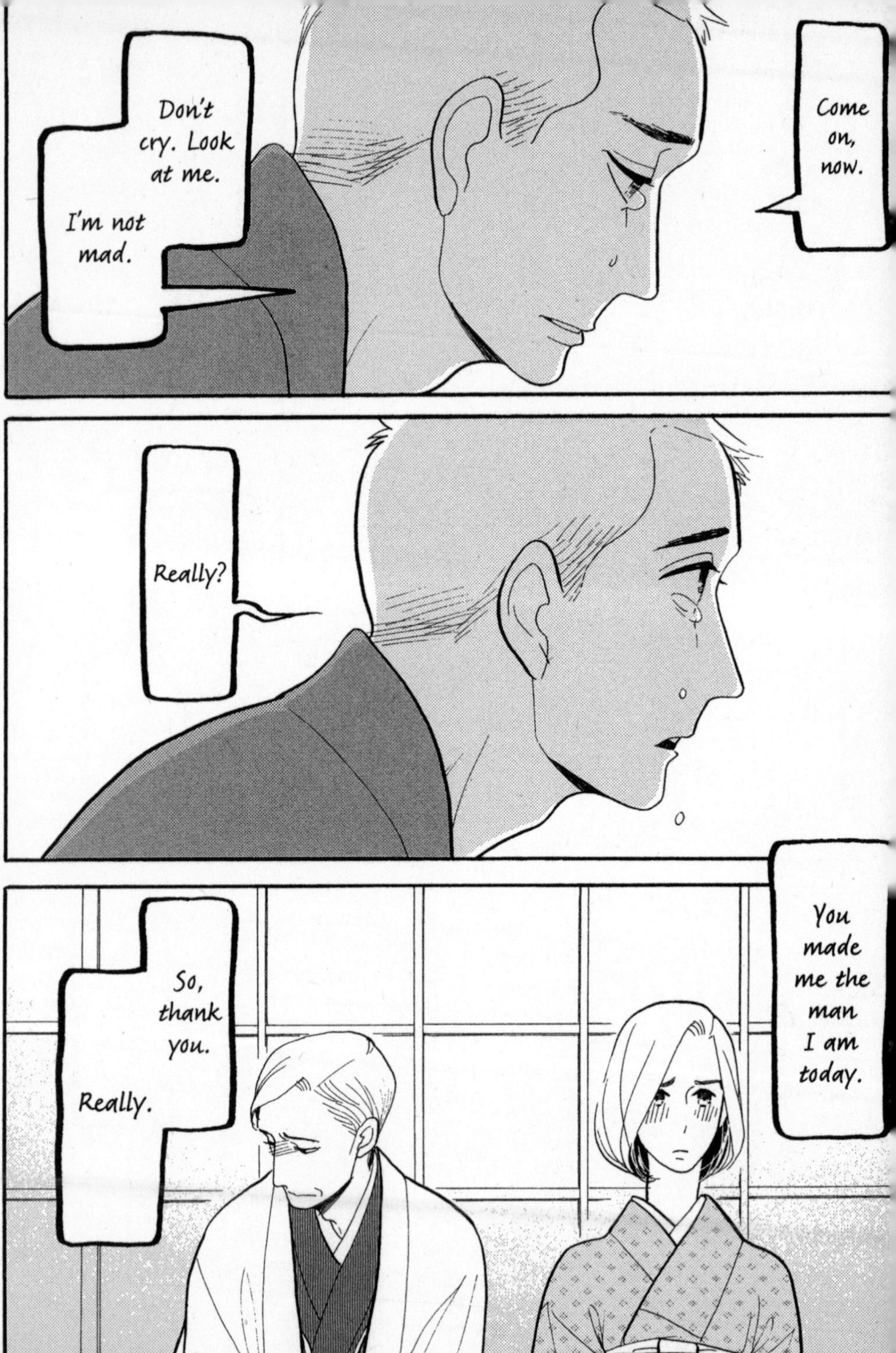
Come on, now.
Don't cry. Look at me.
I'm not mad.
Really?
You made me the man I am today.
So, thank you.
Really.

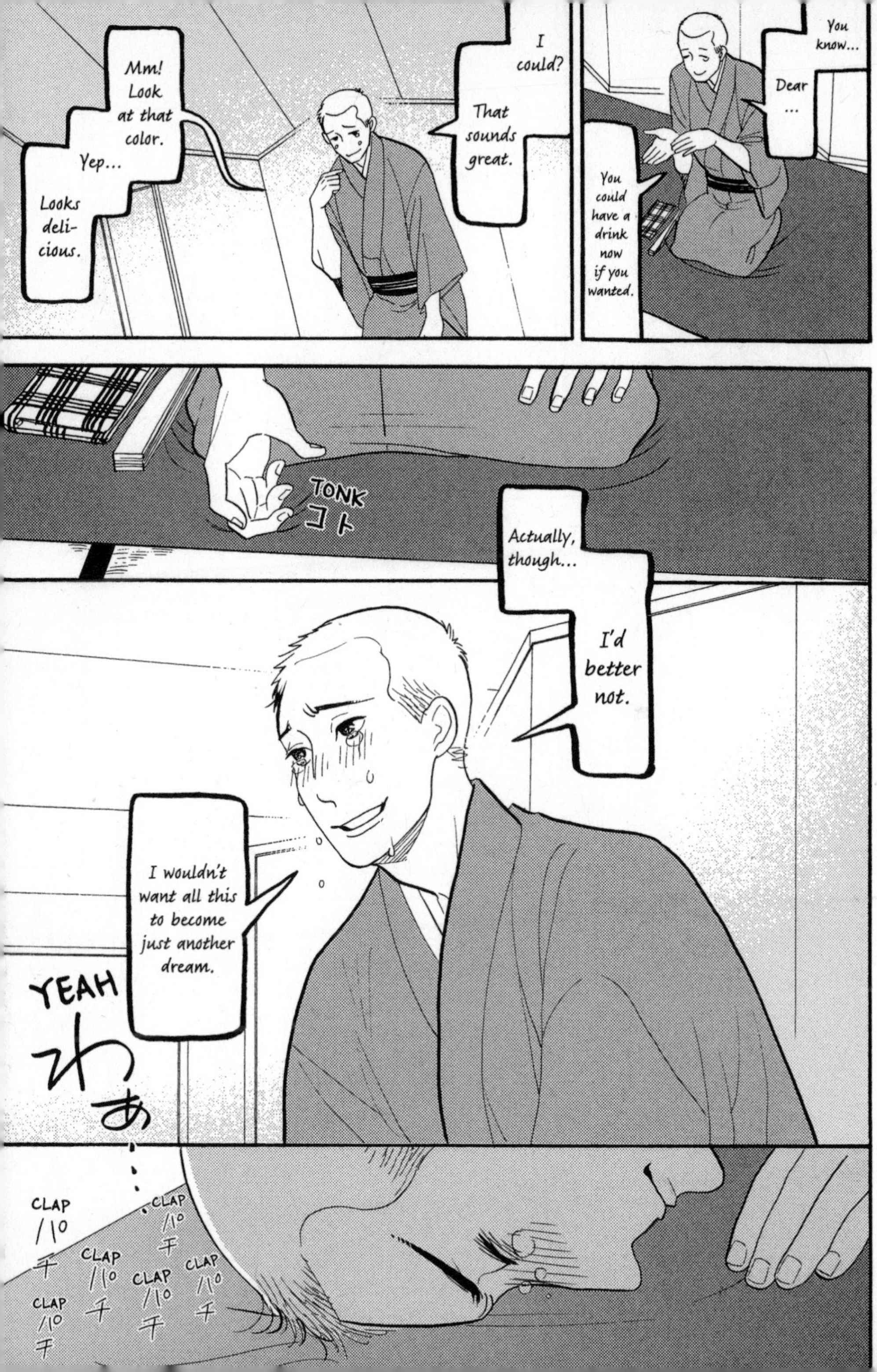
You know...
Dear...
You could have a drink now if you wanted.
I could?
That sounds great.
Mm! Look at that color.
Yep...
Looks delicious.
TONK コト
Actually, though...
I'd better not.
I wouldn't want all this to become just another dream.
YEAH わあ...
CLAP パチ
CLAP パチ
CLAP パチ
CLAP パチ
CLAP パチ
CLAP パチ

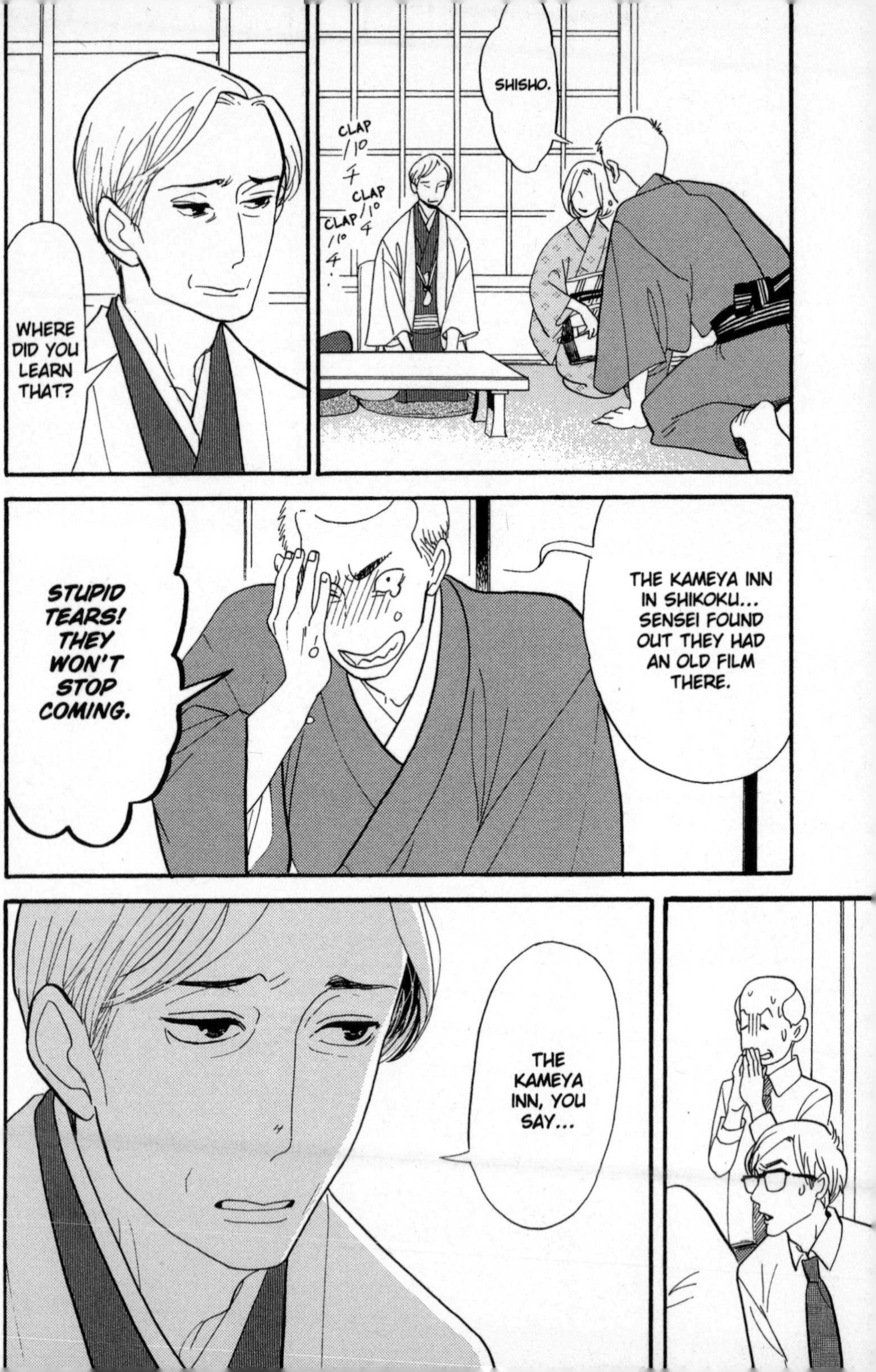
SHISHO.
CLAP CLAP CLAP
WHERE DID YOU LEARN THAT?
THE KAMEYA INN IN SHIKOKU... SENSEI FOUND OUT THEY HAD AN OLD FILM THERE.
STUPID TEARS! THEY WON'T STOP COMING.
THE KAMEYA INN, YOU SAY...

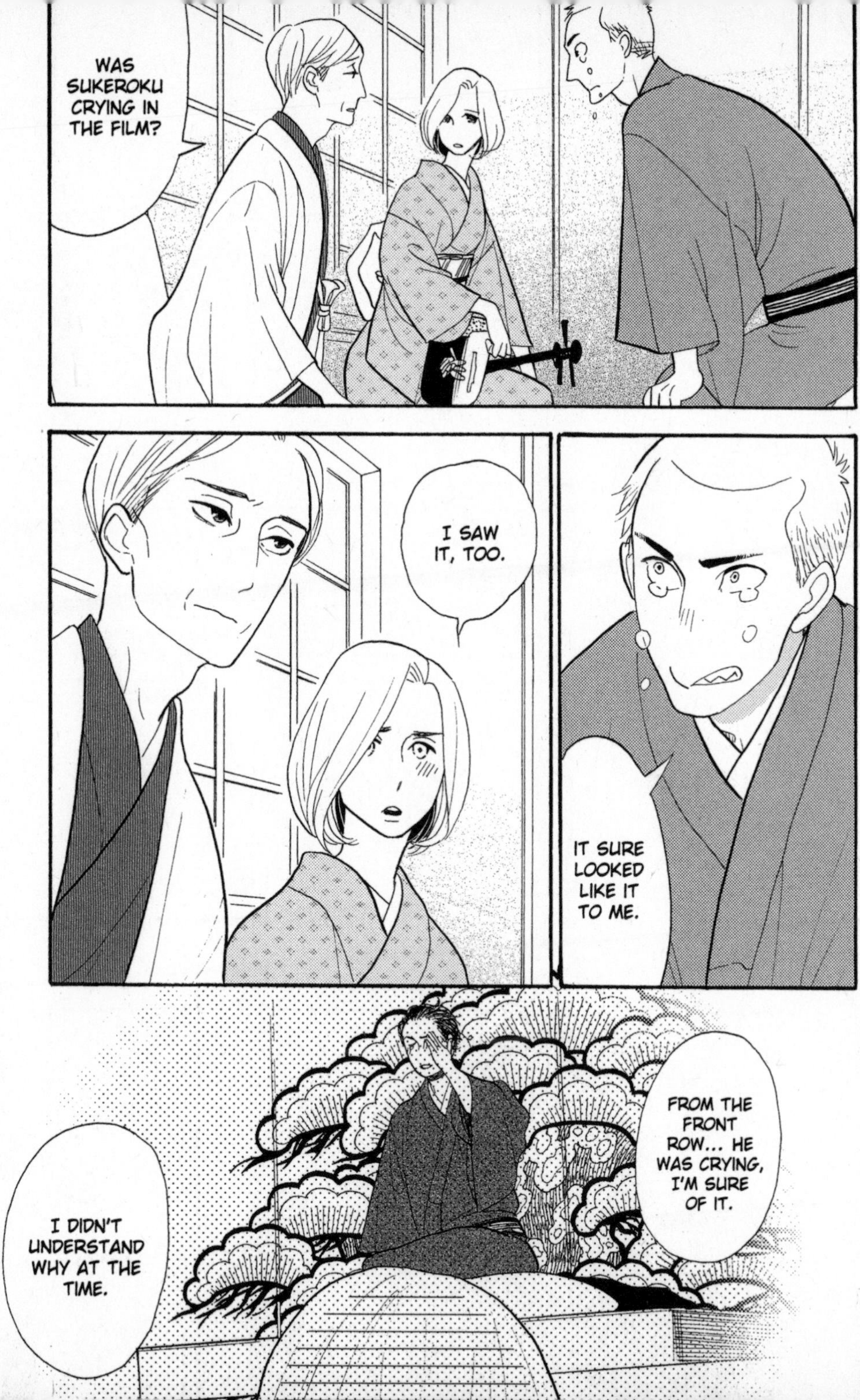
WAS SUKEROKU CRYING IN THE FILM?
IT SURE LOOKED LIKE IT TO ME.
I SAW IT, TOO.
FROM THE FRONT ROW... HE WAS CRYING, I'M SURE OF IT.
I DIDN'T UNDERSTAND WHY AT THE TIME.

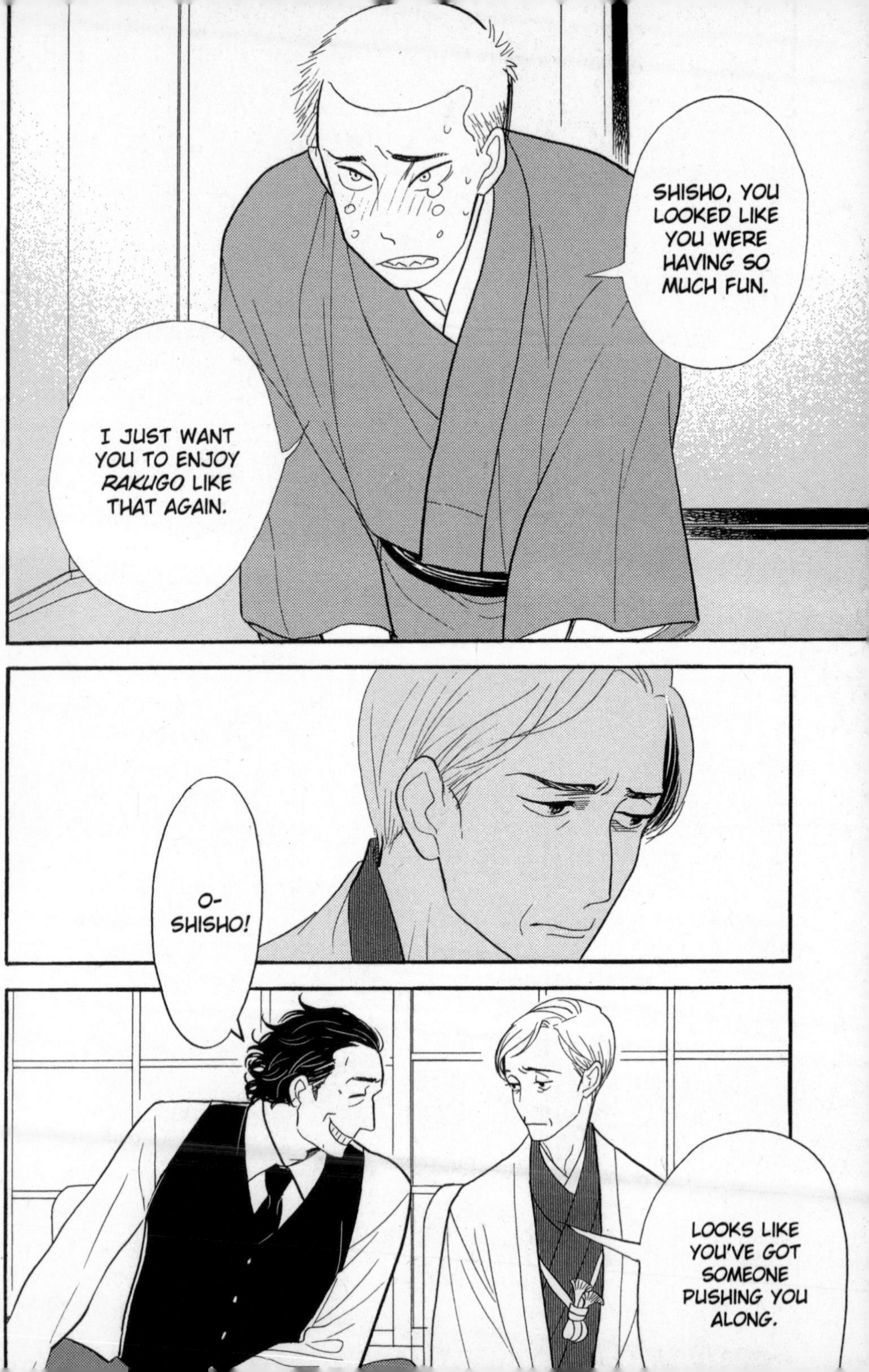
SHISHO, YOU LOOKED LIKE YOU WERE HAVING SO MUCH FUN.
I JUST WANT YOU TO ENJOY *RAKUGO* LIKE THAT AGAIN.
O-SHISHO!
LOOKS LIKE YOU'VE GOT SOMEONE PUSHING YOU ALONG.

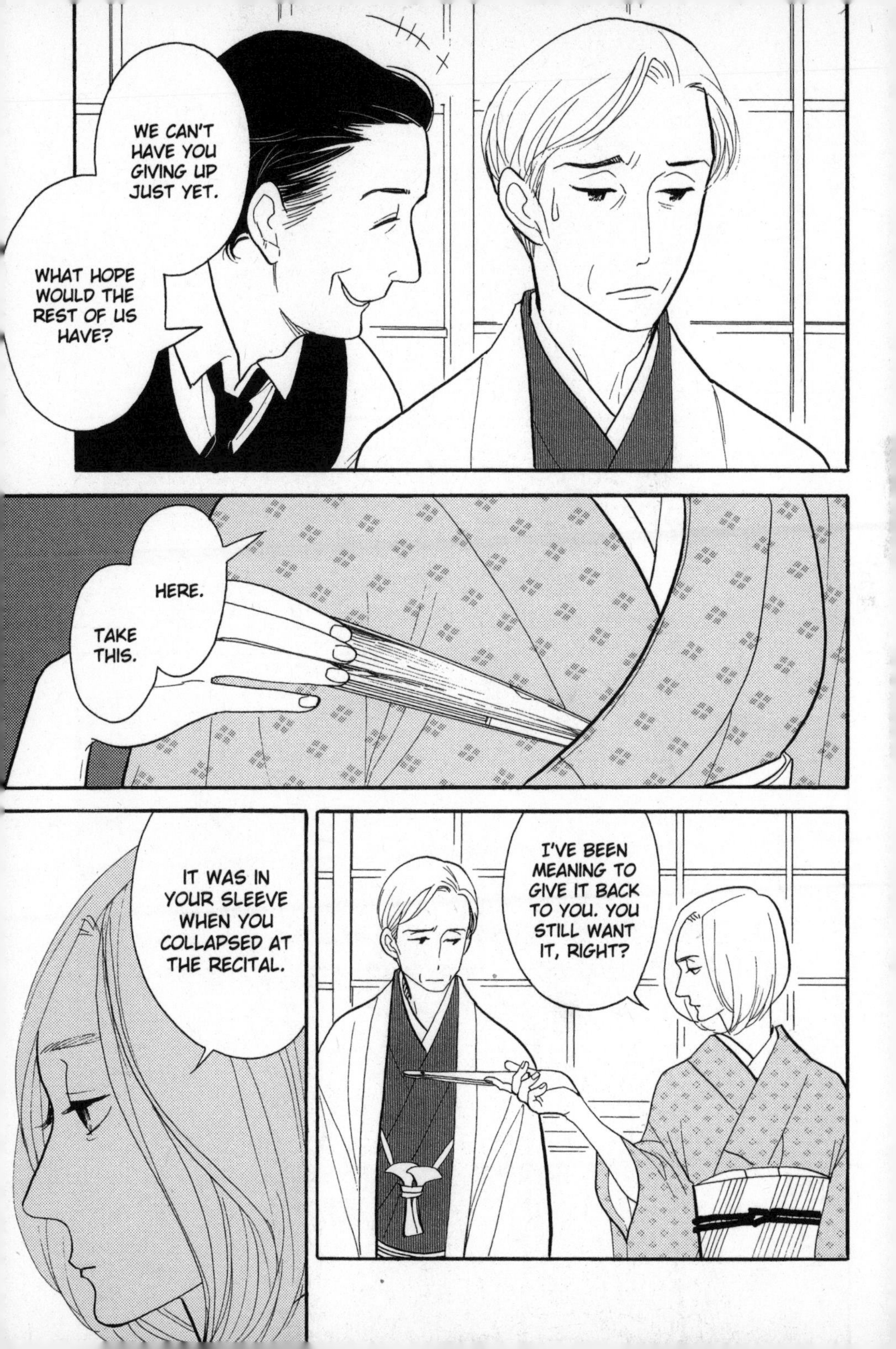
WE CAN'T HAVE YOU GIVING UP JUST YET.
WHAT HOPE WOULD THE REST OF US HAVE?
HERE.
TAKE THIS.
I'VE BEEN MEANING TO GIVE IT BACK TO YOU. YOU STILL WANT IT, RIGHT?
IT WAS IN YOUR SLEEVE WHEN YOU COLLAPSED AT THE RECITAL.

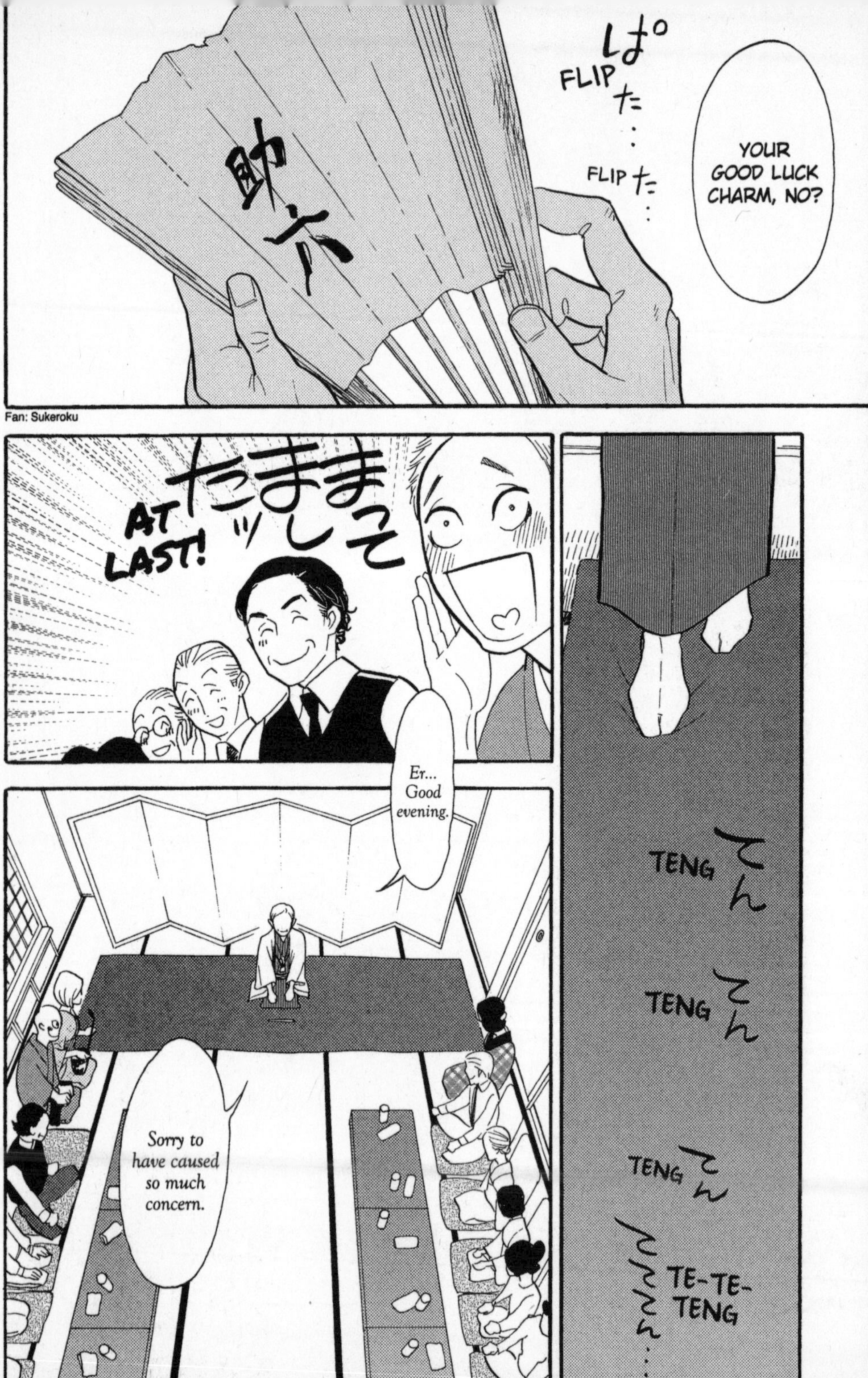
ぱた…
FLIP
た…
FLIP
YOUR GOOD LUCK CHARM, NO?
Fan: Sukeroku
てん
TENG
てん
TENG
てん
TENG
ててて
TE-TE-TENG
AT LAST!
Er... Good evening.
Sorry to have caused so much concern.

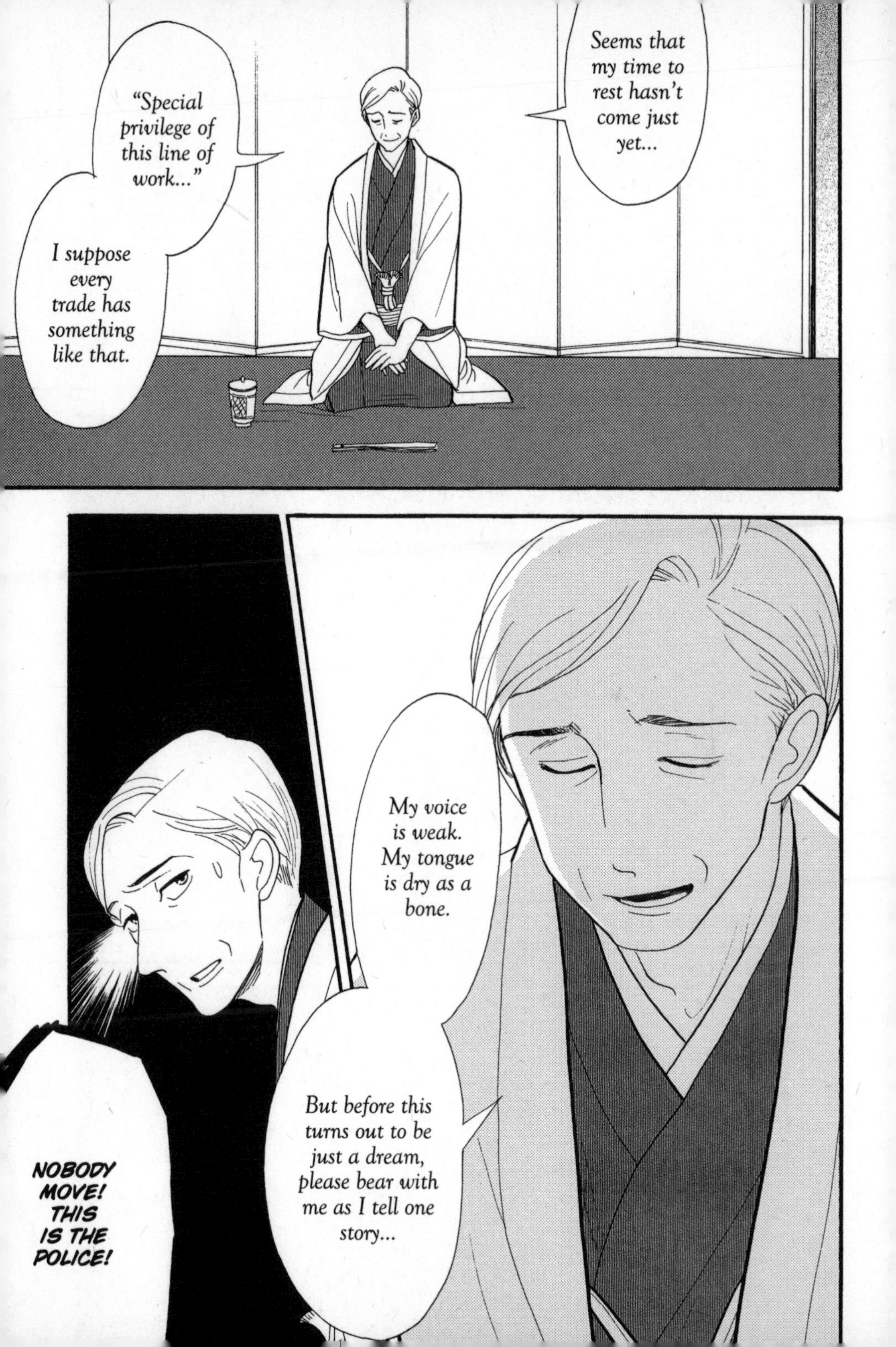
Seems that my time to rest hasn't come just yet...
"Special privilege of this line of work..."
I suppose every trade has something like that.
My voice is weak. My tongue is dry as a bone.
But before this turns out to be just a dream, please bear with me as I tell one story...
NOBODY MOVE! THIS IS THE POLICE!

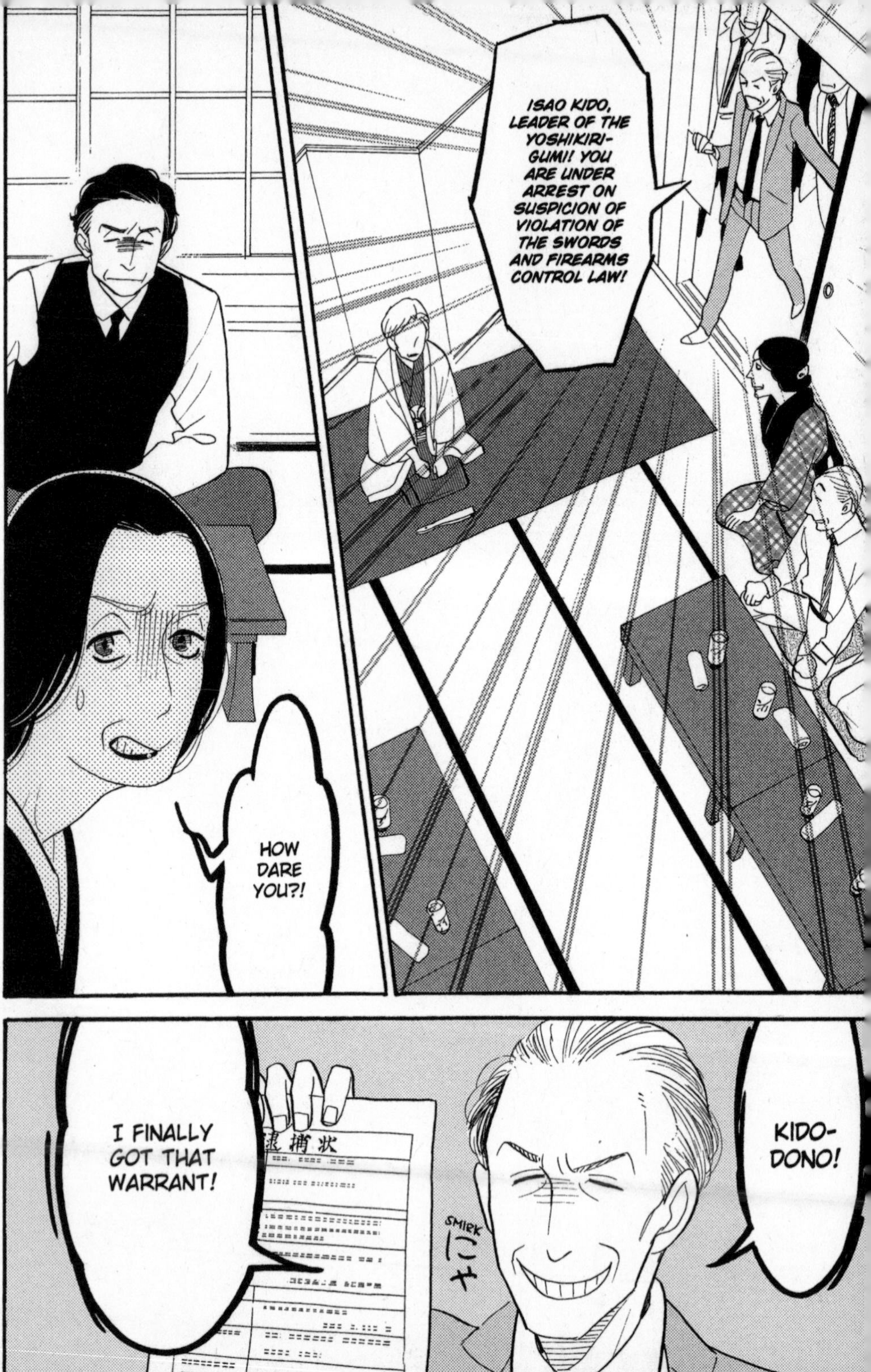
ISAO KIDO, LEADER OF THE YOSHIKIRI-GUMI! YOU ARE UNDER ARREST ON SUSPICION OF VIOLATION OF THE SWORDS AND FIREARMS CONTROL LAW!
HOW DARE YOU?!
KIDO-DONO!
SMIRK
にや
I FINALLY GOT THAT WARRANT!

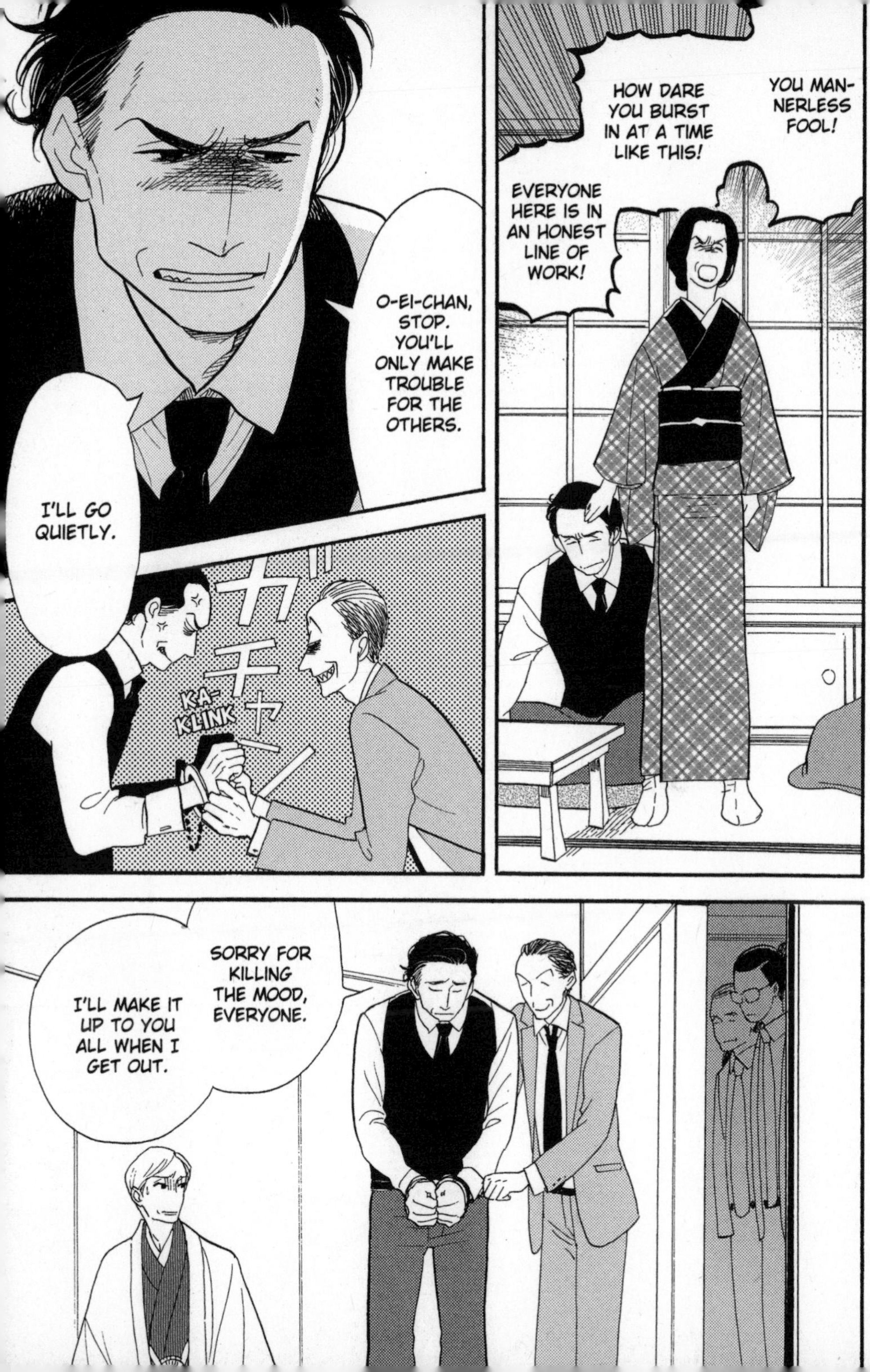
YOU MAN-NERLESS FOOL!
HOW DARE YOU BURST IN AT A TIME LIKE THIS!
EVERYONE HERE IS IN AN HONEST LINE OF WORK!
O-EI-CHAN, STOP. YOU'LL ONLY MAKE TROUBLE FOR THE OTHERS.
I'LL GO QUIETLY.
ガチャー
KA-KLINK
SORRY FOR KILLING THE MOOD, EVERYONE.
I'LL MAKE IT UP TO YOU ALL WHEN I GET OUT.

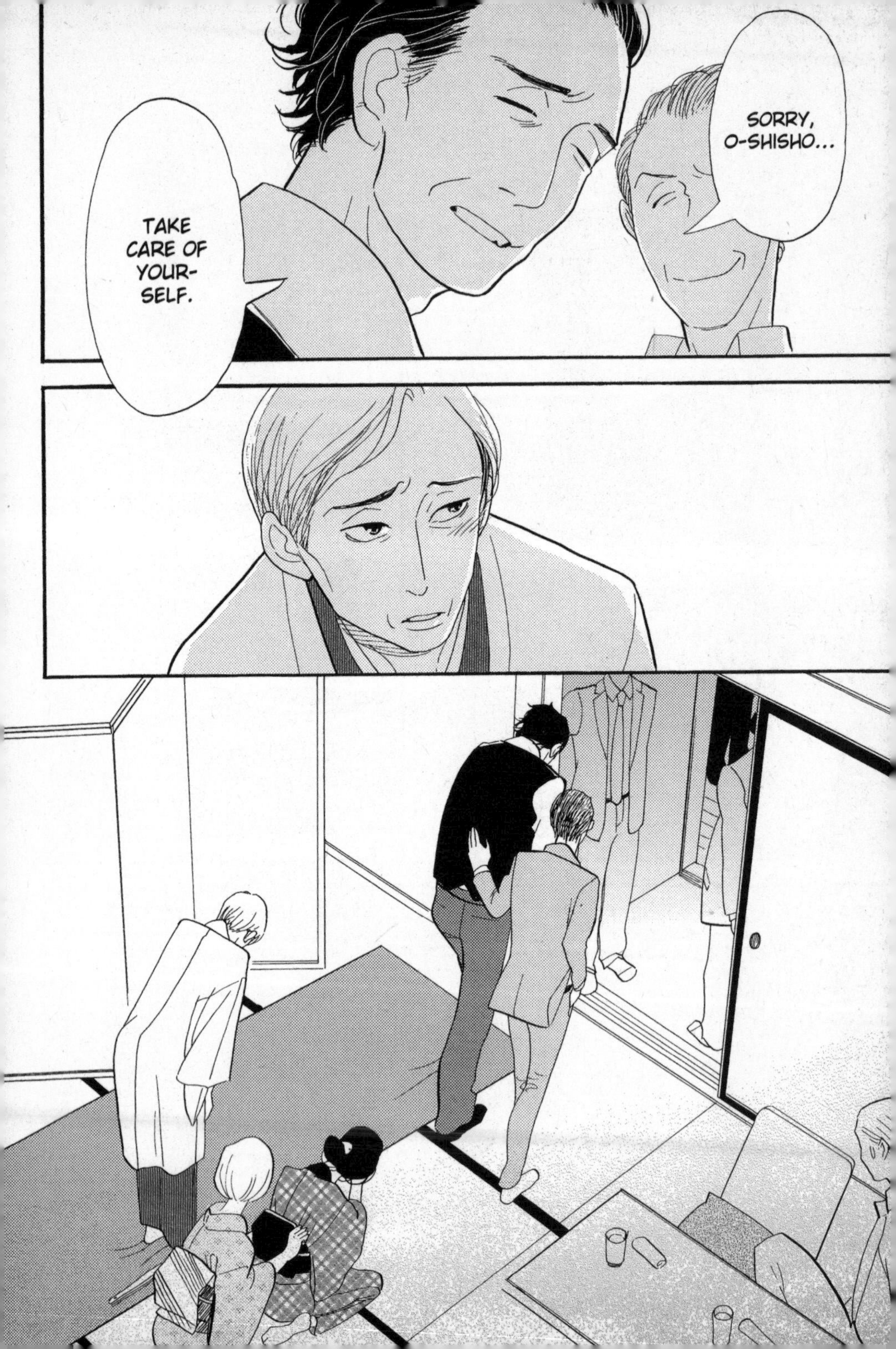
SORRY, O-SHISHO...
TAKE CARE OF YOUR-SELF.

DESCENDING STORIES

SHOWA GENROKU RAKUGO SHINJU

HARUKO KUMOTA

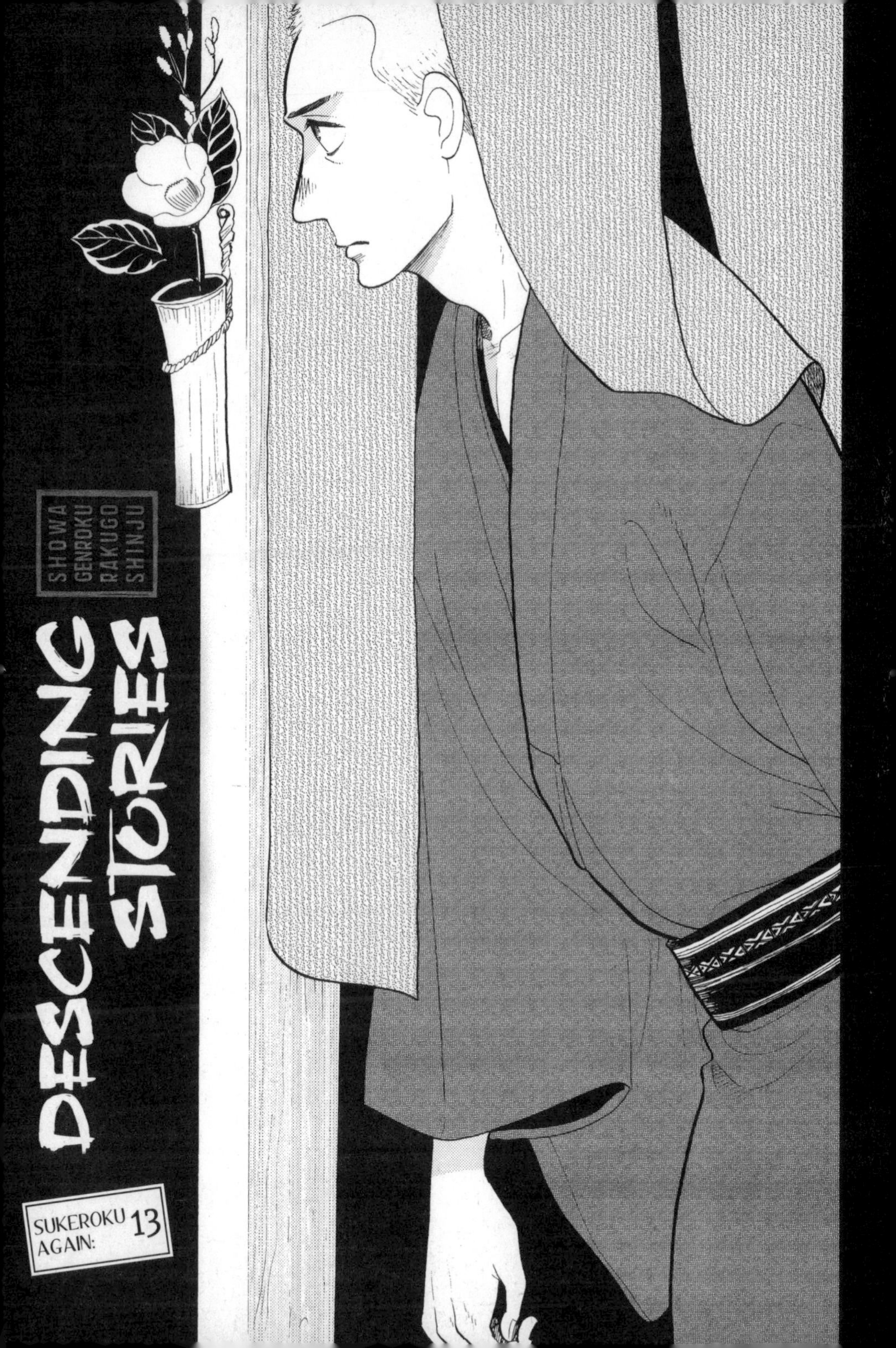
DESCENDING STORIES
SHOWA GENROKU RAKUGO SHINJU
SUKEROKU AGAIN: 13

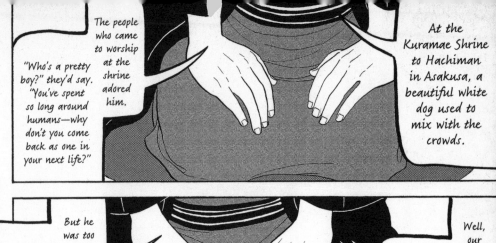

At the Kuramae Shrine to Hachiman in Asakusa, a beautiful white dog used to mix with the crowds.

The people who came to worship at the shrine adored him.

"Who's a pretty boy?" they'd say. "You've spent so long around humans—why don't you come back as one in your next life?"

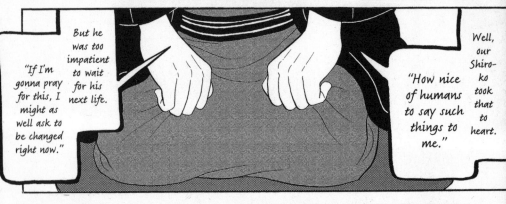

Well, our Shiro-ko took that to heart.

"How nice of humans to say such things to me."

But he was too impatient to wait for his next life.

"If I'm gonna pray for this, I might as well ask to be changed right now."

And so, every day for three weeks he made a barefoot pilgrimage to the shrine...

He was pretty much always barefoot, mind you, being a dog.

Finally, on the morning after the 21st day...

The wind rose and blew all of Shiro's fur off. He was human.

HEE HEE HE

GIGGLE GIGGLE

HA HA

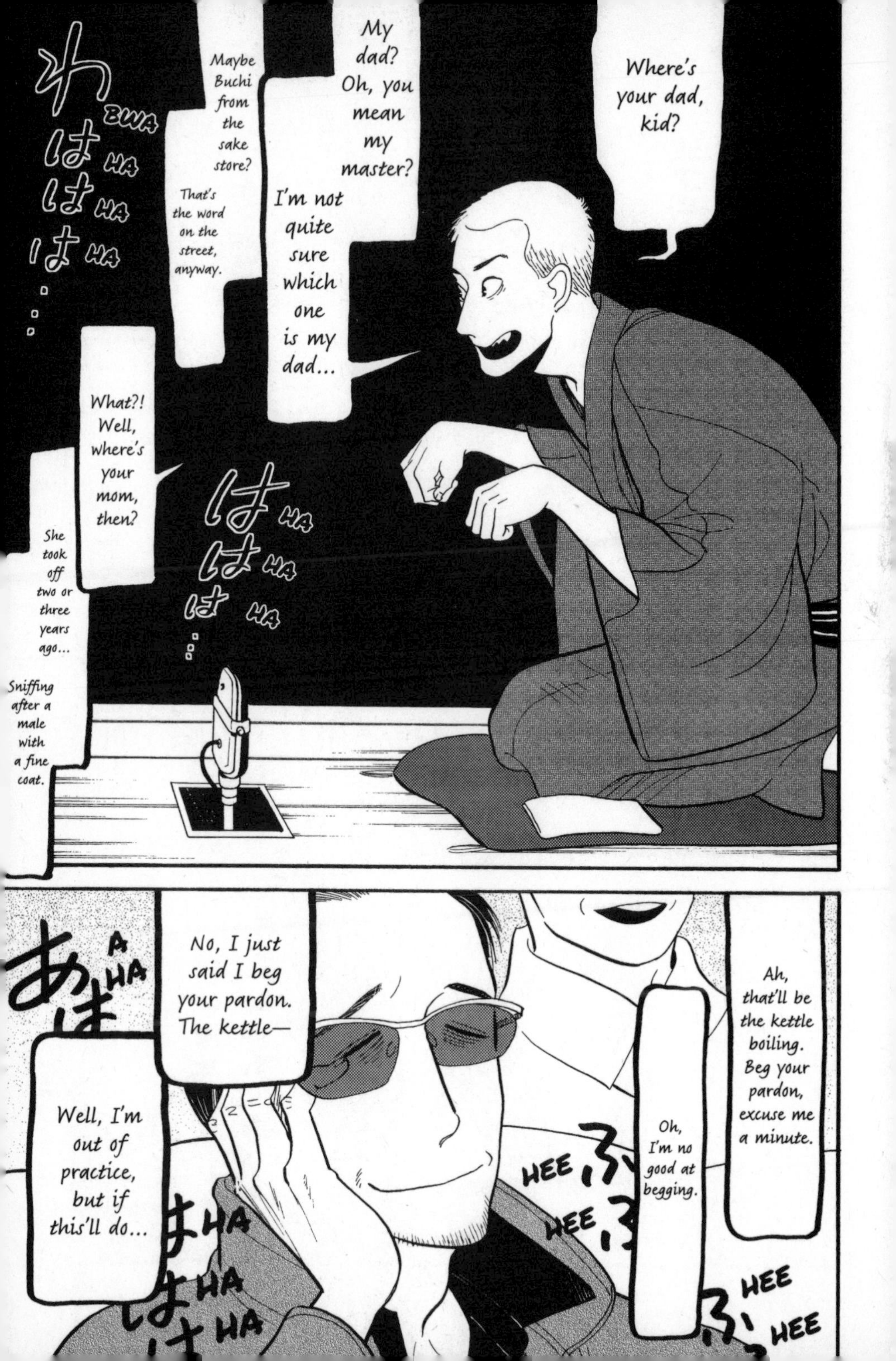
Where's your dad, kid?
My dad? Oh, you mean my master?
I'm not quite sure which one is my dad...
Maybe Buchi from the sake store?
That's the word on the street, anyway.
わははは BWA HA HA HA...
What?! Well, where's your mom, then?
ははは HA HA HA...
She took off two or three years ago...
Sniffing after a male with a fine coat.
Ah, that'll be the kettle boiling. Beg your pardon, excuse me a minute.
Oh, I'm no good at begging.
ふふふ HEE HEE HEE HEE
No, I just said I beg your pardon. The kettle—
あははは A HA HA HA
Well, I'm out of practice, but if this'll do...

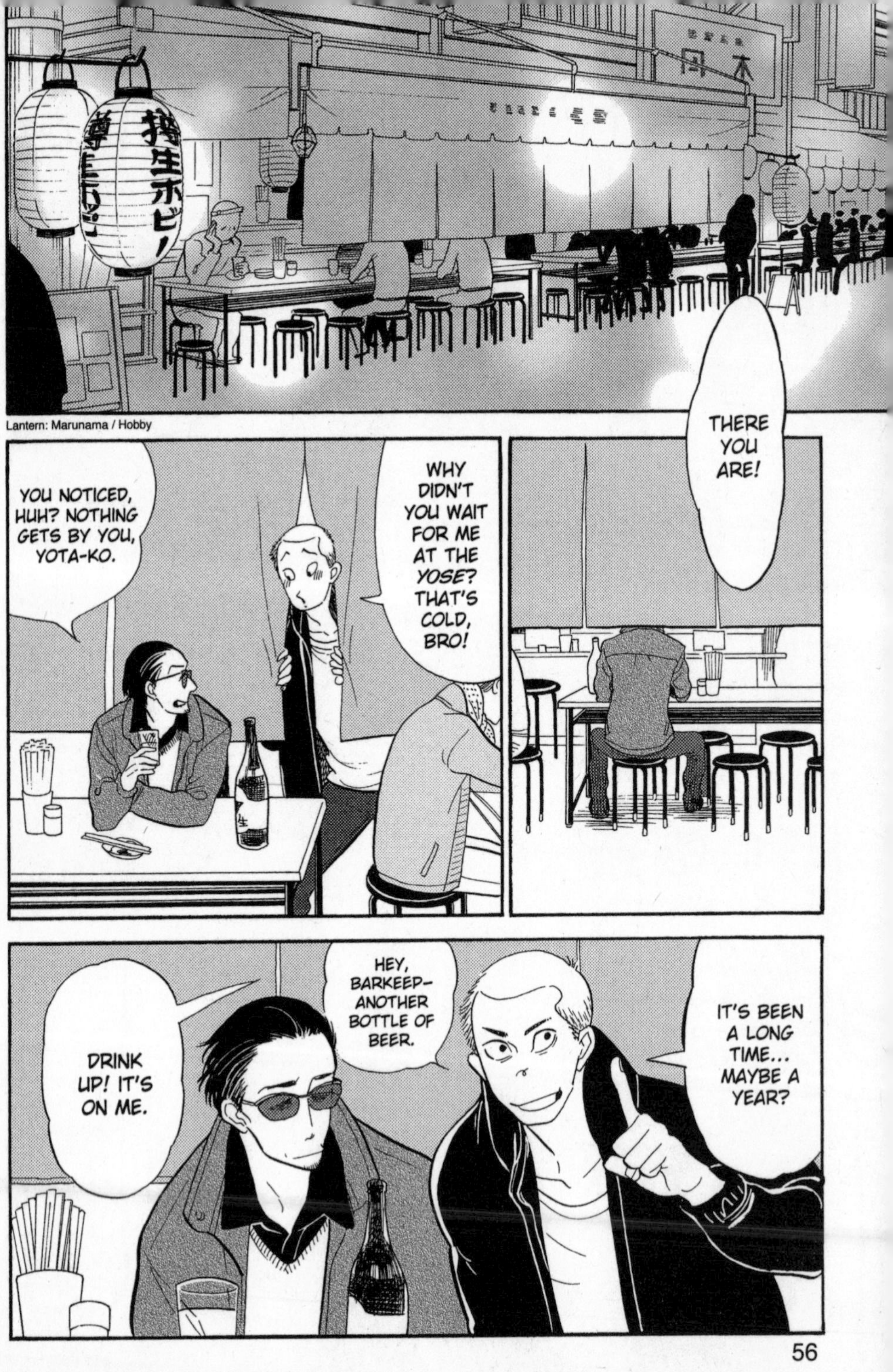
THERE YOU ARE!
WHY DIDN'T YOU WAIT FOR ME AT THE *YOSE*? THAT'S COLD, BRO!
YOU NOTICED, HUH? NOTHING GETS BY YOU, YOTA-KO.
IT'S BEEN A LONG TIME... MAYBE A YEAR?
HEY, BARKEEP– ANOTHER BOTTLE OF BEER.
DRINK UP! IT'S ON ME.
Lantern: Marunama / Hobby

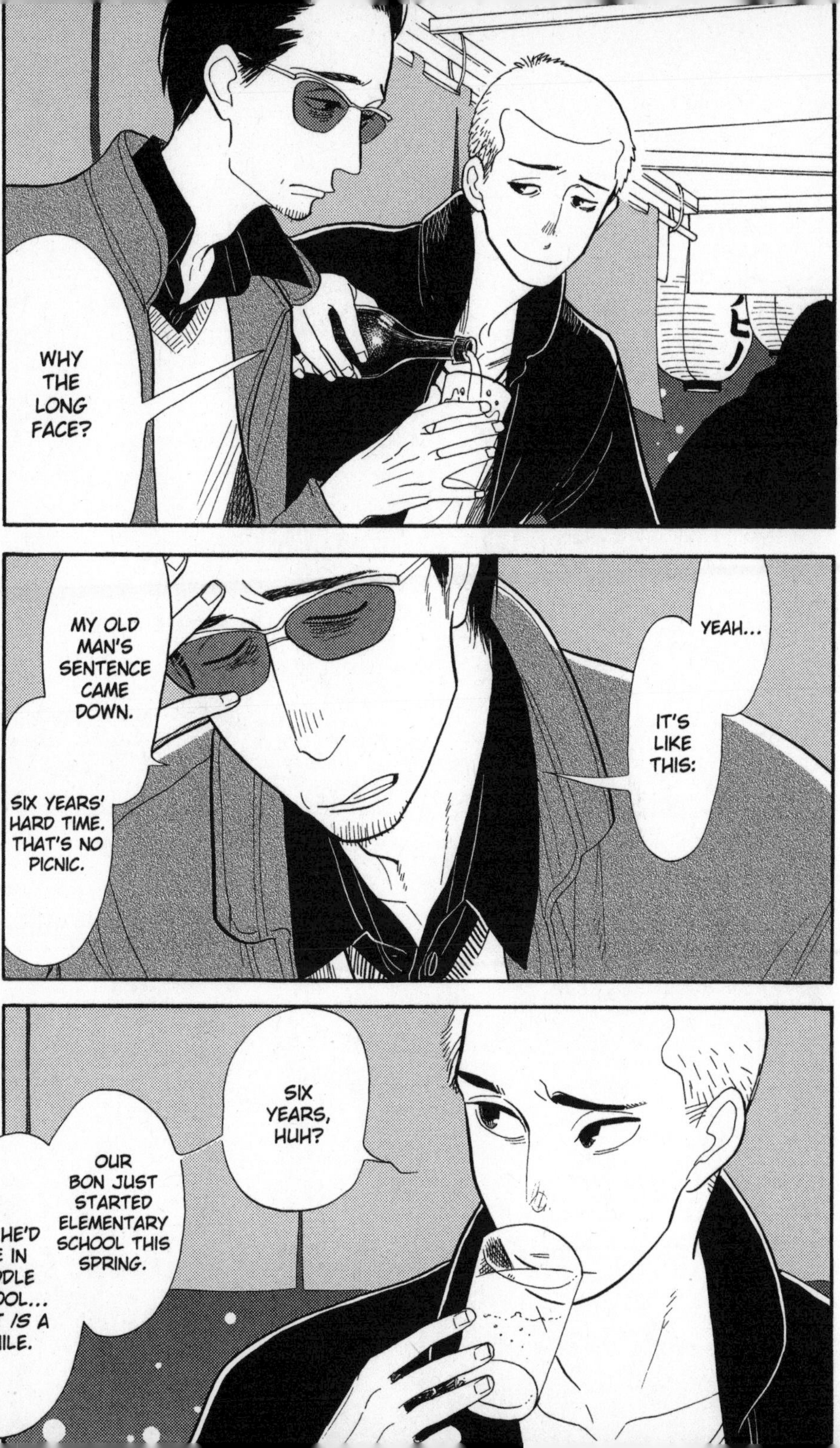
WHY THE LONG FACE?
YEAH...
IT'S LIKE THIS:
MY OLD MAN'S SENTENCE CAME DOWN.
SIX YEARS' HARD TIME. THAT'S NO PICNIC.
SIX YEARS, HUH?
OUR BON JUST STARTED ELEMENTARY SCHOOL THIS SPRING.
SO HE'D BE IN MIDDLE SCHOOL... THAT IS A WHILE.

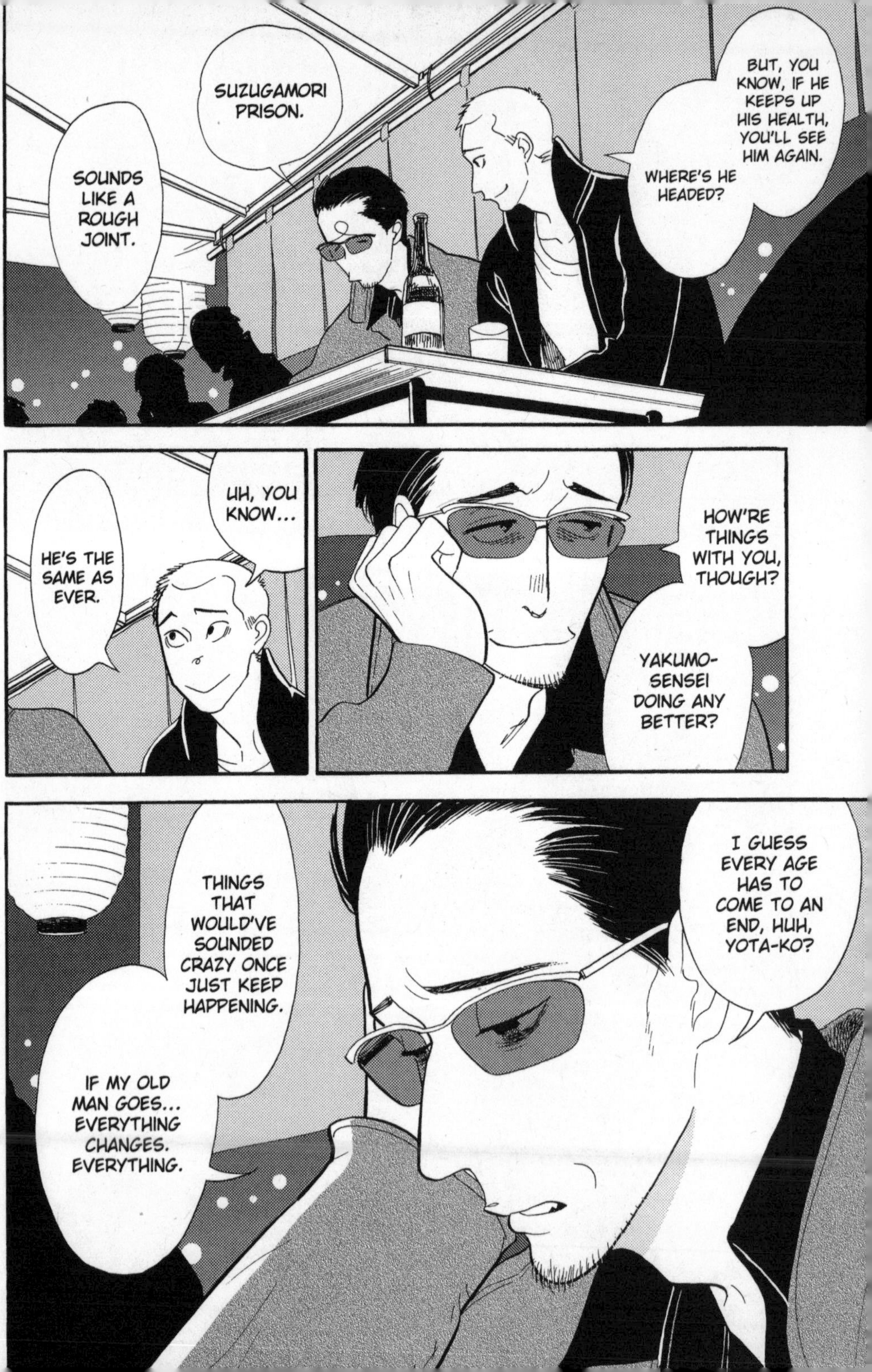
BUT, YOU KNOW, IF HE KEEPS UP HIS HEALTH, YOU'LL SEE HIM AGAIN.
WHERE'S HE HEADED?
SUZUGAMORI PRISON.
SOUNDS LIKE A ROUGH JOINT.
HOW'RE THINGS WITH YOU, THOUGH?
YAKUMO-SENSEI DOING ANY BETTER?
UH, YOU KNOW...
HE'S THE SAME AS EVER.
I GUESS EVERY AGE HAS TO COME TO AN END, HUH, YOTA-KO?
THINGS THAT WOULD'VE SOUNDED CRAZY ONCE JUST KEEP HAPPENING.
IF MY OLD MAN GOES... EVERYTHING CHANGES. EVERYTHING.

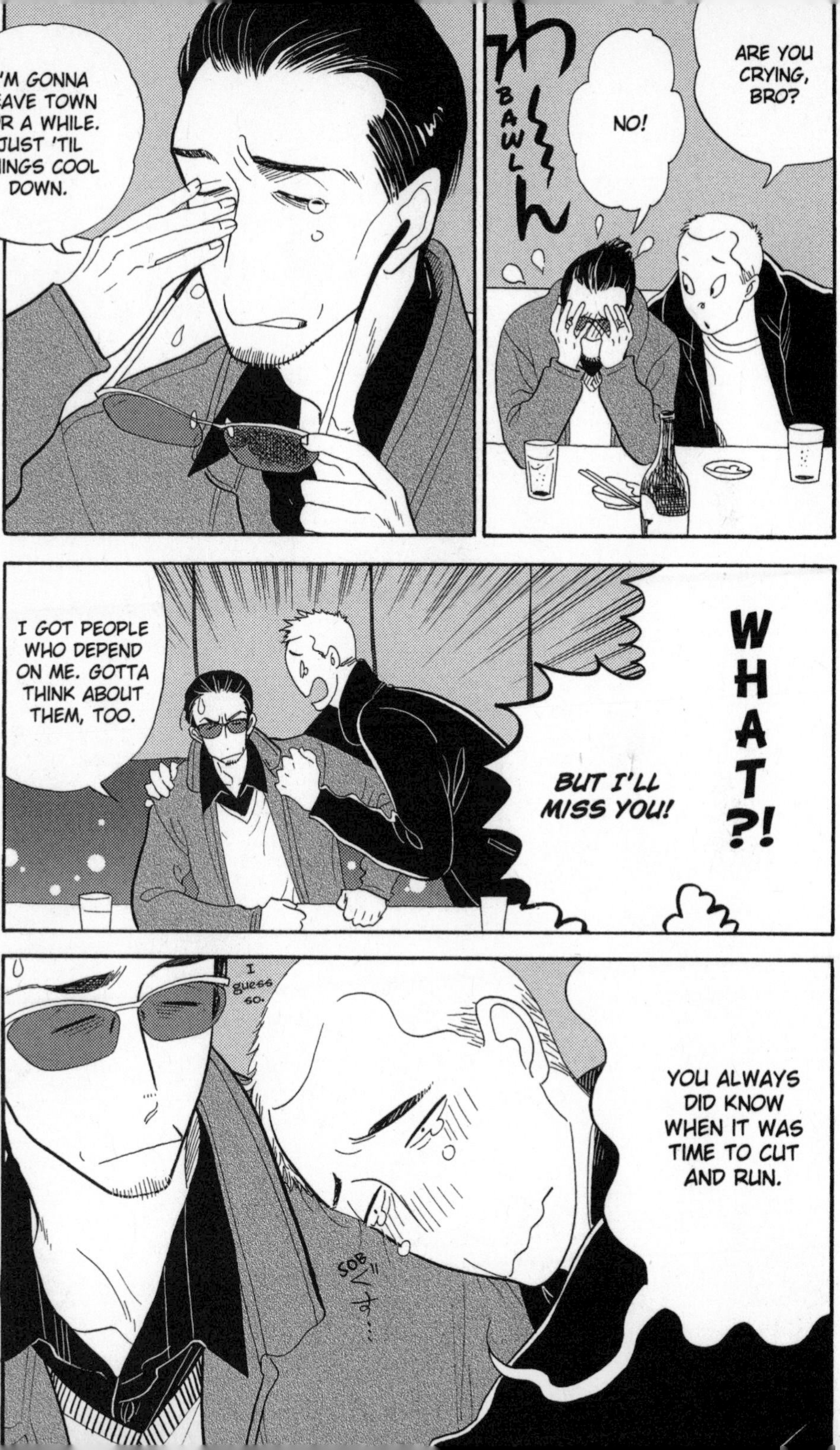
ARE YOU CRYING, BRO?
NO!
BAWL
I'M GONNA LEAVE TOWN FOR A WHILE. JUST 'TIL THINGS COOL DOWN.
WHAT?!
BUT I'LL MISS YOU!
I GOT PEOPLE WHO DEPEND ON ME. GOTTA THINK ABOUT THEM, TOO.
YOU ALWAYS DID KNOW WHEN IT WAS TIME TO CUT AND RUN.
I guess so.
SOB

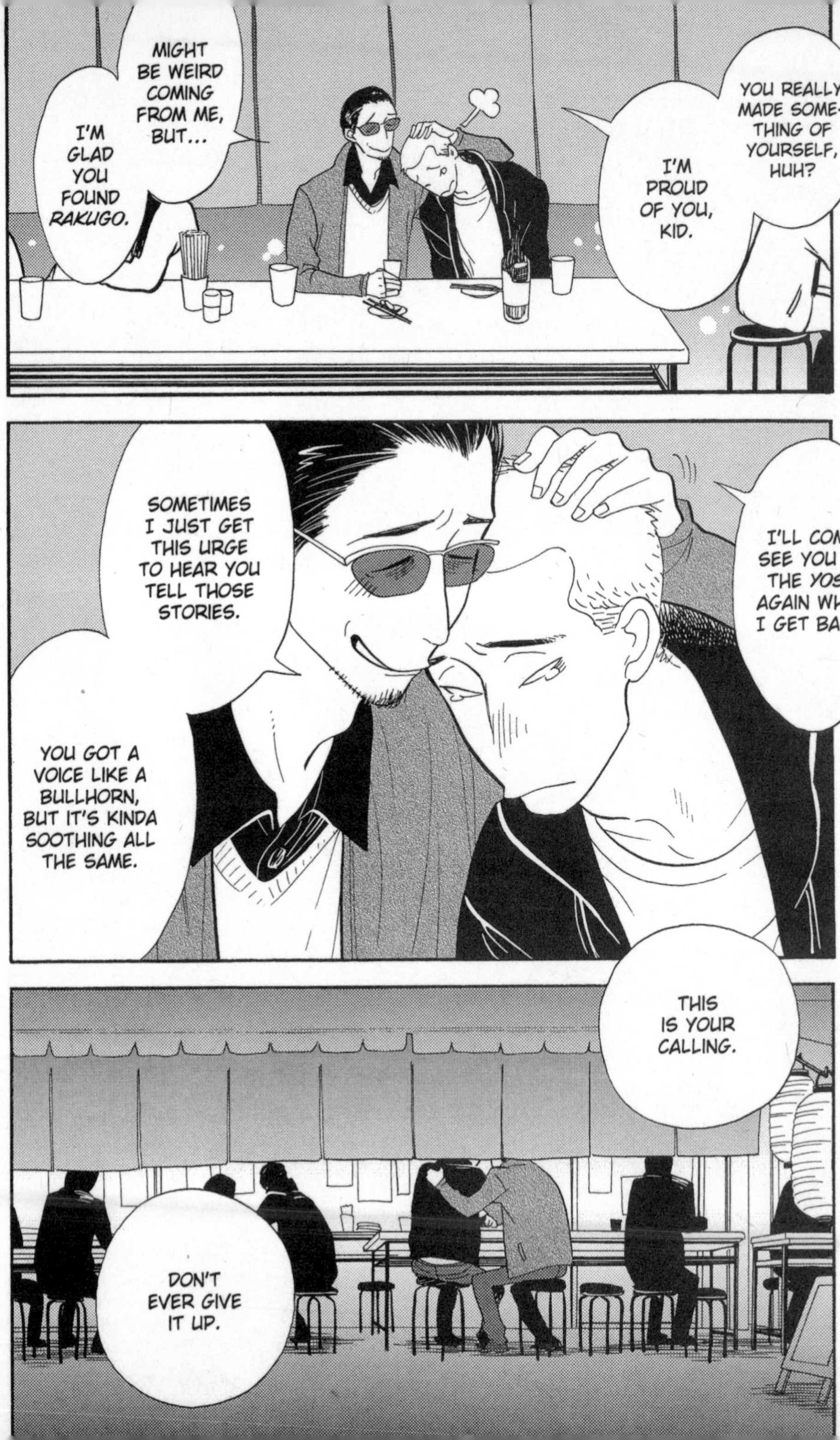
YOU REALLY MADE SOME-THING OF YOURSELF, HUH?
I'M PROUD OF YOU, KID.
MIGHT BE WEIRD COMING FROM ME, BUT...
I'M GLAD YOU FOUND *RAKUGO*.
I'LL COME SEE YOU AT THE *YOSE* AGAIN WHEN I GET BACK.
SOMETIMES I JUST GET THIS URGE TO HEAR YOU TELL THOSE STORIES.
YOU GOT A VOICE LIKE A BULLHORN, BUT IT'S KINDA SOOTHING ALL THE SAME.
THIS IS YOUR CALLING.
DON'T EVER GIVE IT UP.

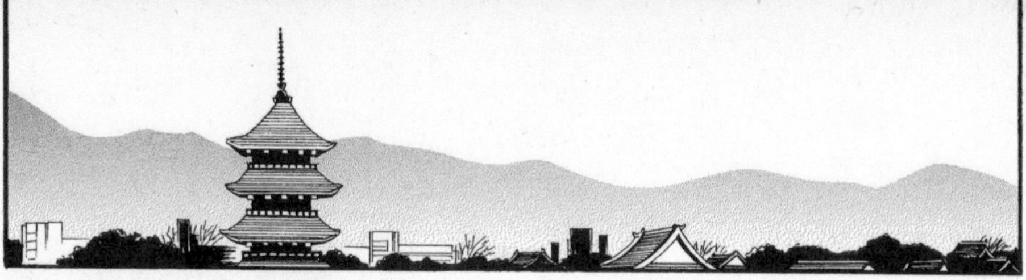

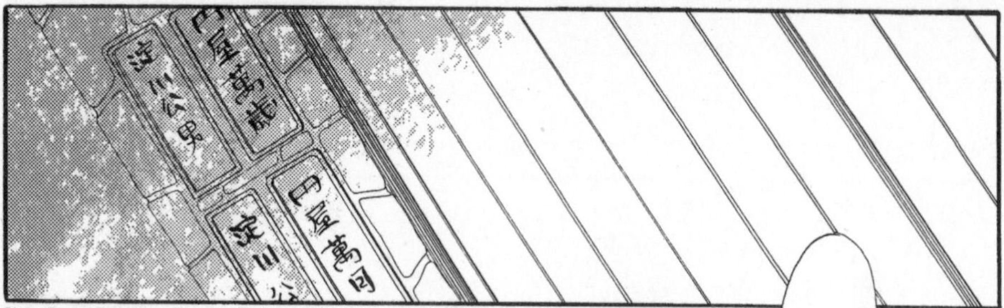
円屋萬歳
淀川公男

Signs: Bansai Tsuburaya, Mangetsu Tsuburaya, (Kimi–) Yodogawa, Kimio Yodogawa

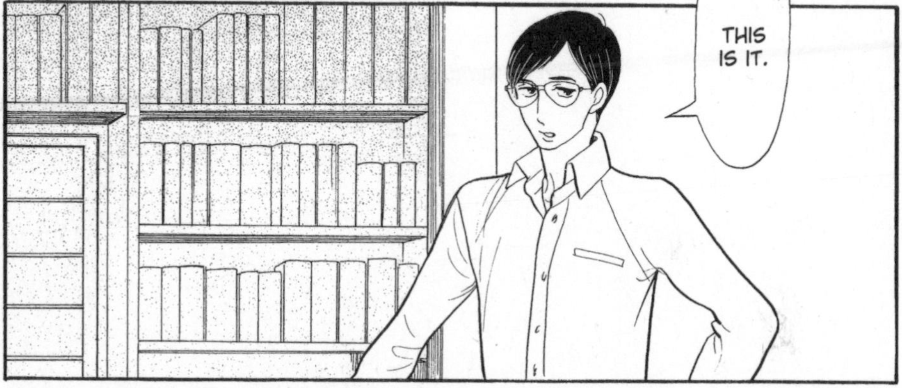
THIS IS IT.

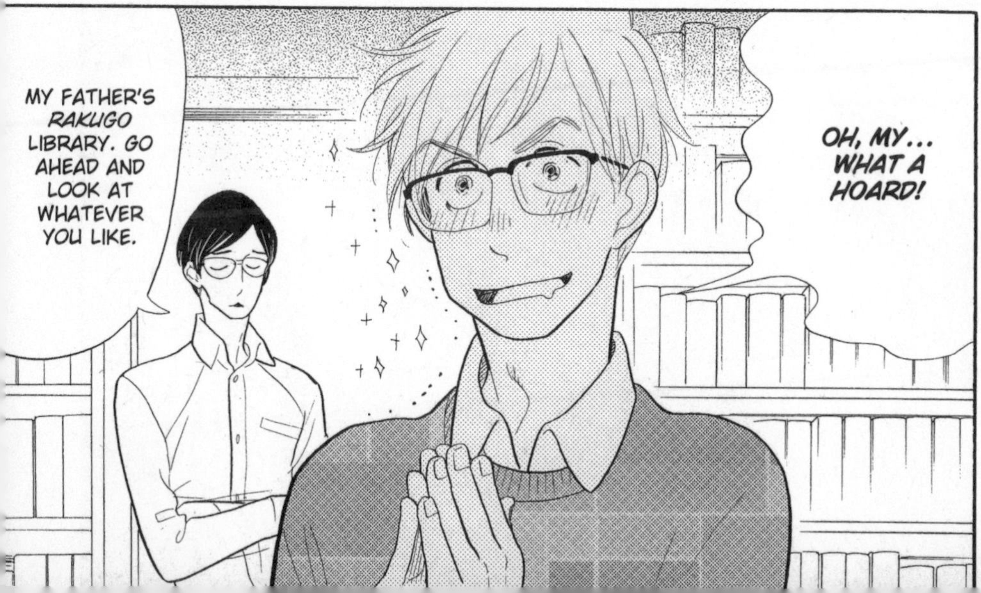
OH, MY... WHAT A HOARD!
MY FATHER'S *RAKUGO* LIBRARY. GO AHEAD AND LOOK AT WHATEVER YOU LIKE.

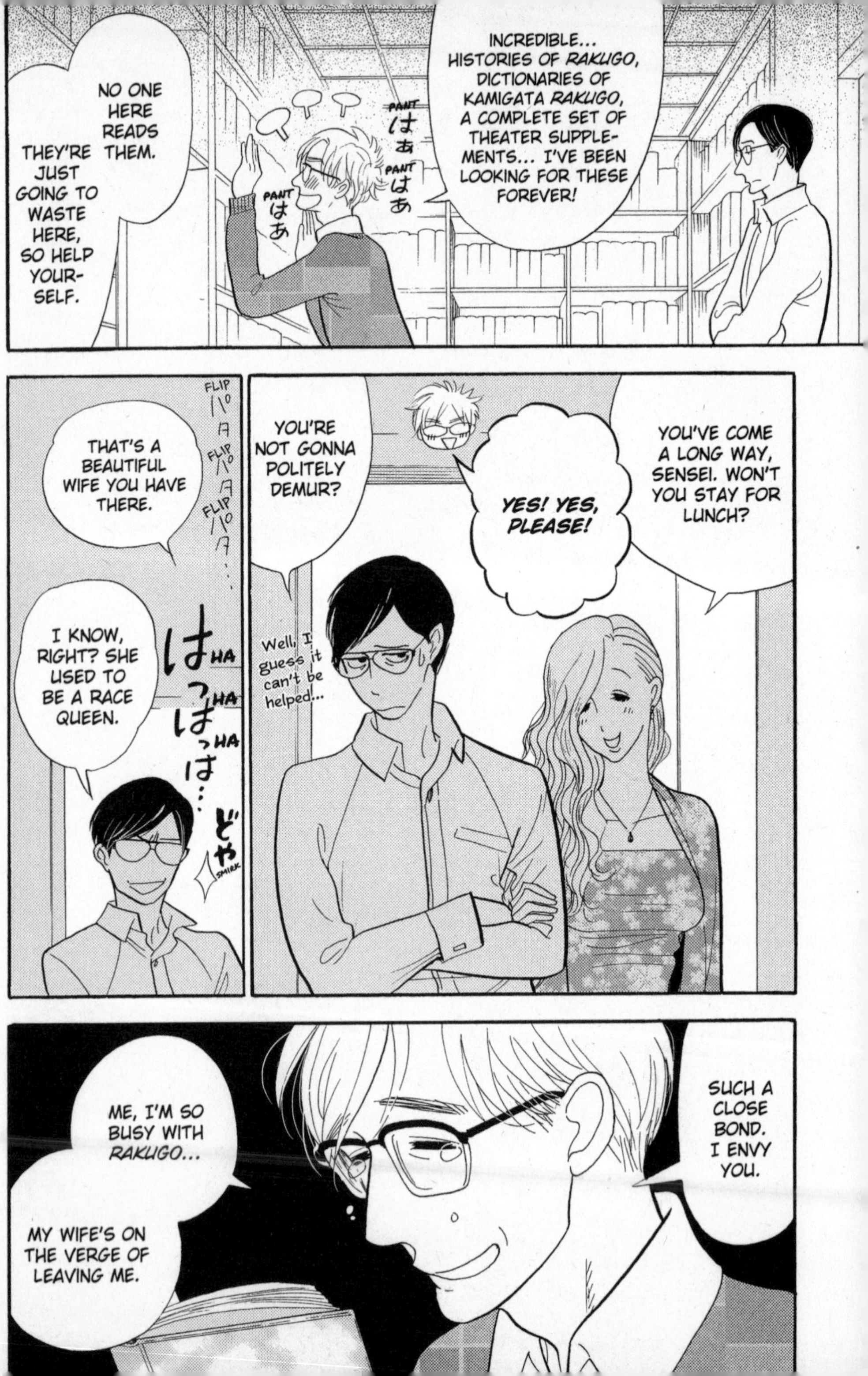
INCREDIBLE... HISTORIES OF RAKUGO, DICTIONARIES OF KAMIGATA RAKUGO, A COMPLETE SET OF THEATER SUPPLEMENTS... I'VE BEEN LOOKING FOR THESE FOREVER!
PANT はぁ PANT はぁ PANT はぁ
NO ONE HERE READS THEM.
THEY'RE JUST GOING TO WASTE HERE, SO HELP YOURSELF.
YOU'VE COME A LONG WAY, SENSEI. WON'T YOU STAY FOR LUNCH?
YES! YES, PLEASE!
YOU'RE NOT GONNA POLITELY DEMUR?
Well, I guess it can't be helped!...
THAT'S A BEAUTIFUL WIFE YOU HAVE THERE.
FLIP パ ラ FLIP パ ラ FLIP パ ラ...
I KNOW, RIGHT? SHE USED TO BE A RACE QUEEN.
は HA っ HA ぱ っ HA ぱ...
どや SMIRK
SUCH A CLOSE BOND. I ENVY YOU.
ME, I'M SO BUSY WITH RAKUGO...
MY WIFE'S ON THE VERGE OF LEAVING ME.

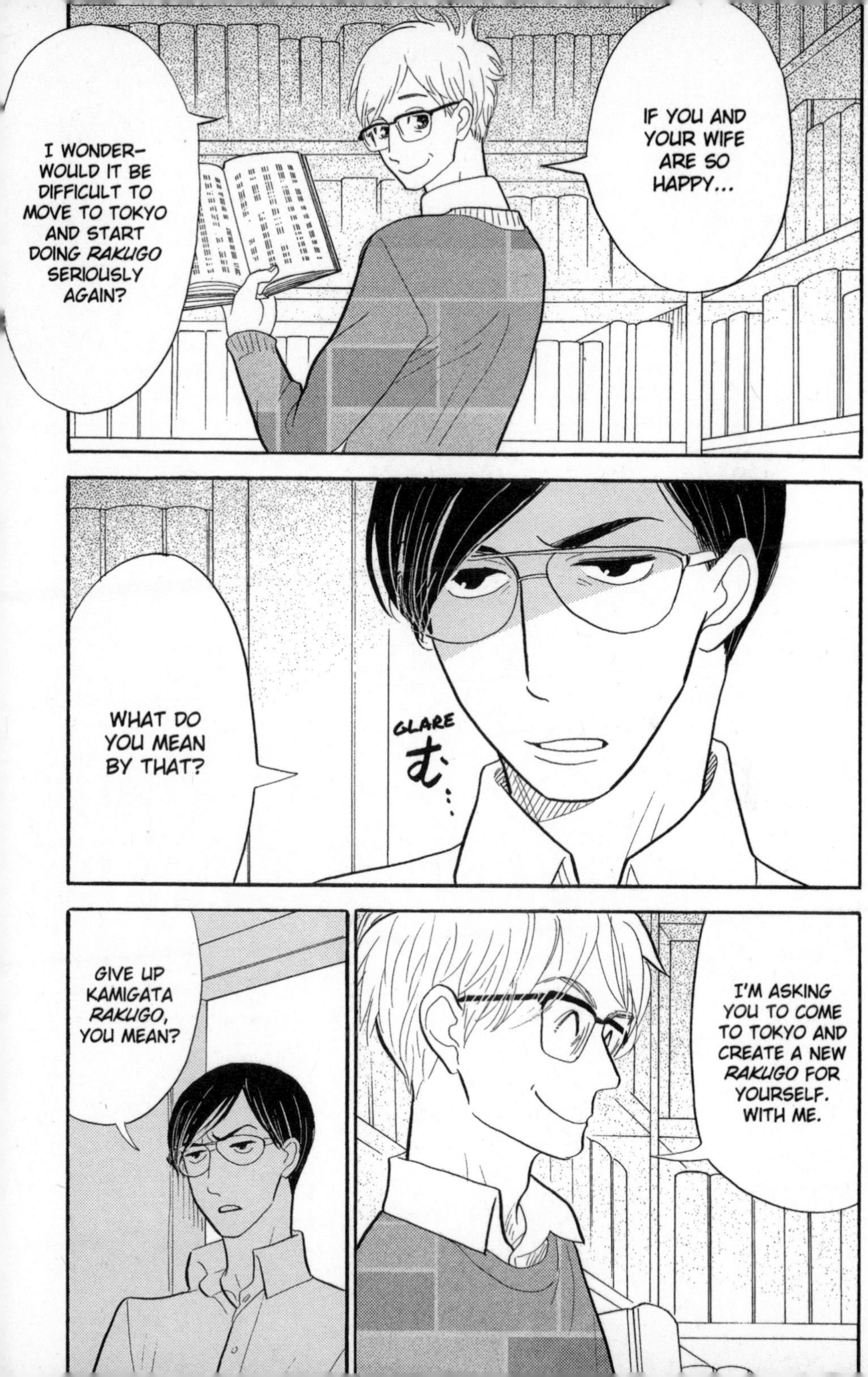
IF YOU AND YOUR WIFE ARE SO HAPPY...
I WONDER—WOULD IT BE DIFFICULT TO MOVE TO TOKYO AND START DOING *RAKUGO* SERIOUSLY AGAIN?
GLARE む
WHAT DO YOU MEAN BY THAT?
I'M ASKING YOU TO COME TO TOKYO AND CREATE A NEW *RAKUGO* FOR YOURSELF. WITH ME.
GIVE UP KAMIGATA *RAKUGO*, YOU MEAN?

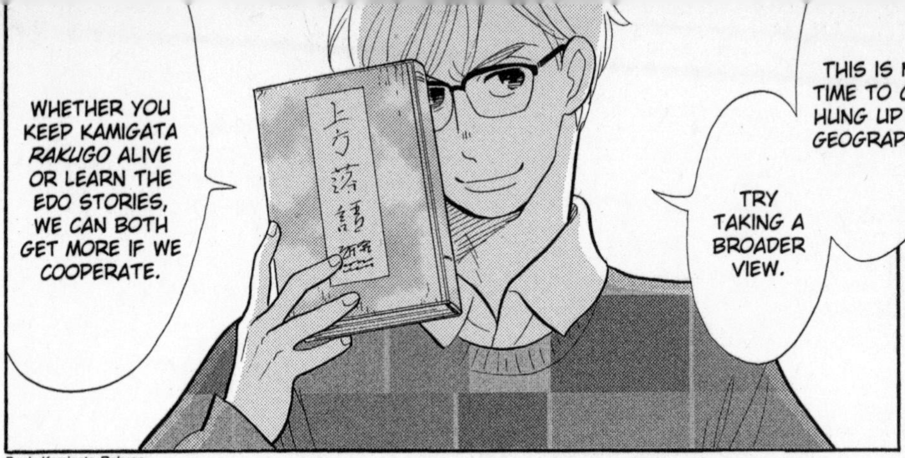
THIS IS NO TIME TO GET HUNG UP ON GEOGRAPHY.
TRY TAKING A BROADER VIEW.
WHETHER YOU KEEP KAMIGATA *RAKUGO* ALIVE OR LEARN THE EDO STORIES, WE CAN BOTH GET MORE IF WE COOPERATE.

Book: Kamigata *Rakugo*

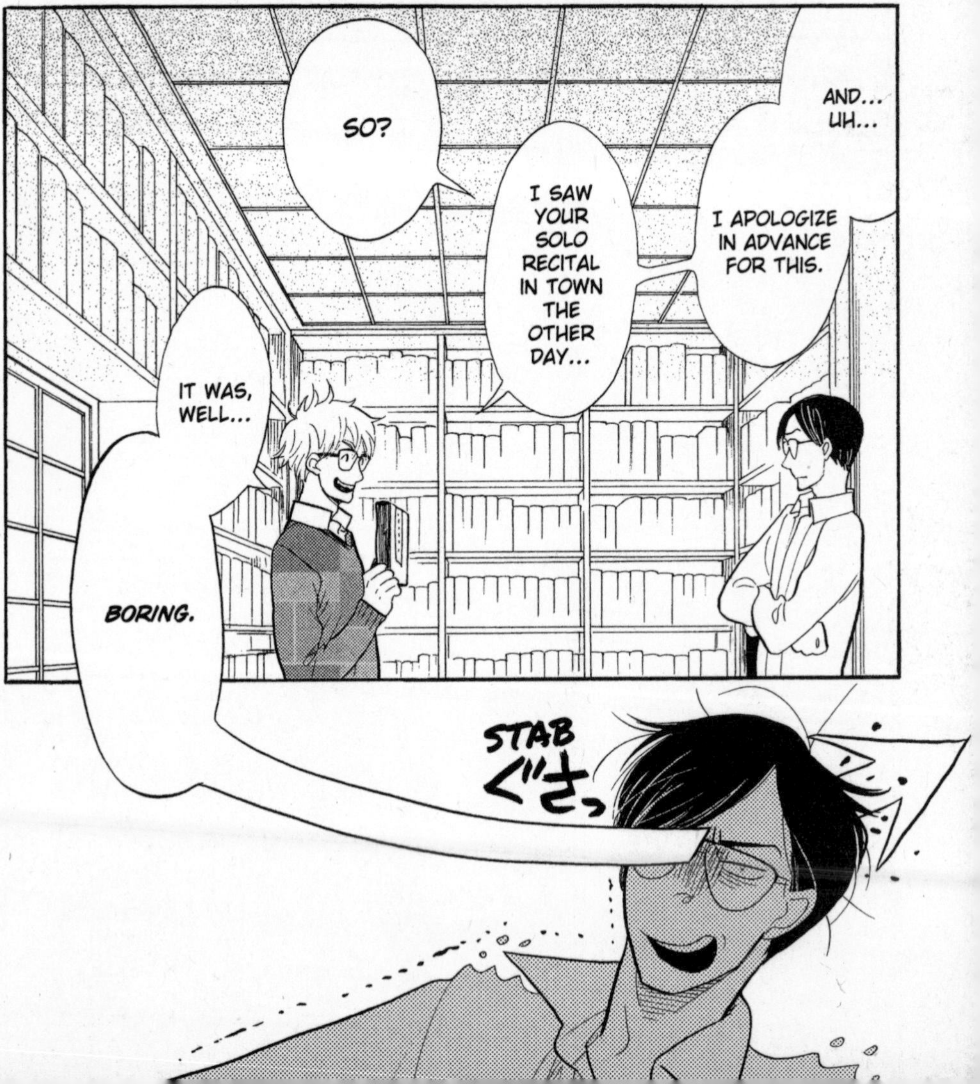
AND... UH...
I APOLOGIZE IN ADVANCE FOR THIS.
SO?
I SAW YOUR SOLO RECITAL IN TOWN THE OTHER DAY...
IT WAS, WELL...
BORING.
STAB
ぐさっ

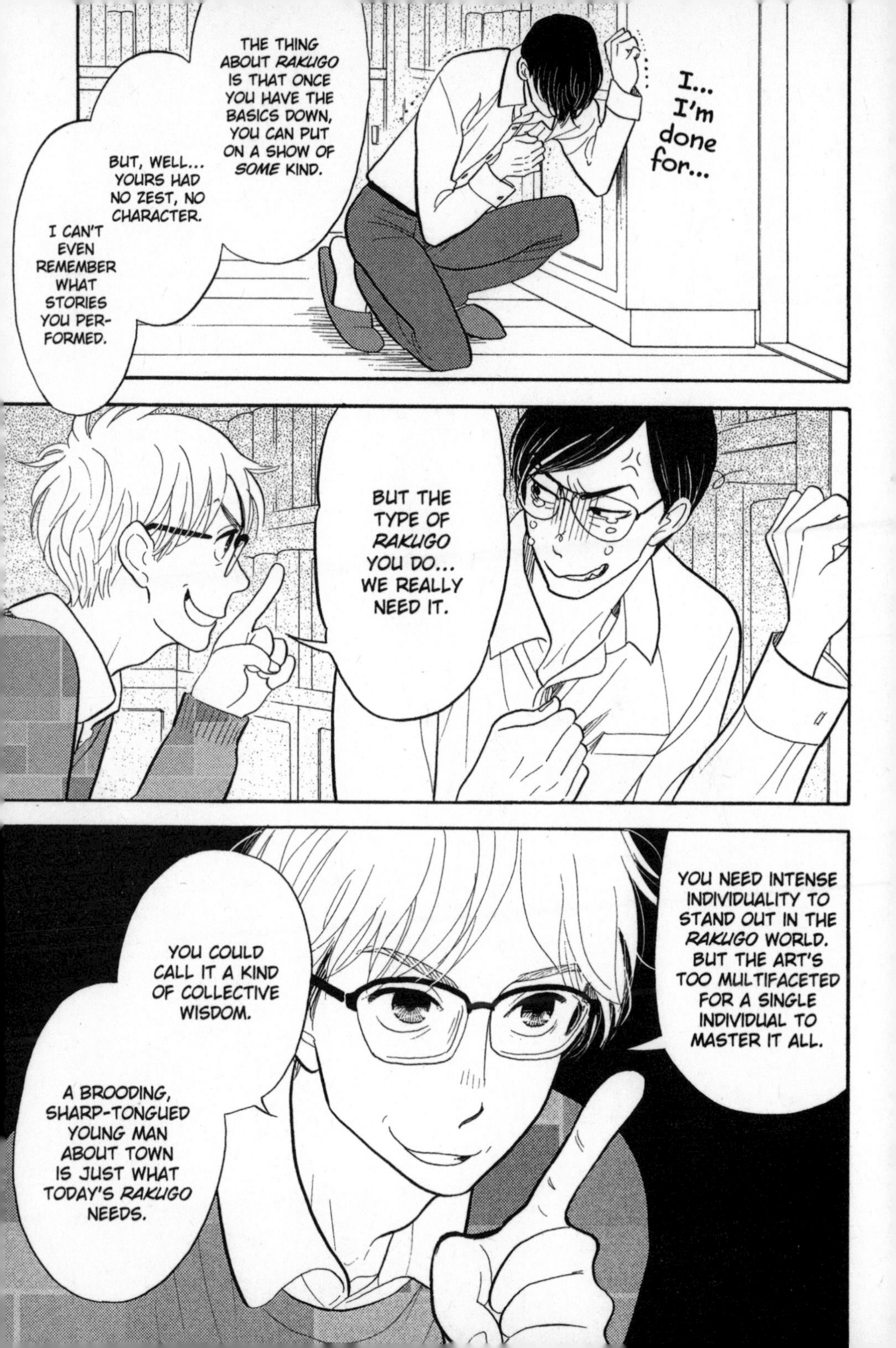

I... I'm done for...
THE THING ABOUT *RAKUGO* IS THAT ONCE YOU HAVE THE BASICS DOWN, YOU CAN PUT ON A SHOW OF *SOME* KIND.
BUT, WELL... YOURS HAD NO ZEST, NO CHARACTER.
I CAN'T EVEN REMEMBER WHAT STORIES YOU PER-FORMED.
BUT THE TYPE OF *RAKUGO* YOU DO... WE REALLY NEED IT.
YOU NEED INTENSE INDIVIDUALITY TO STAND OUT IN THE *RAKUGO* WORLD. BUT THE ART'S TOO MULTIFACETED FOR A SINGLE INDIVIDUAL TO MASTER IT ALL.
YOU COULD CALL IT A KIND OF COLLECTIVE WISDOM.
A BROODING, SHARP-TONGUED YOUNG MAN ABOUT TOWN IS JUST WHAT TODAY'S *RAKUGO* NEEDS.

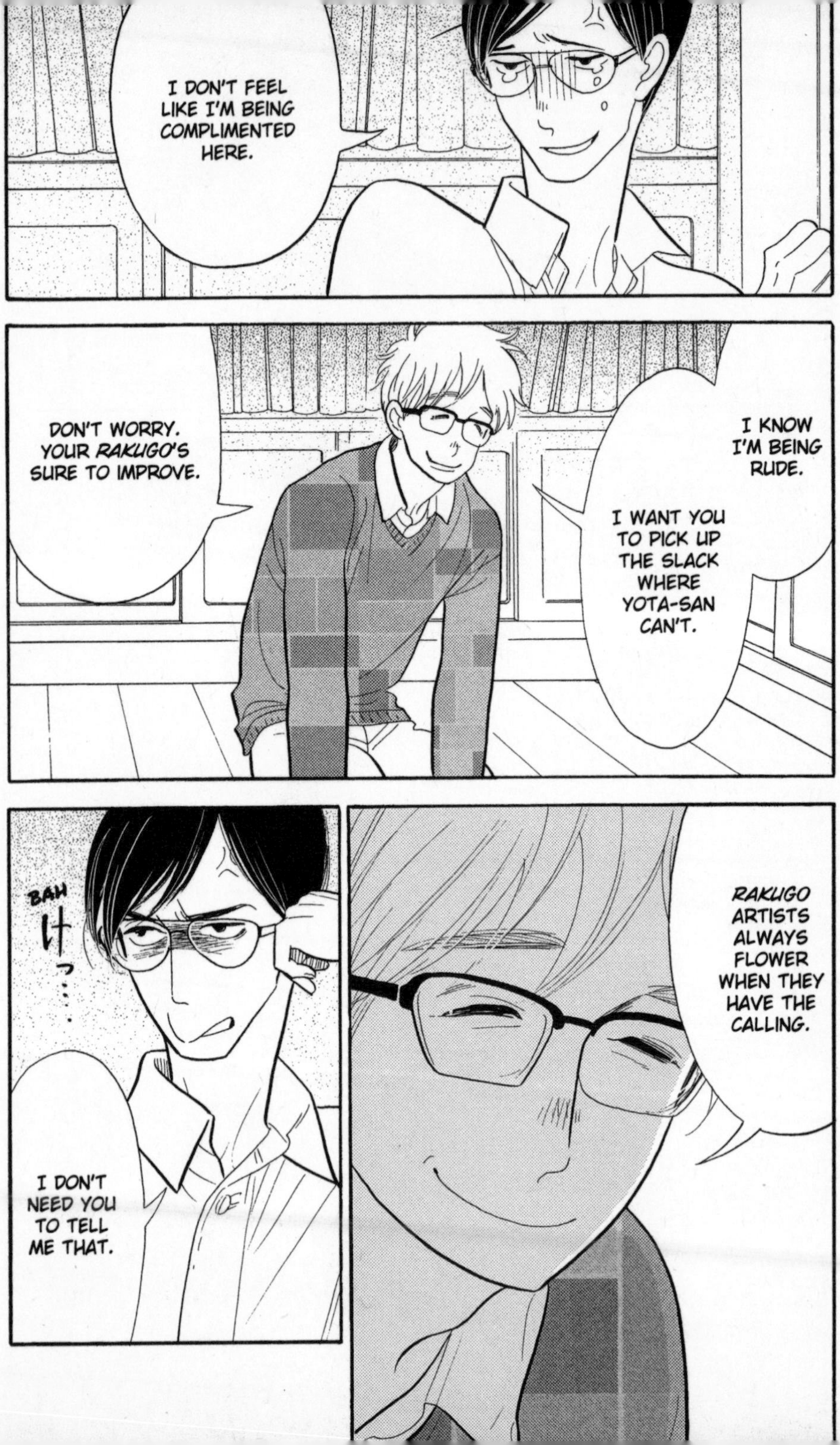
I DON'T FEEL LIKE I'M BEING COMPLIMENTED HERE.
I KNOW I'M BEING RUDE.
I WANT YOU TO PICK UP THE SLACK WHERE YOTA-SAN CAN'T.
DON'T WORRY. YOUR *RAKUGO*'S SURE TO IMPROVE.
RAKUGO ARTISTS ALWAYS FLOWER WHEN THEY HAVE THE CALLING.
BAH
I DON'T NEED YOU TO TELL ME THAT.

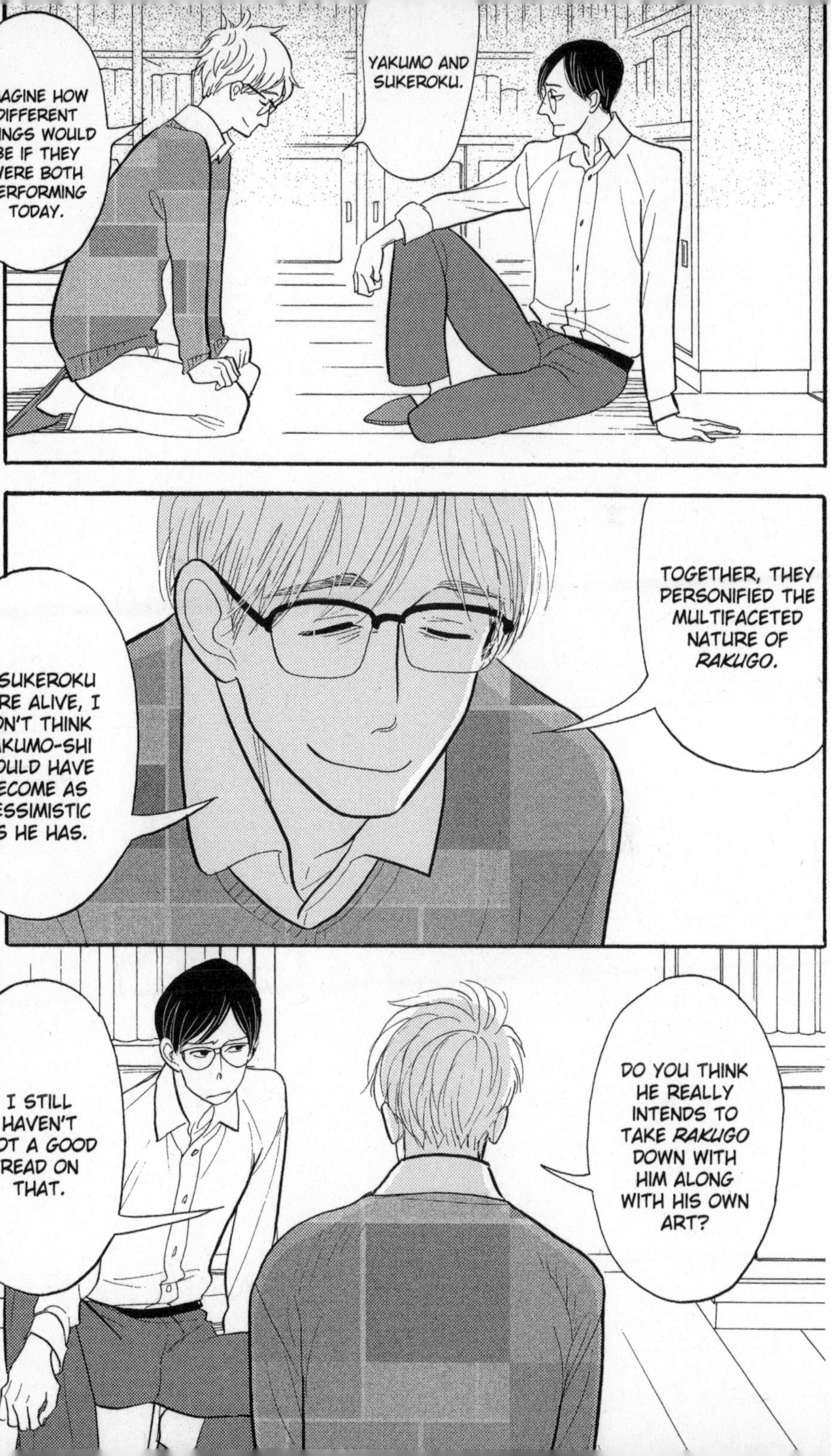
YAKUMO AND SUKEROKU.
IMAGINE HOW DIFFERENT THINGS WOULD BE IF THEY WERE BOTH PERFORMING TODAY.
TOGETHER, THEY PERSONIFIED THE MULTIFACETED NATURE OF *RAKUGO*.
IF SUKEROKU WERE ALIVE, I DON'T THINK YAKUMO-SHI WOULD HAVE BECOME AS PESSIMISTIC AS HE HAS.
DO YOU THINK HE REALLY INTENDS TO TAKE *RAKUGO* DOWN WITH HIM ALONG WITH HIS OWN ART?
I STILL HAVEN'T GOT A GOOD READ ON THAT.

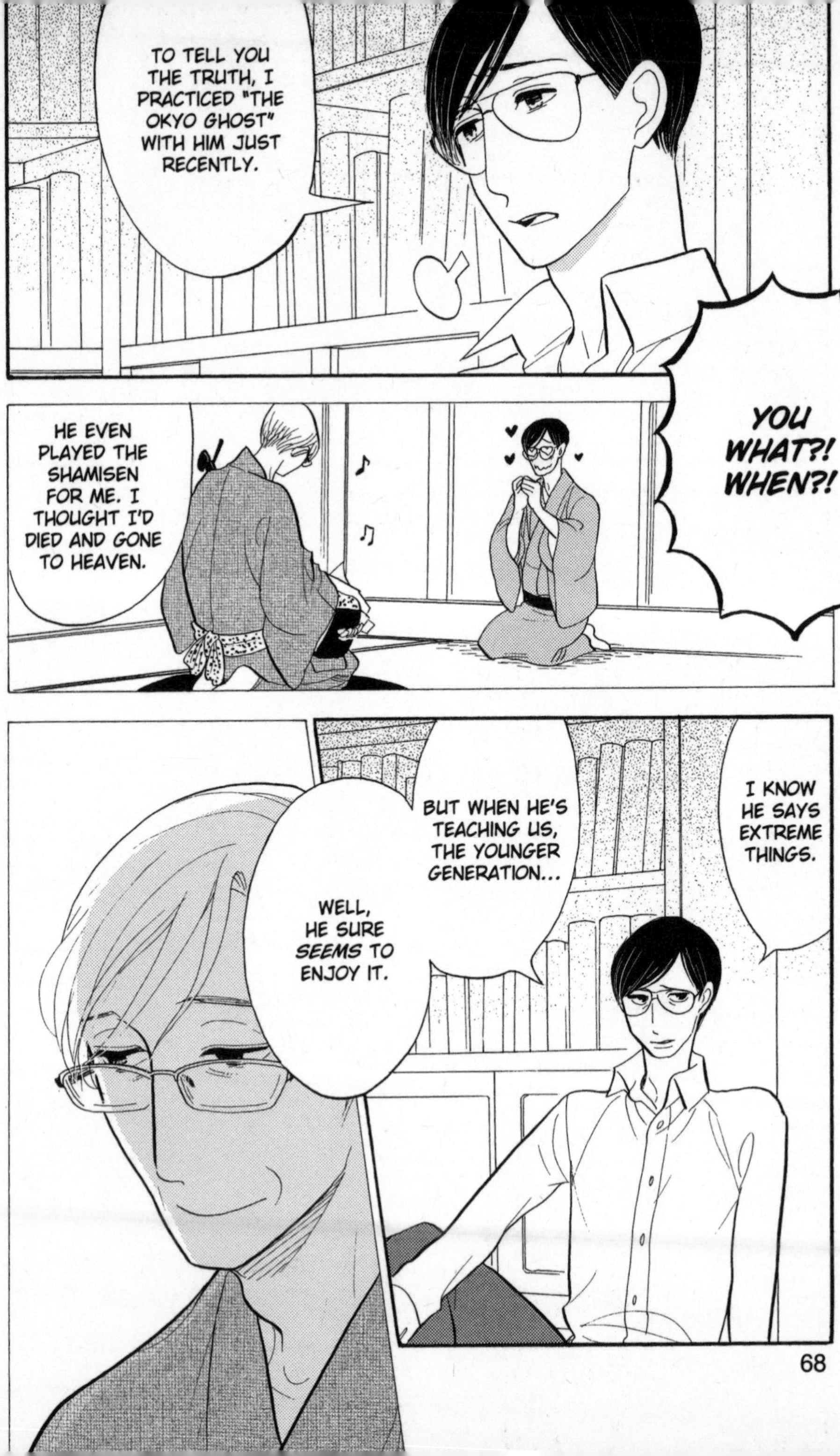
TO TELL YOU THE TRUTH, I PRACTICED "THE OKYO GHOST" WITH HIM JUST RECENTLY.
YOU WHAT?! WHEN?!
HE EVEN PLAYED THE SHAMISEN FOR ME. I THOUGHT I'D DIED AND GONE TO HEAVEN.
I KNOW HE SAYS EXTREME THINGS.
BUT WHEN HE'S TEACHING US, THE YOUNGER GENERATION...
WELL, HE SURE *SEEMS* TO ENJOY IT.

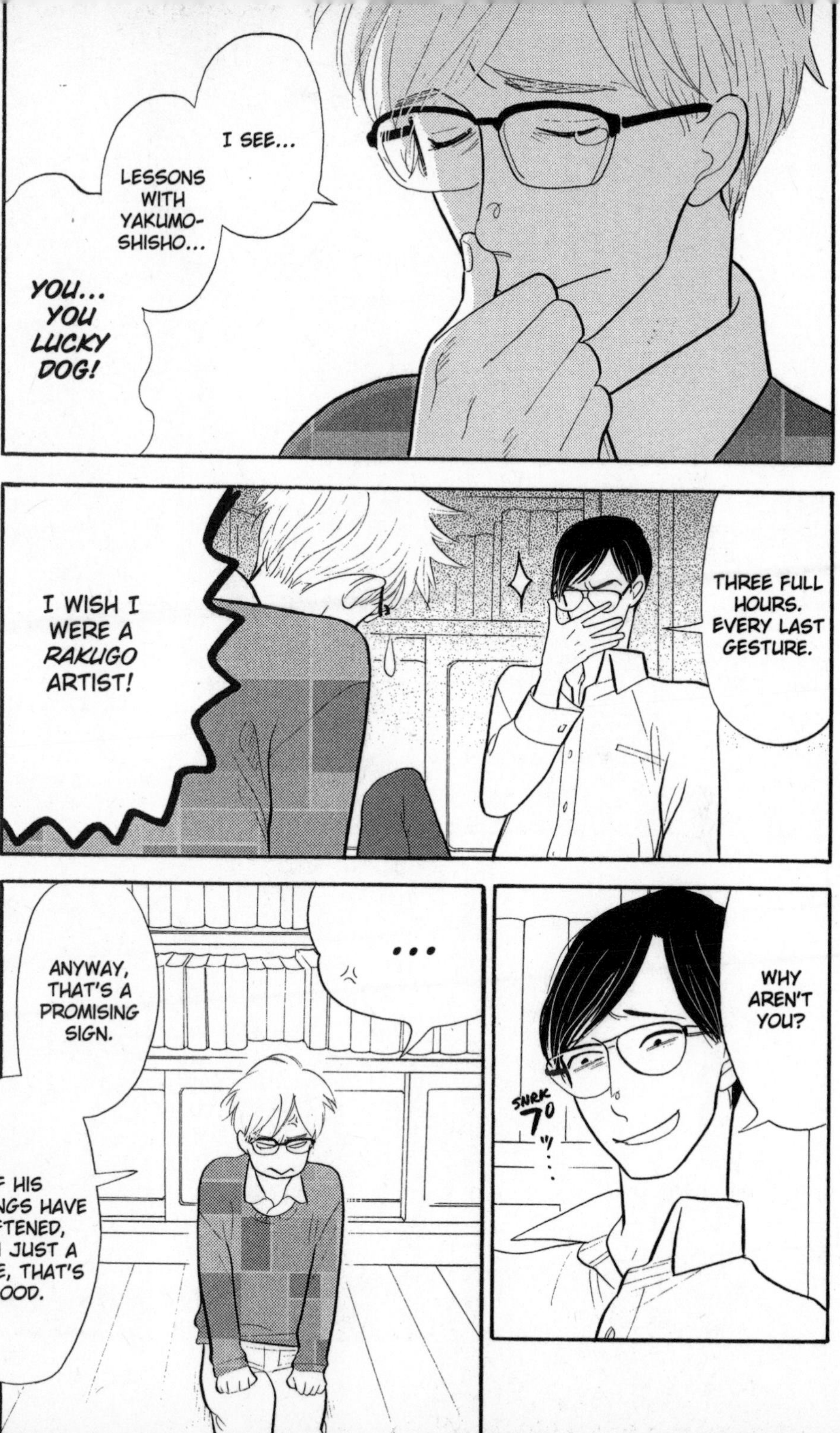
I SEE... LESSONS WITH YAKUMO-SHISHO...
YOU... YOU LUCKY DOG!
THREE FULL HOURS. EVERY LAST GESTURE.
I WISH I WERE A *RAKUGO* ARTIST!
WHY AREN'T YOU?
SNRK
...
ANYWAY, THAT'S A PROMISING SIGN.
IF HIS FEELINGS HAVE SOFTENED, EVEN JUST A LITTLE, THAT'S GOOD.

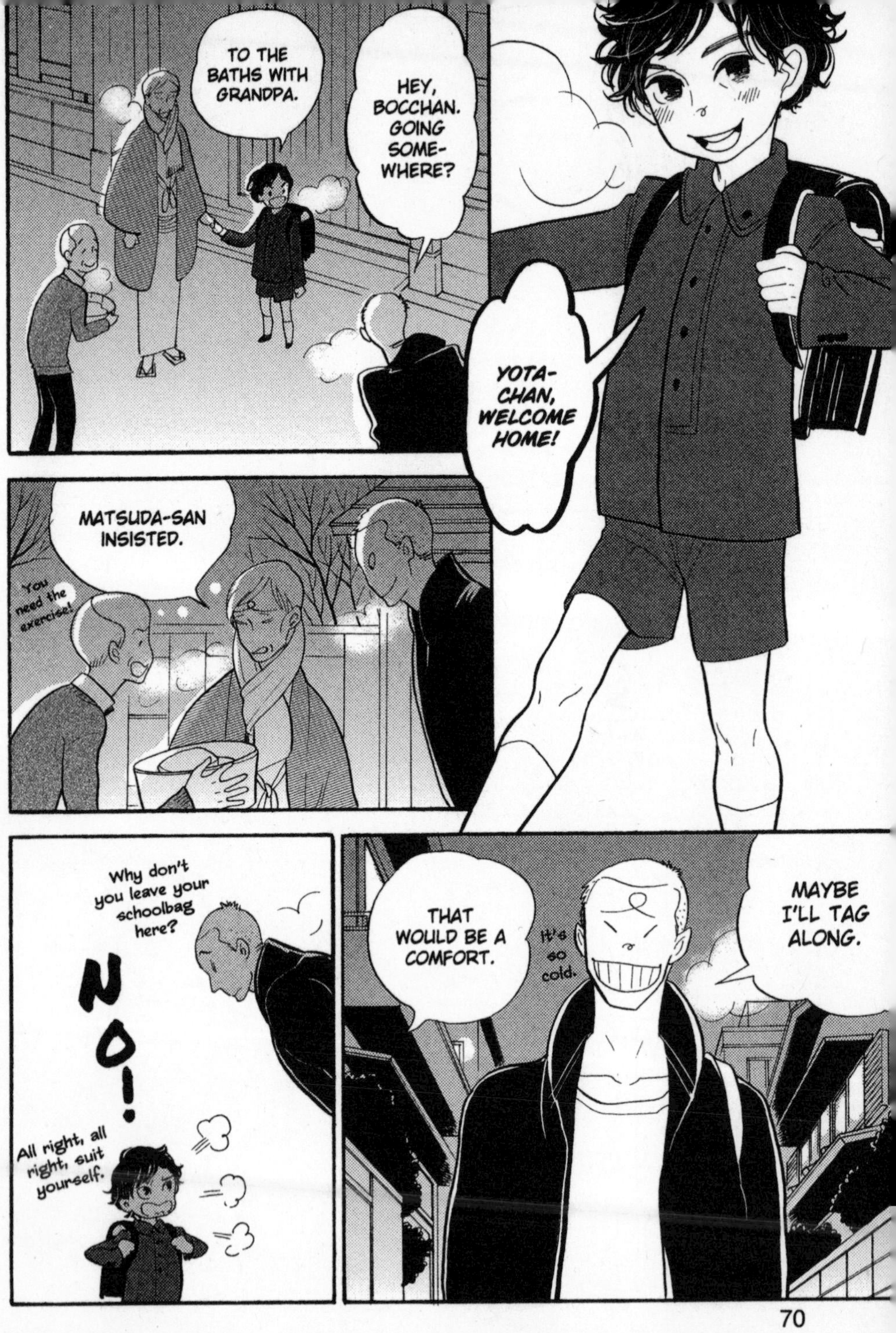
YOTA-CHAN, WELCOME HOME!
HEY, BOCCHAN. GOING SOME-WHERE?
TO THE BATHS WITH GRANDPA.
MATSUDA-SAN INSISTED.
You need the exercise!
MAYBE I'LL TAG ALONG.
THAT WOULD BE A COMFORT.
It's so cold.
Why don't you leave your schoolbag here?
NO!
All right, all right, suit yourself.

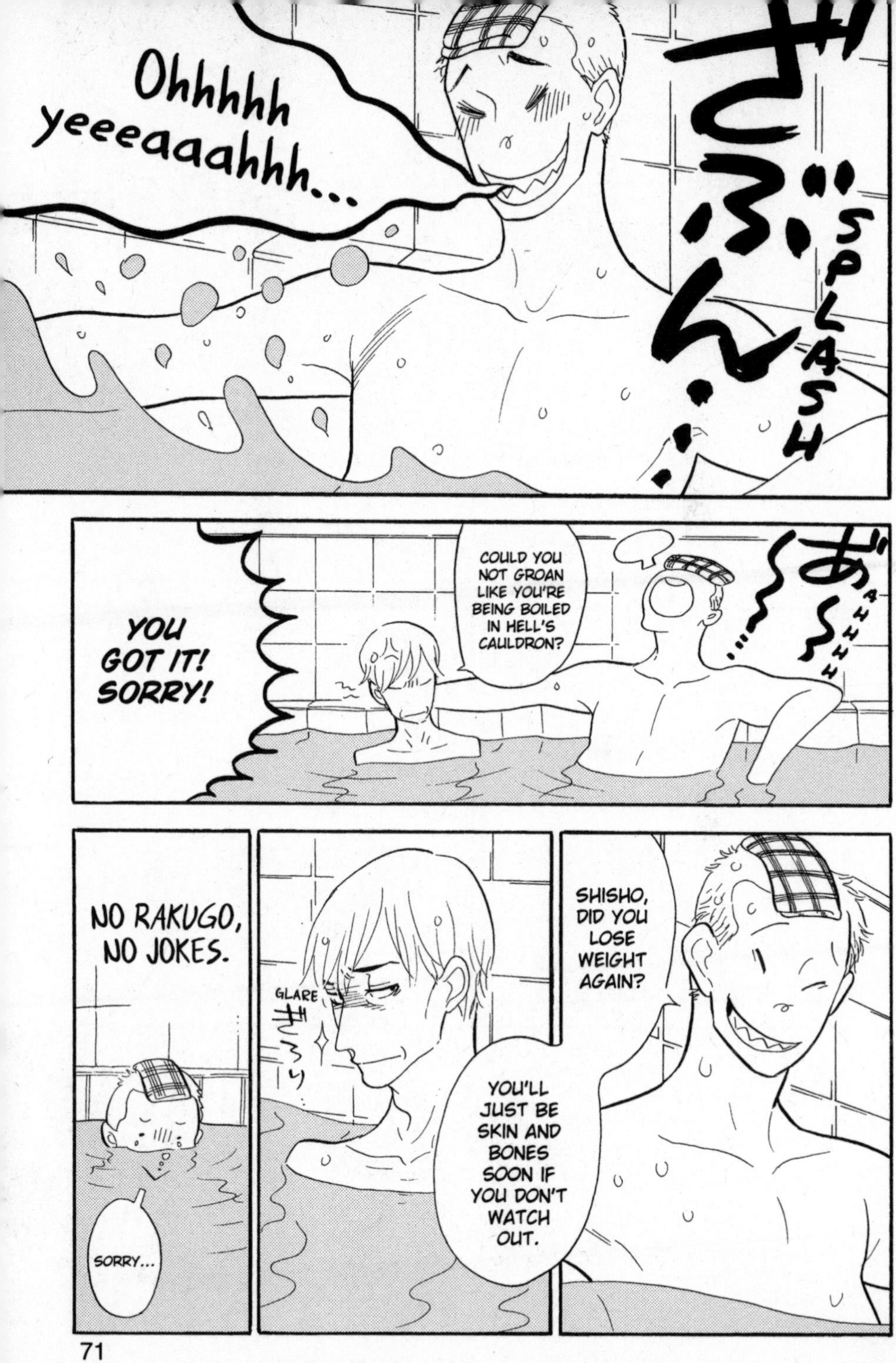
ざぶん
SPLASH
Ohhhhh yeeeaaahhh...
あ〜〜…
AHHHHH
COULD YOU NOT GROAN LIKE YOU'RE BEING BOILED IN HELL'S CAULDRON?
YOU GOT IT! SORRY!
SHISHO, DID YOU LOSE WEIGHT AGAIN?
YOU'LL JUST BE SKIN AND BONES SOON IF YOU DON'T WATCH OUT.
GLARE
ぎろり
NO RAKUGO, NO JOKES.
SORRY...

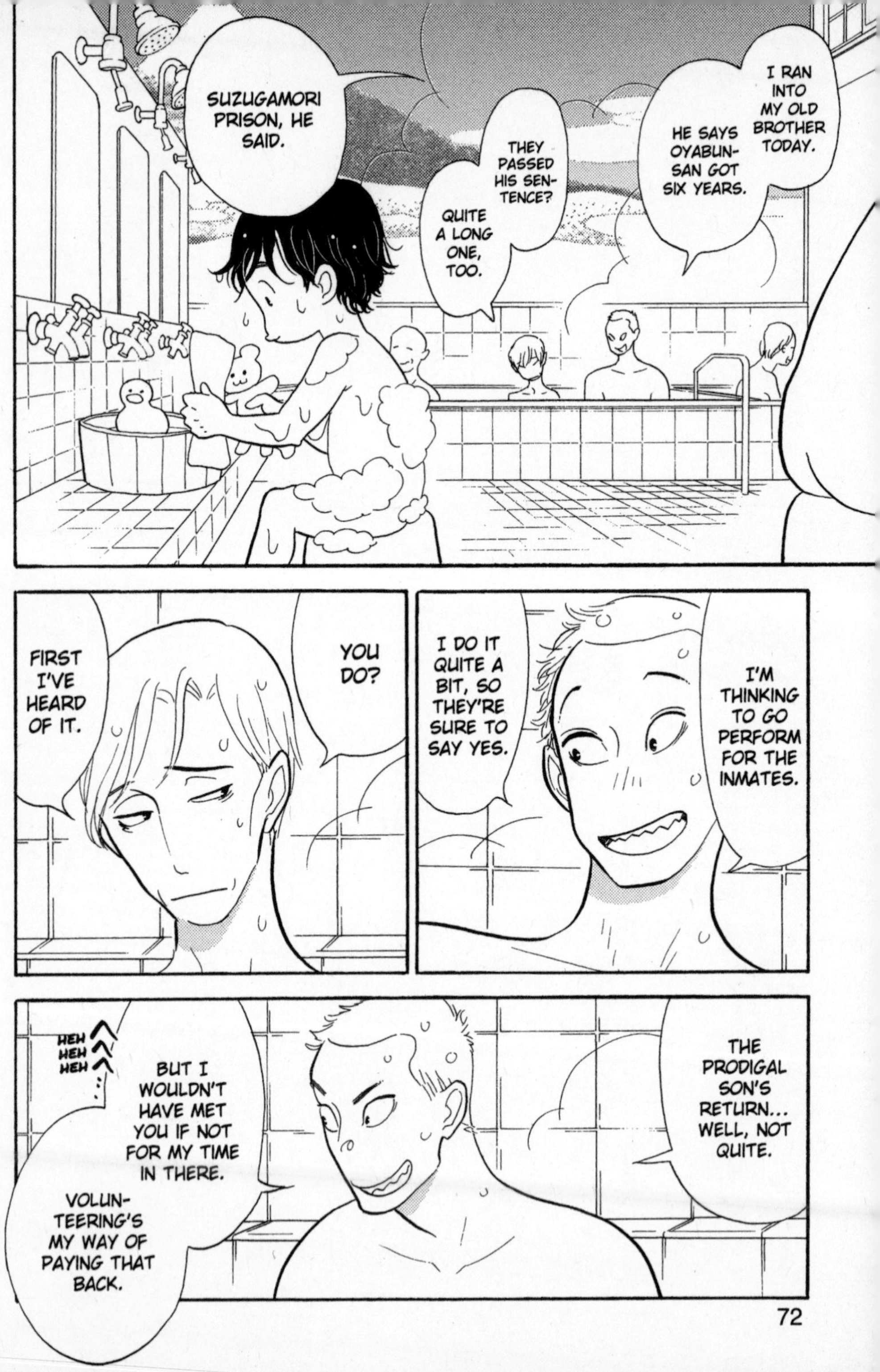
I RAN INTO MY OLD BROTHER TODAY.
HE SAYS OYABUN-SAN GOT SIX YEARS.
THEY PASSED HIS SENTENCE?
QUITE A LONG ONE, TOO.
SUZUGAMORI PRISON, HE SAID.
I'M THINKING TO GO PERFORM FOR THE INMATES.
I DO IT QUITE A BIT, SO THEY'RE SURE TO SAY YES.
YOU DO?
FIRST I'VE HEARD OF IT.
THE PRODIGAL SON'S RETURN... WELL, NOT QUITE.
HEH HEH HEH
...
BUT I WOULDN'T HAVE MET YOU IF NOT FOR MY TIME IN THERE.
VOLUNTEERING'S MY WAY OF PAYING THAT BACK.

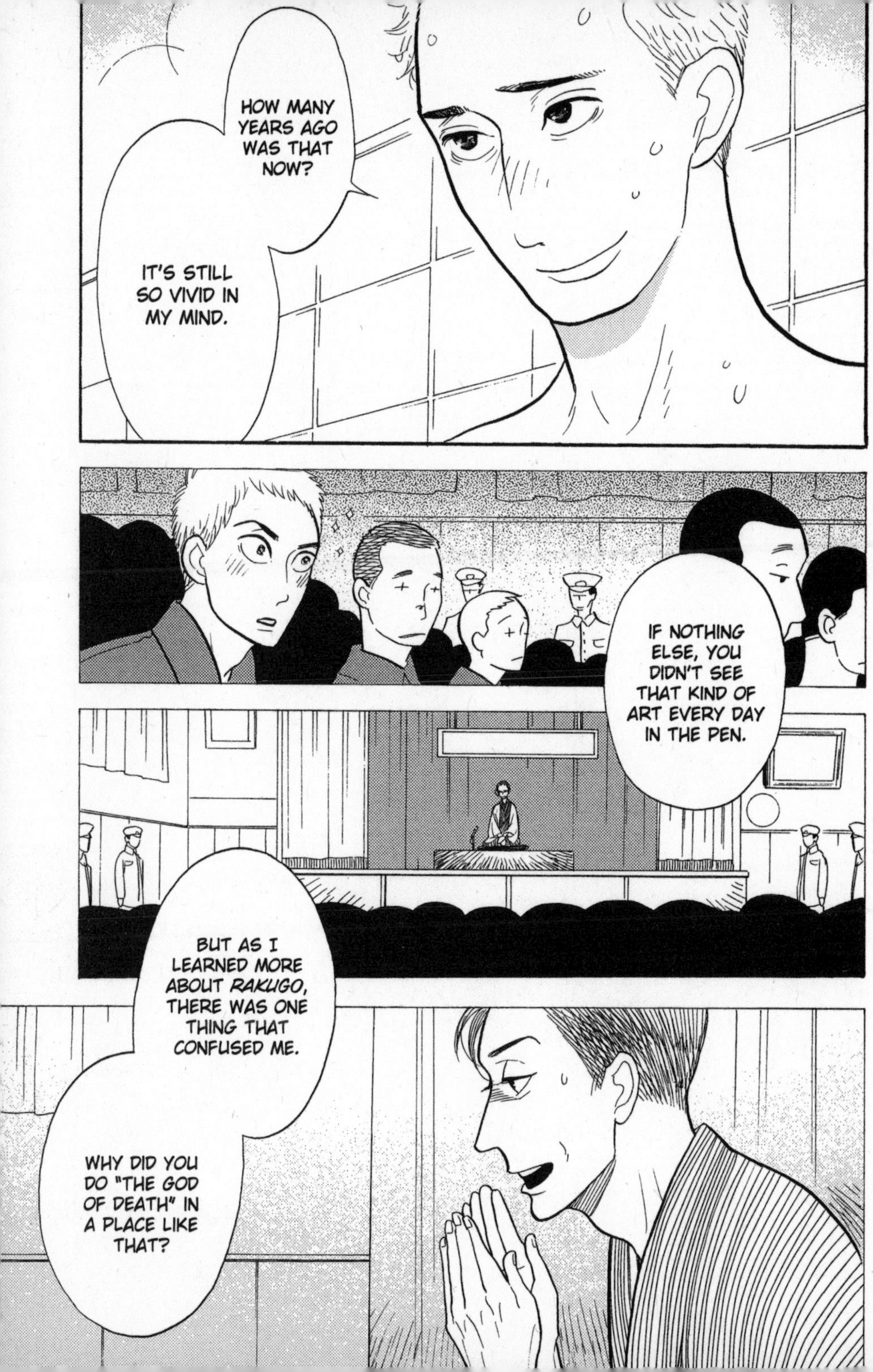
HOW MANY YEARS AGO WAS THAT NOW?
IT'S STILL SO VIVID IN MY MIND.
IF NOTHING ELSE, YOU DIDN'T SEE THAT KIND OF ART EVERY DAY IN THE PEN.
BUT AS I LEARNED MORE ABOUT *RAKUGO*, THERE WAS ONE THING THAT CONFUSED ME.
WHY DID YOU DO "THE GOD OF DEATH" IN A PLACE LIKE THAT?

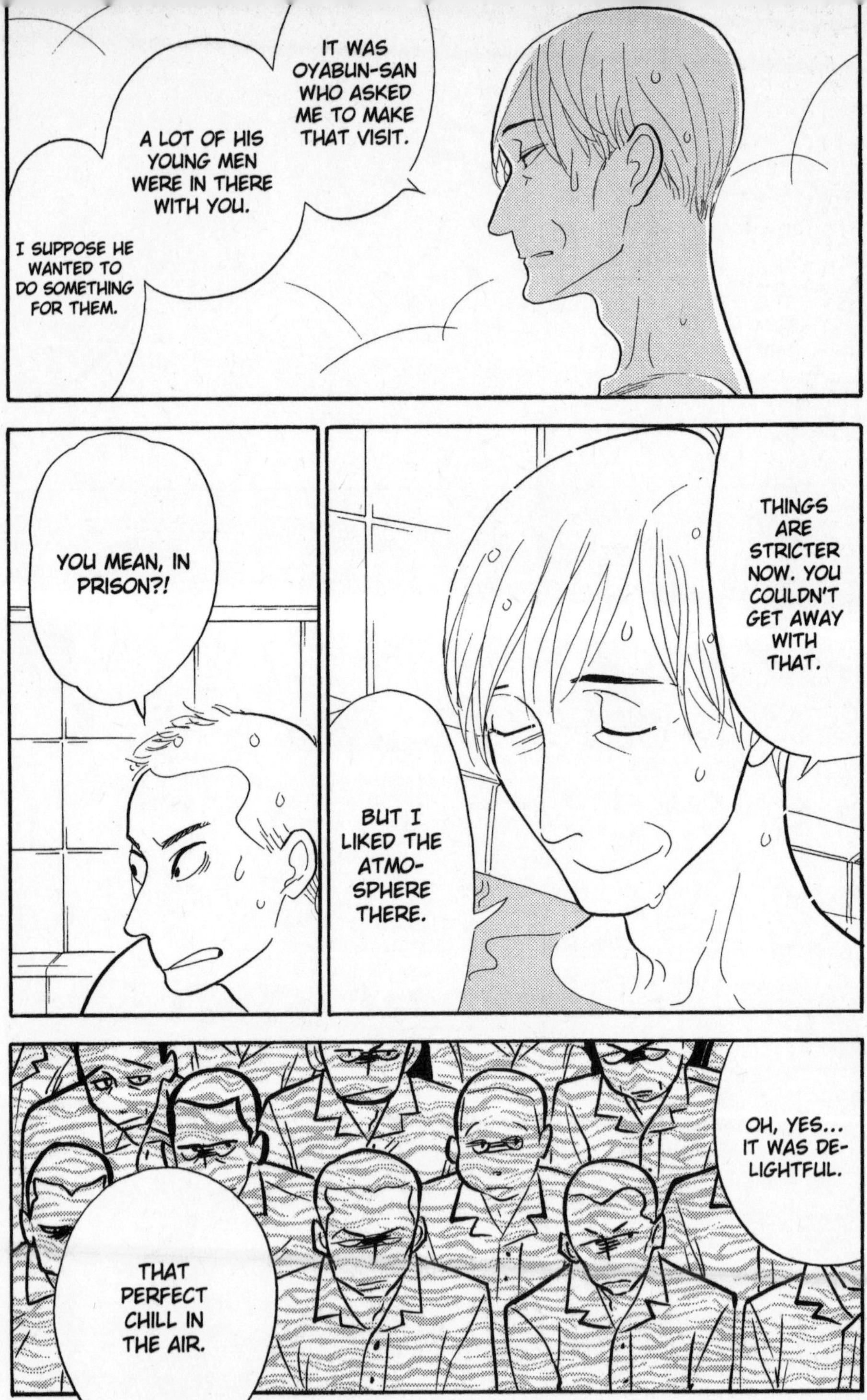
IT WAS OYABUN-SAN WHO ASKED ME TO MAKE THAT VISIT.
A LOT OF HIS YOUNG MEN WERE IN THERE WITH YOU.
I SUPPOSE HE WANTED TO DO SOMETHING FOR THEM.
THINGS ARE STRICTER NOW. YOU COULDN'T GET AWAY WITH THAT.
BUT I LIKED THE ATMO-SPHERE THERE.
YOU MEAN, IN PRISON?!
OH, YES... IT WAS DE-LIGHTFUL.
THAT PERFECT CHILL IN THE AIR.

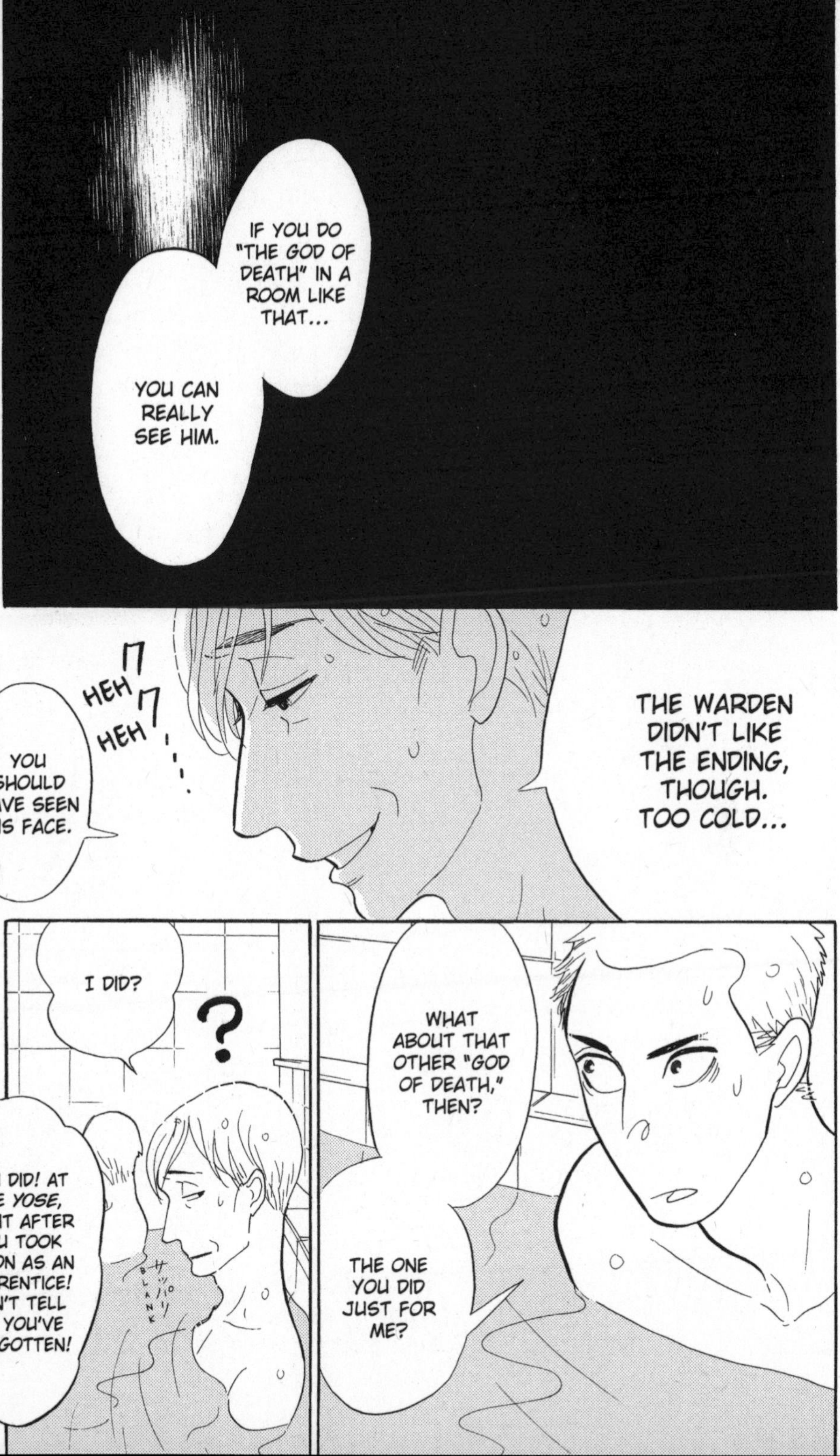
IF YOU DO "THE GOD OF DEATH" IN A ROOM LIKE THAT...
YOU CAN REALLY SEE HIM.
THE WARDEN DIDN'T LIKE THE ENDING, THOUGH. TOO COLD...
HEH HEH
YOU SHOULD HAVE SEEN HIS FACE.
WHAT ABOUT THAT OTHER "GOD OF DEATH," THEN?
THE ONE YOU DID JUST FOR ME?
I DID?
?
BLANK
YOU DID! AT THE YOSE, RIGHT AFTER YOU TOOK ME ON AS AN APPRENTICE! DON'T TELL ME YOU'VE FORGOTTEN!

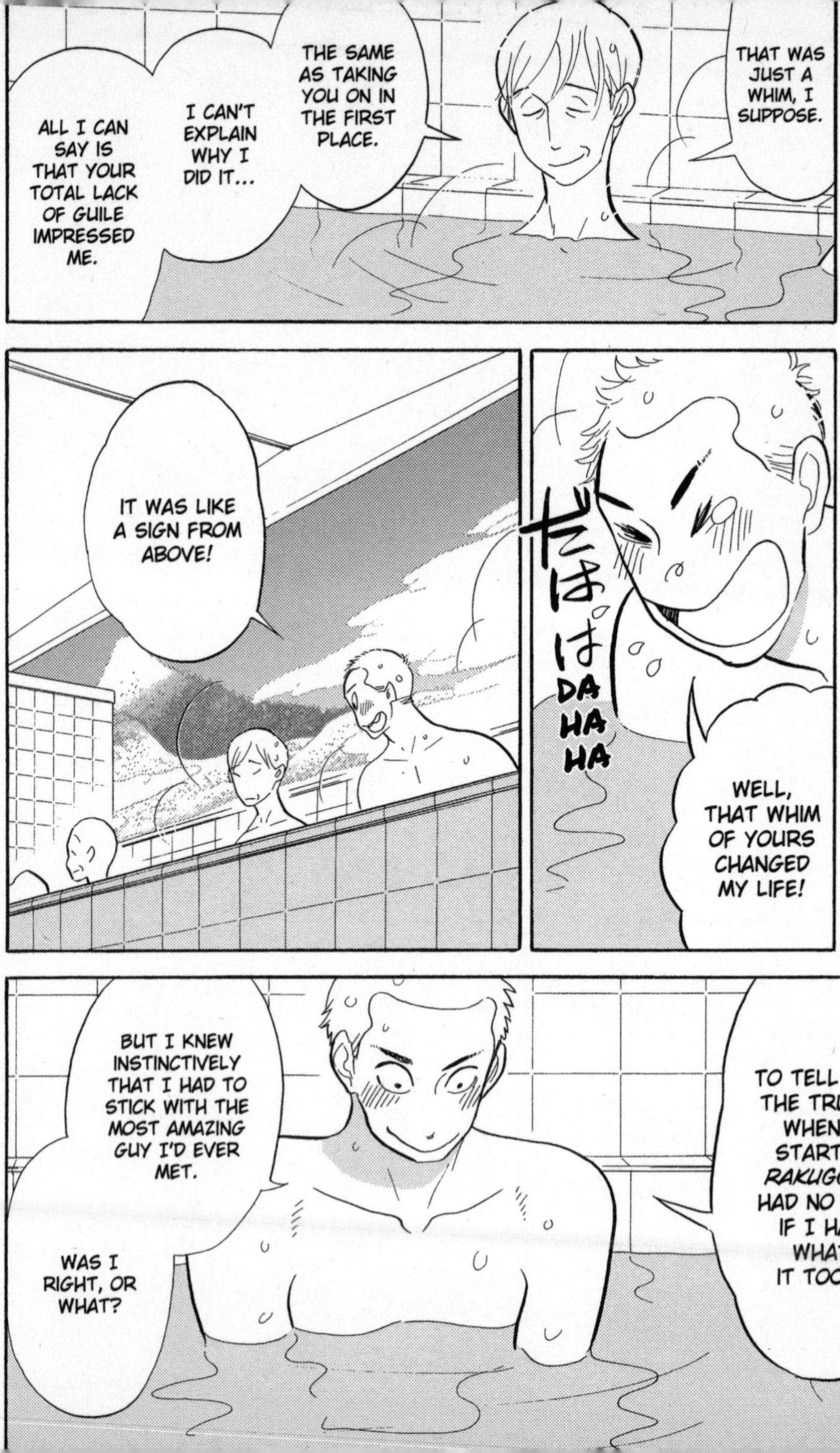
THAT WAS JUST A WHIM, I SUPPOSE.
THE SAME AS TAKING YOU ON IN THE FIRST PLACE.
I CAN'T EXPLAIN WHY I DID IT...
ALL I CAN SAY IS THAT YOUR TOTAL LACK OF GUILE IMPRESSED ME.
だはは
DA HA HA
WELL, THAT WHIM OF YOURS CHANGED MY LIFE!
IT WAS LIKE A SIGN FROM ABOVE!
TO TELL YOU THE TRUTH, WHEN I STARTED *RAKUGO*, I HAD NO IDEA IF I HAD WHAT IT TOOK.
BUT I KNEW INSTINCTIVELY THAT I HAD TO STICK WITH THE MOST AMAZING GUY I'D EVER MET.
WAS I RIGHT, OR WHAT?

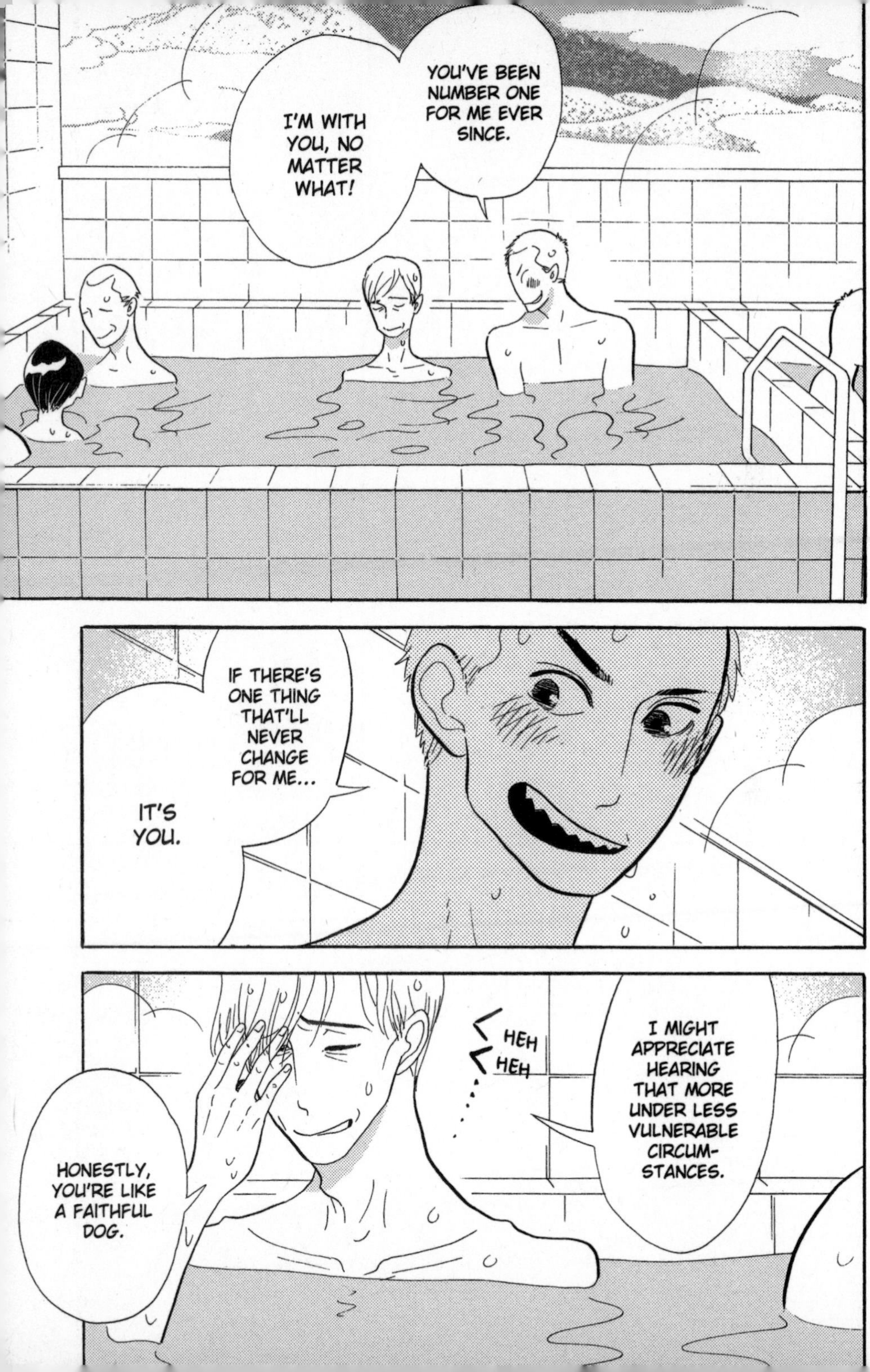
YOU'VE BEEN NUMBER ONE FOR ME EVER SINCE.
I'M WITH YOU, NO MATTER WHAT!
IF THERE'S ONE THING THAT'LL NEVER CHANGE FOR ME...
IT'S YOU.
I MIGHT APPRECIATE HEARING THAT MORE UNDER LESS VULNERABLE CIRCUM-STANCES.
HEH HEH
...
HONESTLY, YOU'RE LIKE A FAITHFUL DOG.

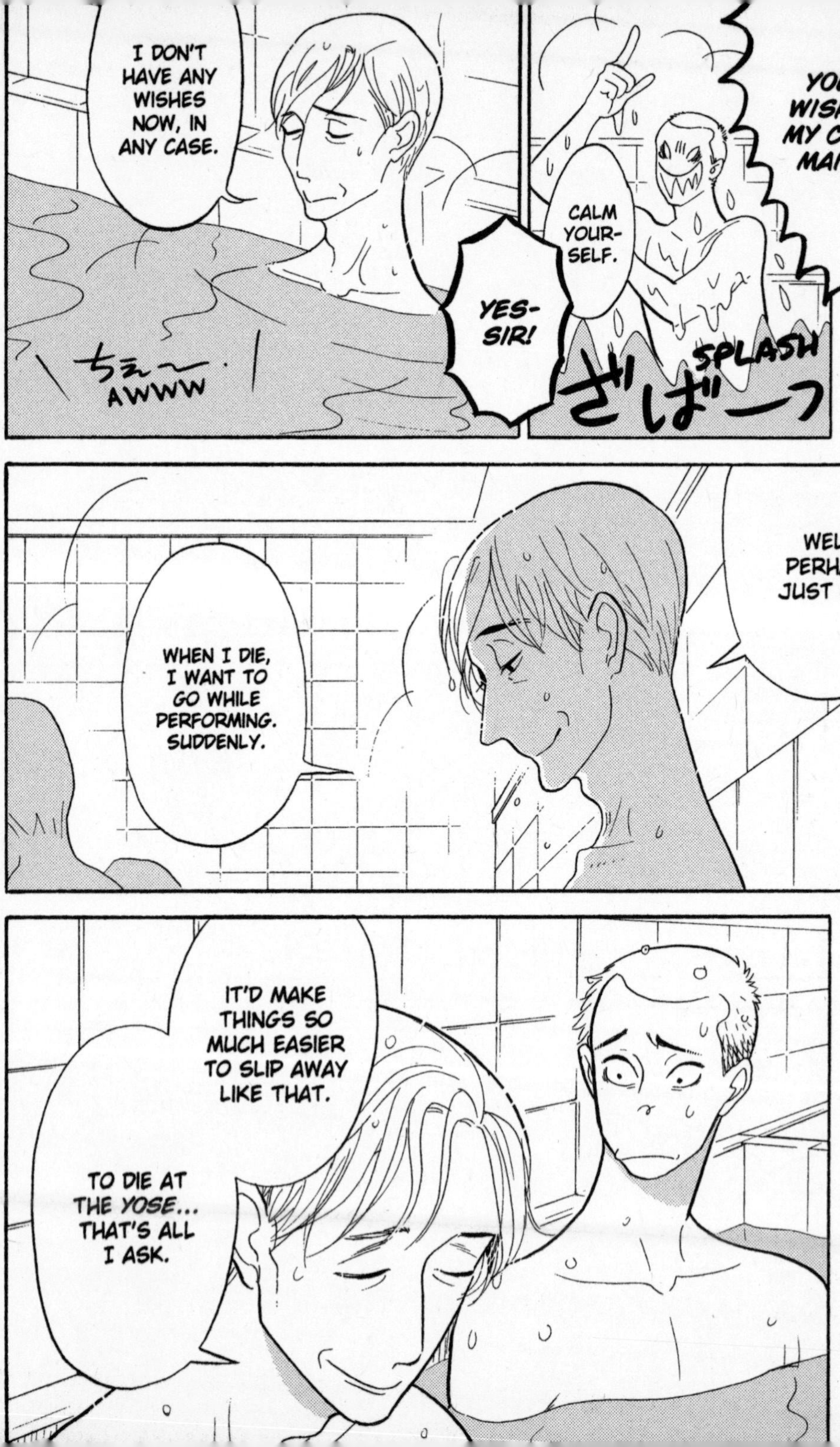
YOUR WISH IS MY COM-MAND!
CALM YOUR-SELF.
YES-SIR!
SPLASH
ざばーっ
I DON'T HAVE ANY WISHES NOW, IN ANY CASE.
ちぇ〜
AWWW
WELL, PERHAPS JUST ONE.
WHEN I DIE, I WANT TO GO WHILE PERFORMING. SUDDENLY.
IT'D MAKE THINGS SO MUCH EASIER TO SLIP AWAY LIKE THAT.
TO DIE AT THE *YOSE*... THAT'S ALL I ASK.

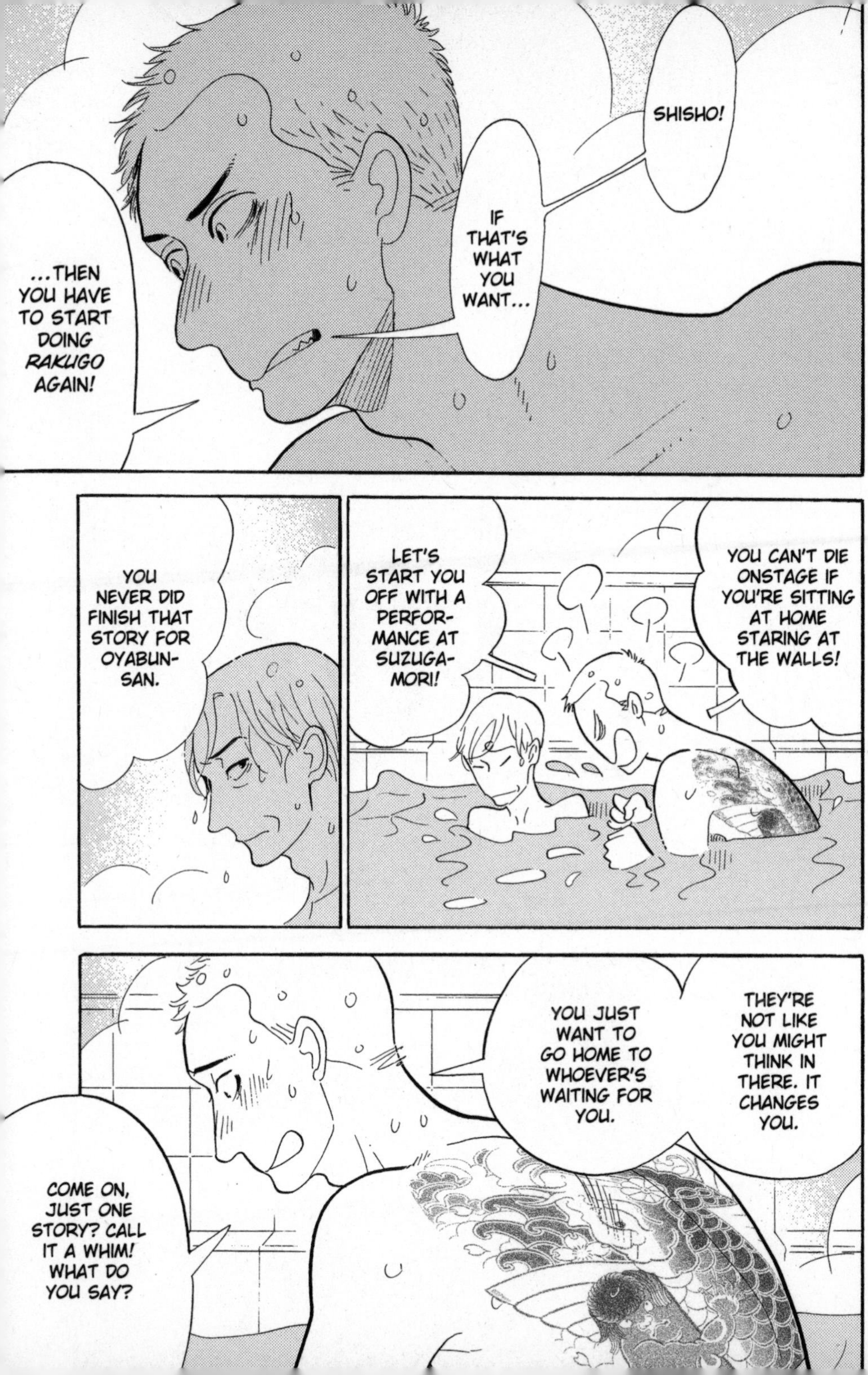
SHISHO!
IF THAT'S WHAT YOU WANT...
...THEN YOU HAVE TO START DOING *RAKUGO* AGAIN!
YOU CAN'T DIE ONSTAGE IF YOU'RE SITTING AT HOME STARING AT THE WALLS!
LET'S START YOU OFF WITH A PERFORMANCE AT SUZUGAMORI!
YOU NEVER DID FINISH THAT STORY FOR OYABUN-SAN.
THEY'RE NOT LIKE YOU MIGHT THINK IN THERE. IT CHANGES YOU.
YOU JUST WANT TO GO HOME TO WHOEVER'S WAITING FOR YOU.
COME ON, JUST ONE STORY? CALL IT A WHIM! WHAT DO YOU SAY?

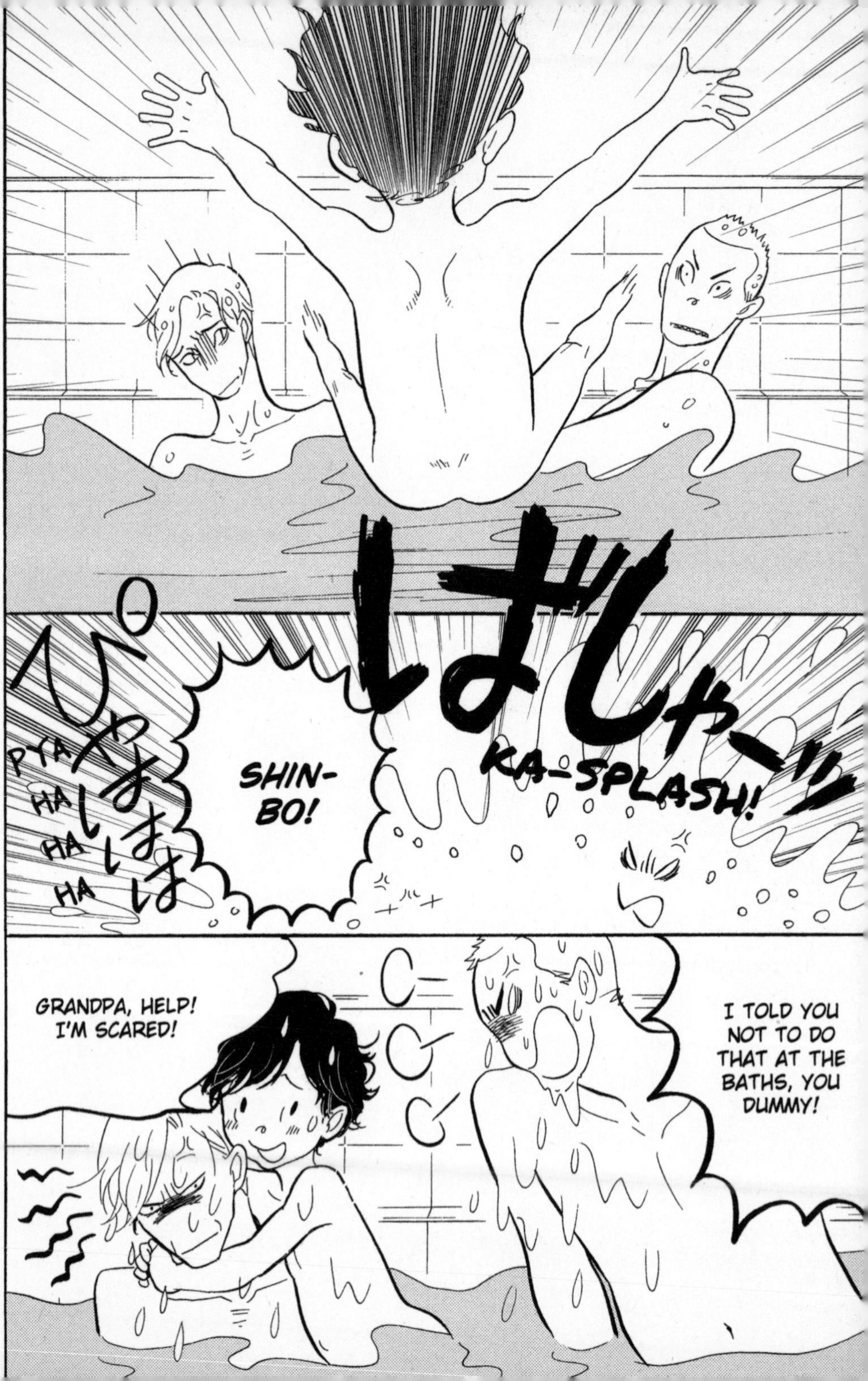
ばしゃーッ!!
KA-SPLASH!
SHIN-BO!
ぴゃははは
PYA HA HA HA
I TOLD YOU NOT TO DO THAT AT THE BATHS, YOU DUMMY!
GRANDPA, HELP! I'M SCARED!

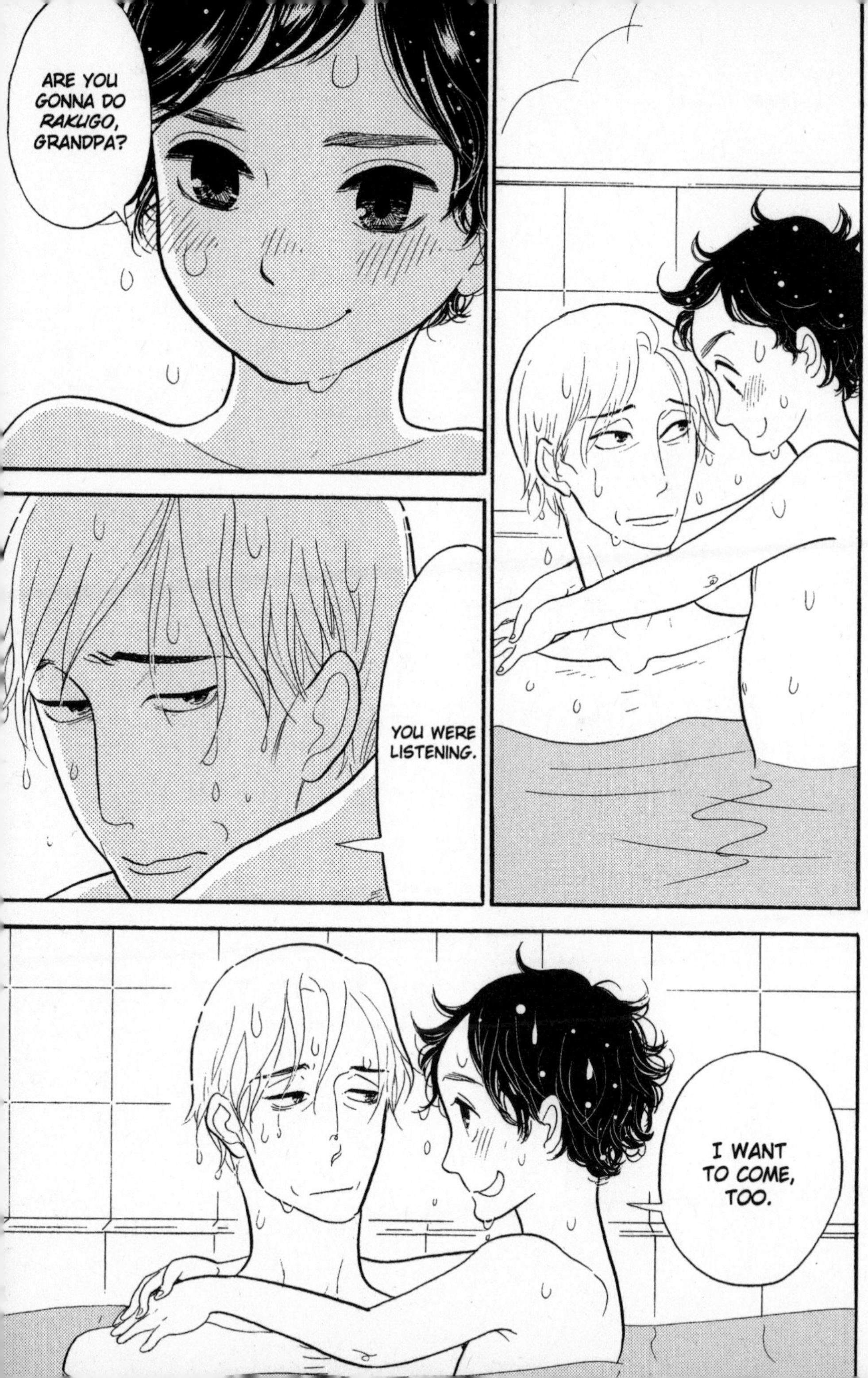
ARE YOU GONNA DO *RAKUGO*, GRANDPA?
YOU WERE LISTENING.
I WANT TO COME, TOO.

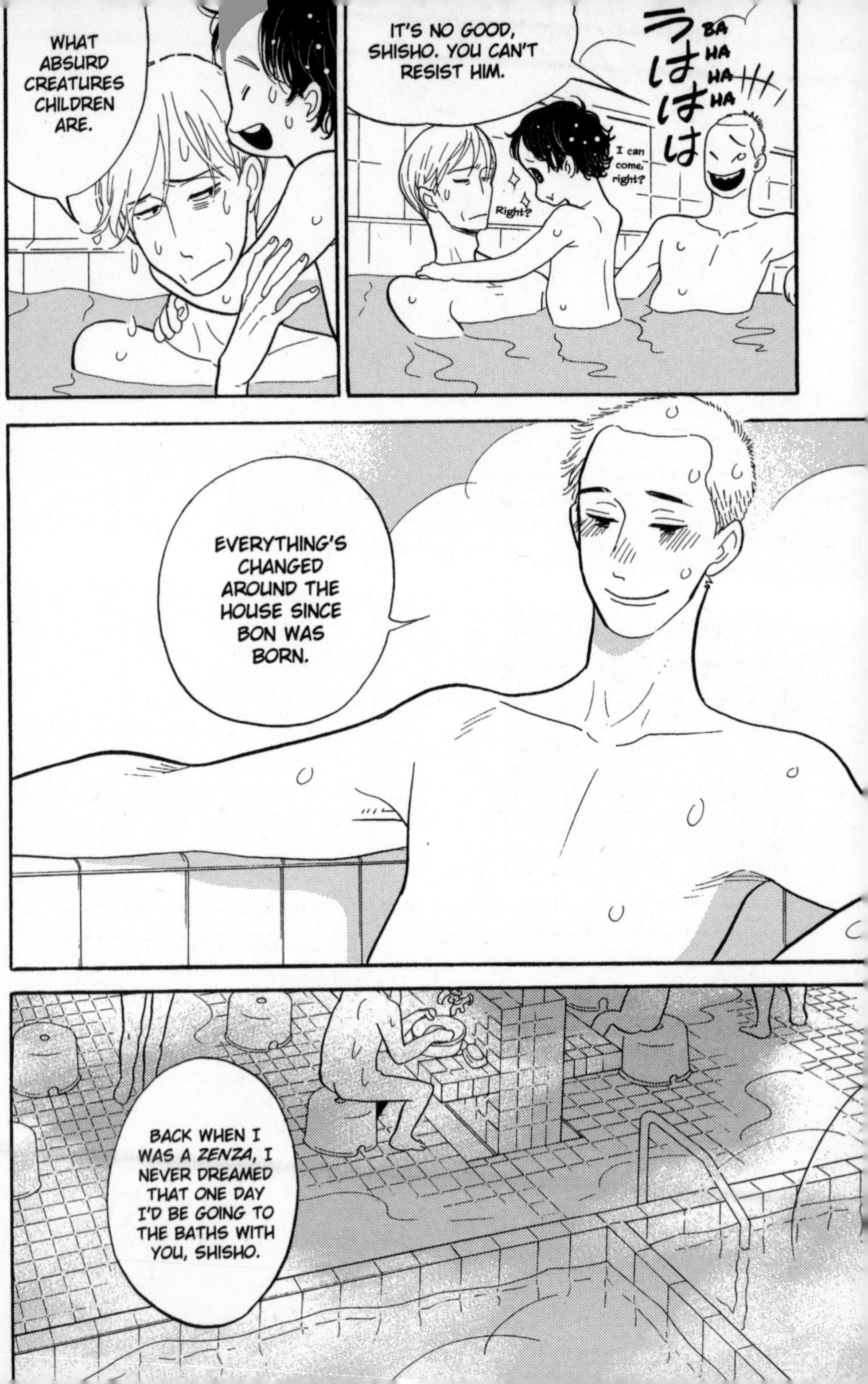
うははは
BA HA HA HA
IT'S NO GOOD, SHISHO. YOU CAN'T RESIST HIM.
I can come, right?
Right?
WHAT ABSURD CREATURES CHILDREN ARE.
EVERYTHING'S CHANGED AROUND THE HOUSE SINCE BON WAS BORN.
BACK WHEN I WAS A *ZENZA*, I NEVER DREAMED THAT ONE DAY I'D BE GOING TO THE BATHS WITH YOU, SHISHO.

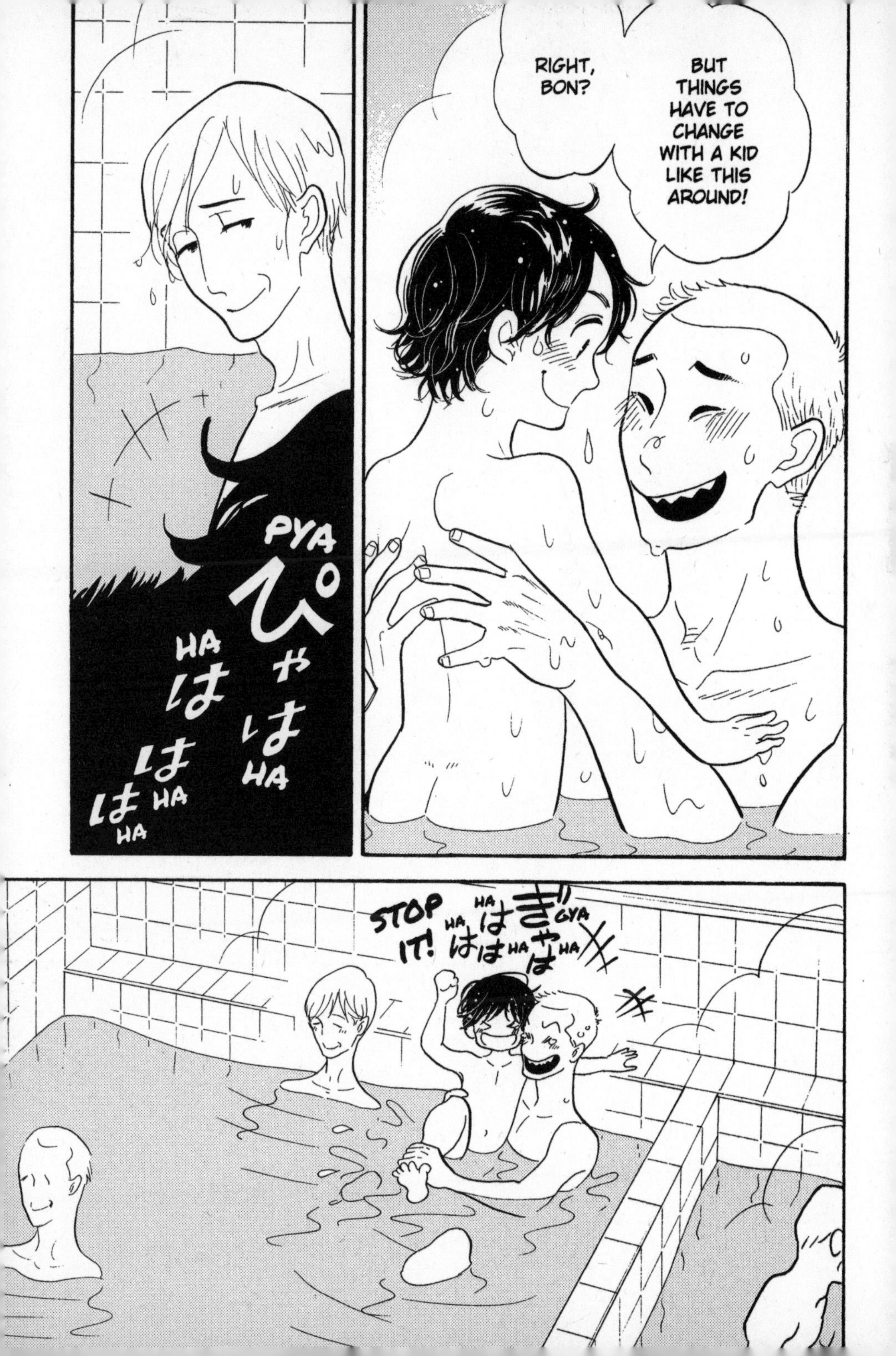
BUT THINGS HAVE TO CHANGE WITH A KID LIKE THIS AROUND!
RIGHT, BON?
ぴゃははは
PYA HA HA HA HA
ぎゃははは
GYA HA HA HA HA
STOP IT!

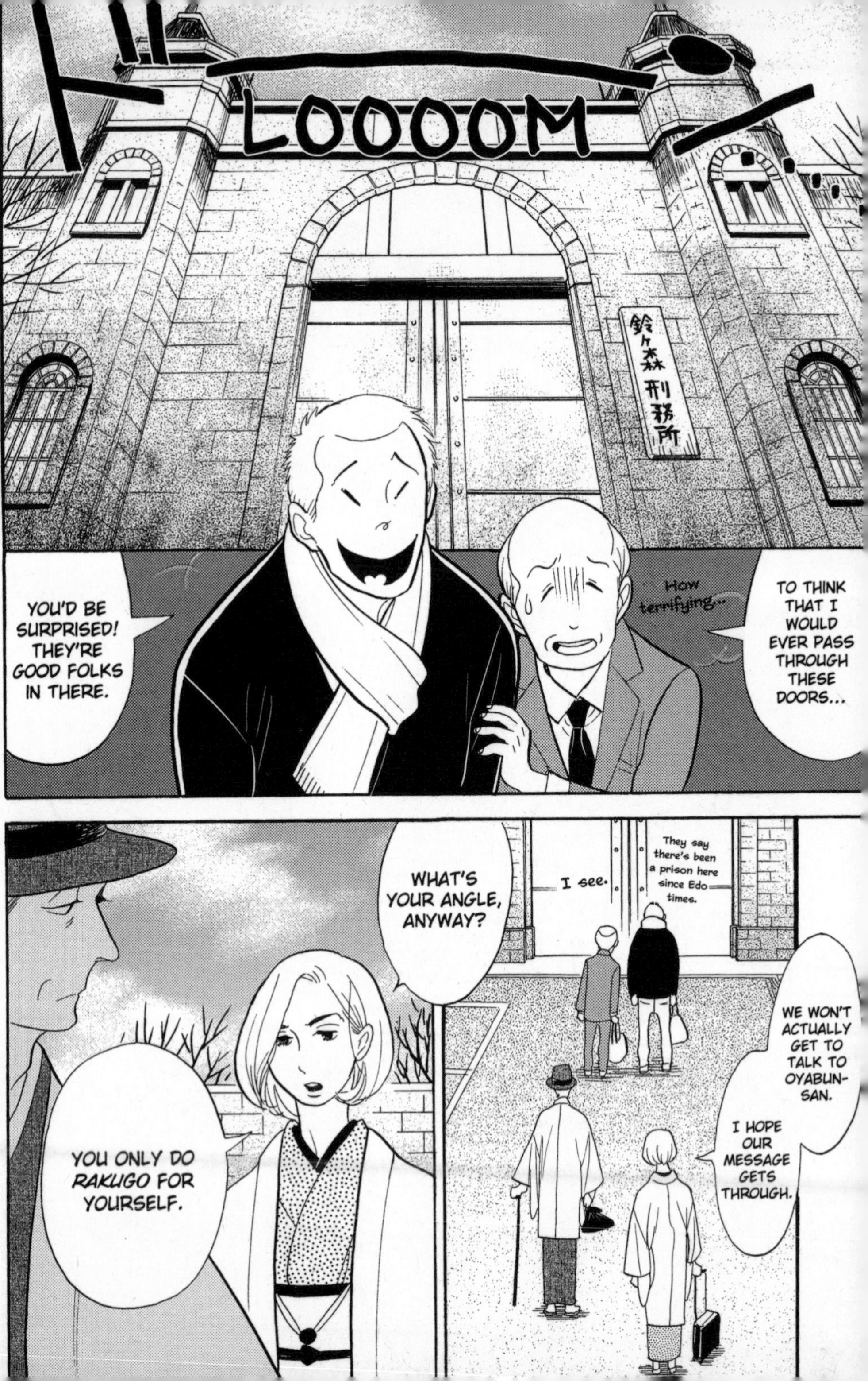
LOOOOM
鈴ヶ森刑務所
TO THINK THAT I WOULD EVER PASS THROUGH THESE DOORS...
How terrifying...
YOU'D BE SURPRISED! THEY'RE GOOD FOLKS IN THERE.
They say there's been a prison here since Edo times.
I see.
WE WON'T ACTUALLY GET TO TALK TO OYABUN-SAN.
I HOPE OUR MESSAGE GETS THROUGH.
WHAT'S YOUR ANGLE, ANYWAY?
YOU ONLY DO *RAKUGO* FOR YOURSELF.

Sign: Suzugamori Prison

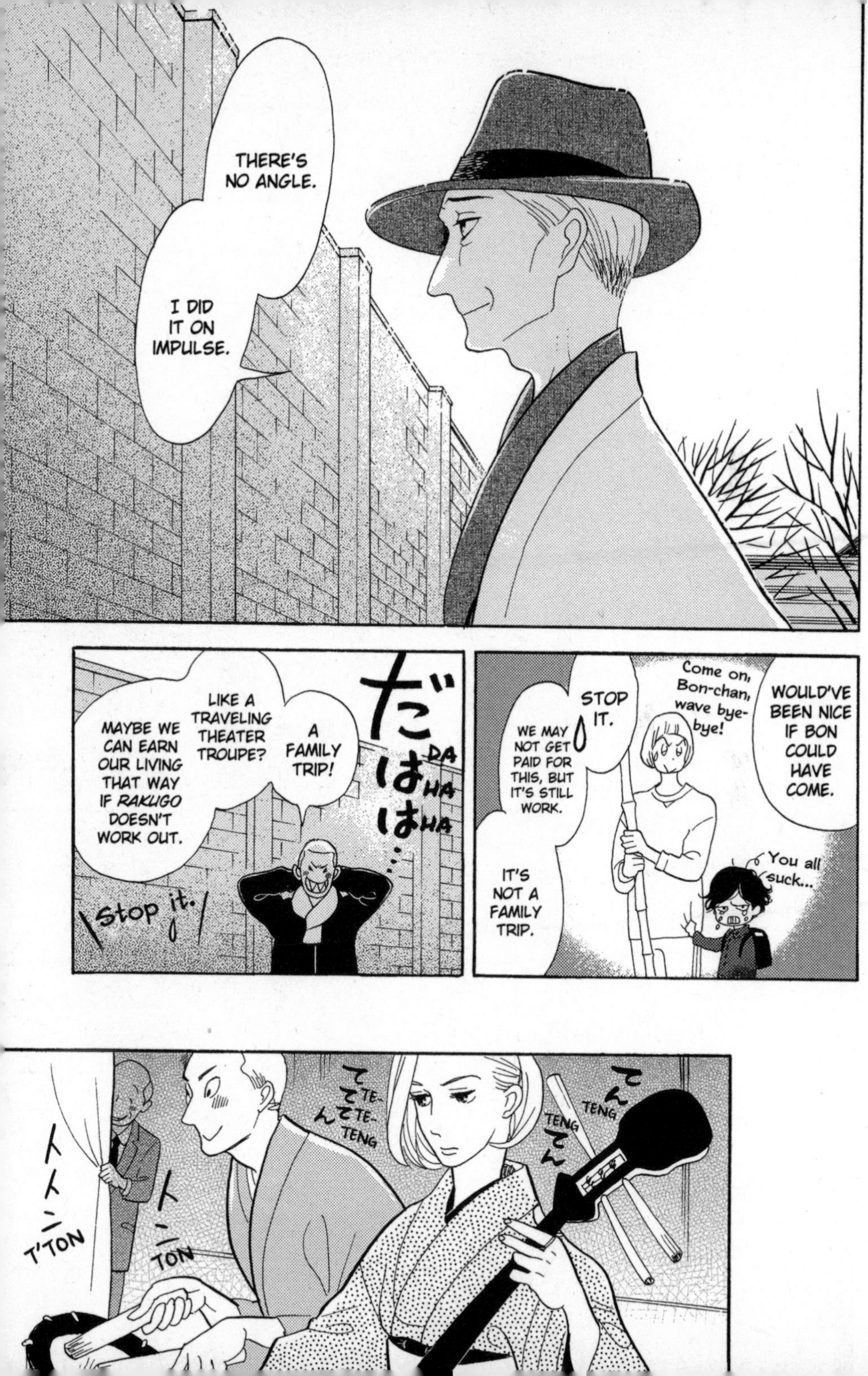
THERE'S NO ANGLE.
I DID IT ON IMPULSE.
WOULD'VE BEEN NICE IF BON COULD HAVE COME.
Come on, Bon-chan, wave bye-bye!
STOP IT.
WE MAY NOT GET PAID FOR THIS, BUT IT'S STILL WORK.
You all suck...
IT'S NOT A FAMILY TRIP.
A FAMILY TRIP!
だはは DA HA HA...
LIKE A TRAVELING THEATER TROUPE?
MAYBE WE CAN EARN OUR LIVING THAT WAY IF *RAKUGO* DOESN'T WORK OUT.
Stop it.
てん TENG
てん TENG
てててん TE-TE-TENG
トン TON
トトン T'TON

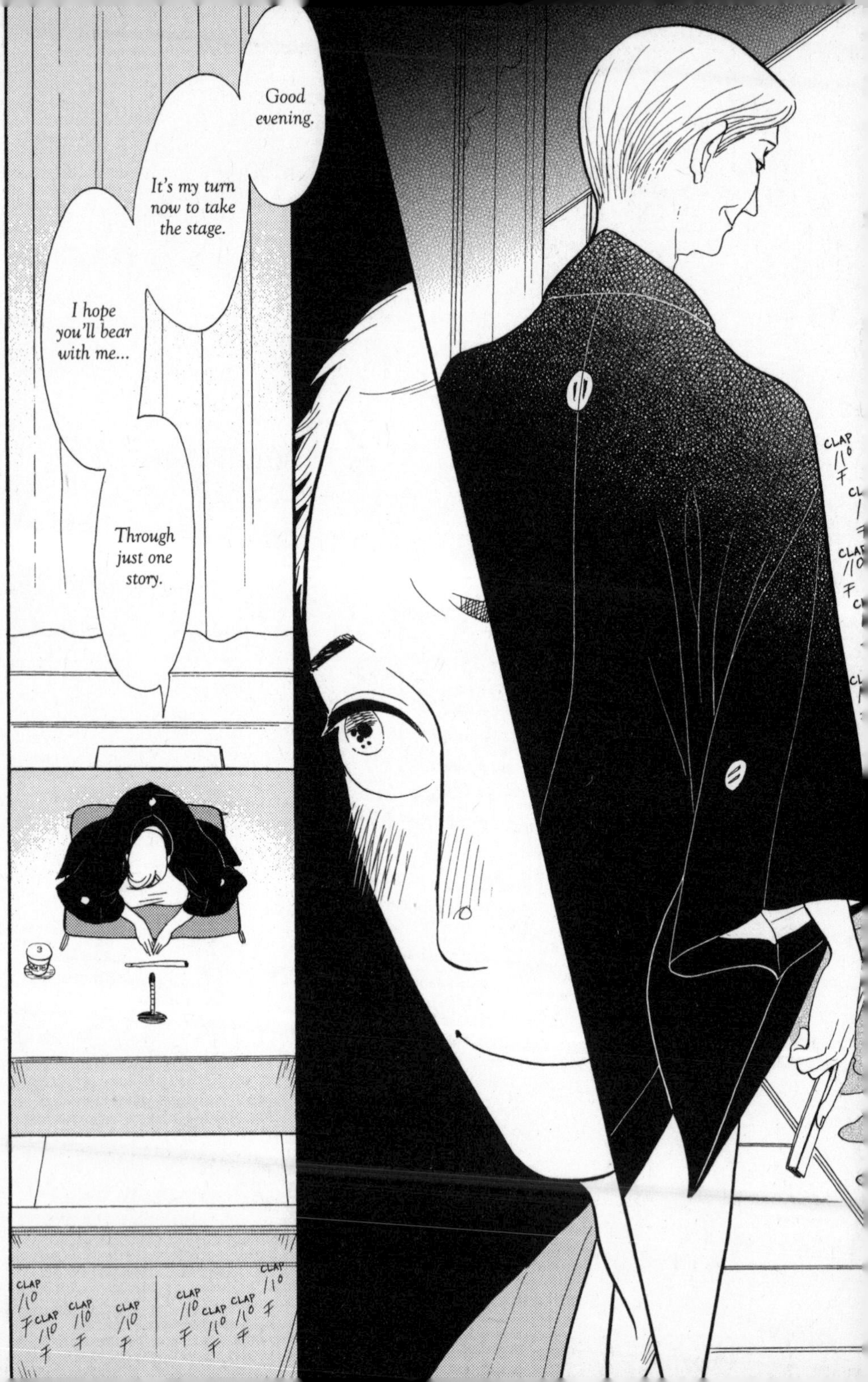
CLAP
Good evening.
It's my turn now to take the stage.
I hope you'll bear with me...
Through just one story.
CLAP
CLAP
CLAP
CLAP
CLAP
CLAP
CLAP
CLAP

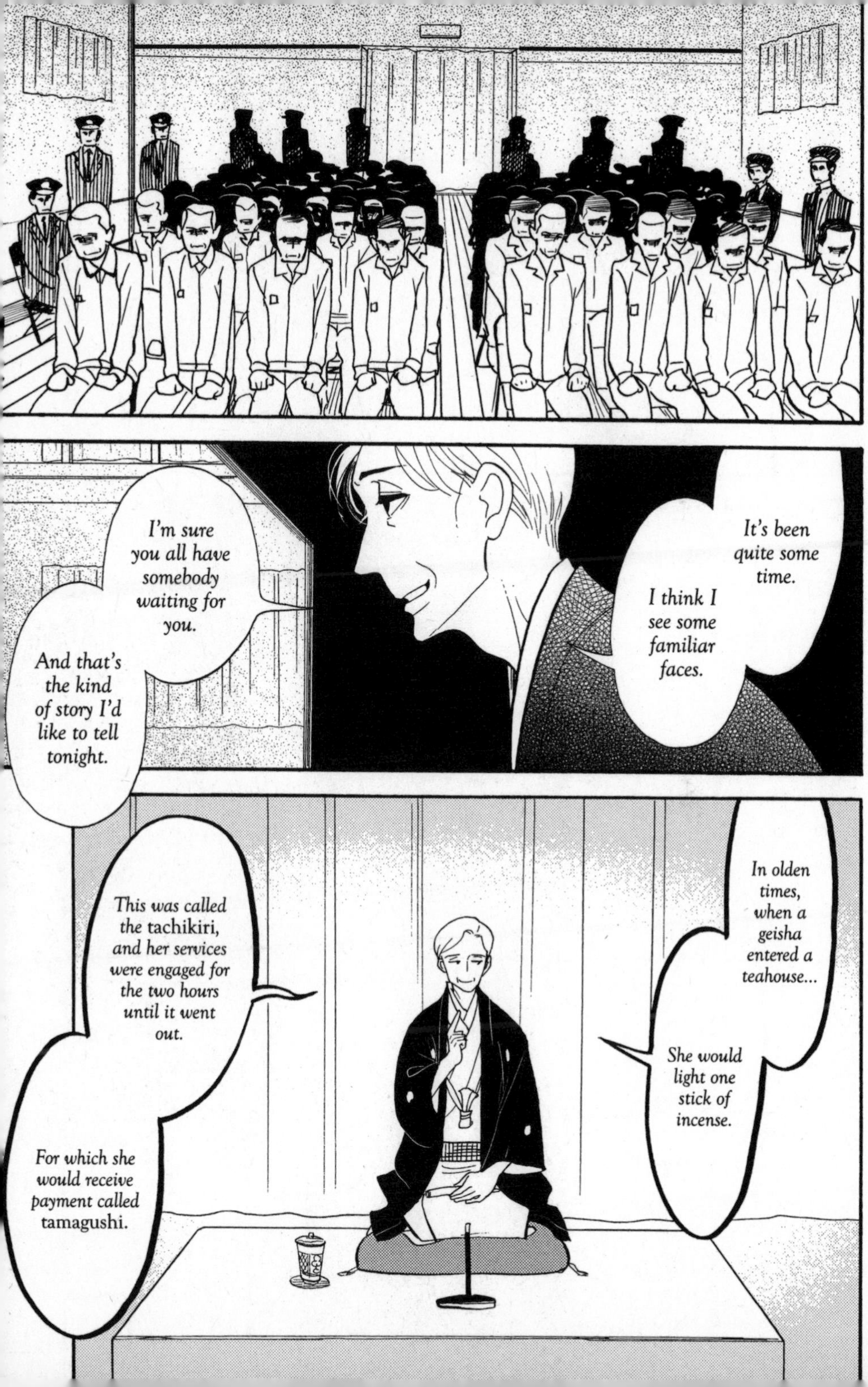
It's been quite some time.
I think I see some familiar faces.
I'm sure you all have somebody waiting for you.
And that's the kind of story I'd like to tell tonight.
In olden times, when a geisha entered a teahouse...
She would light one stick of incense.
This was called the tachikiri, and her services were engaged for the two hours until it went out.
For which she would receive payment called tamagushi.

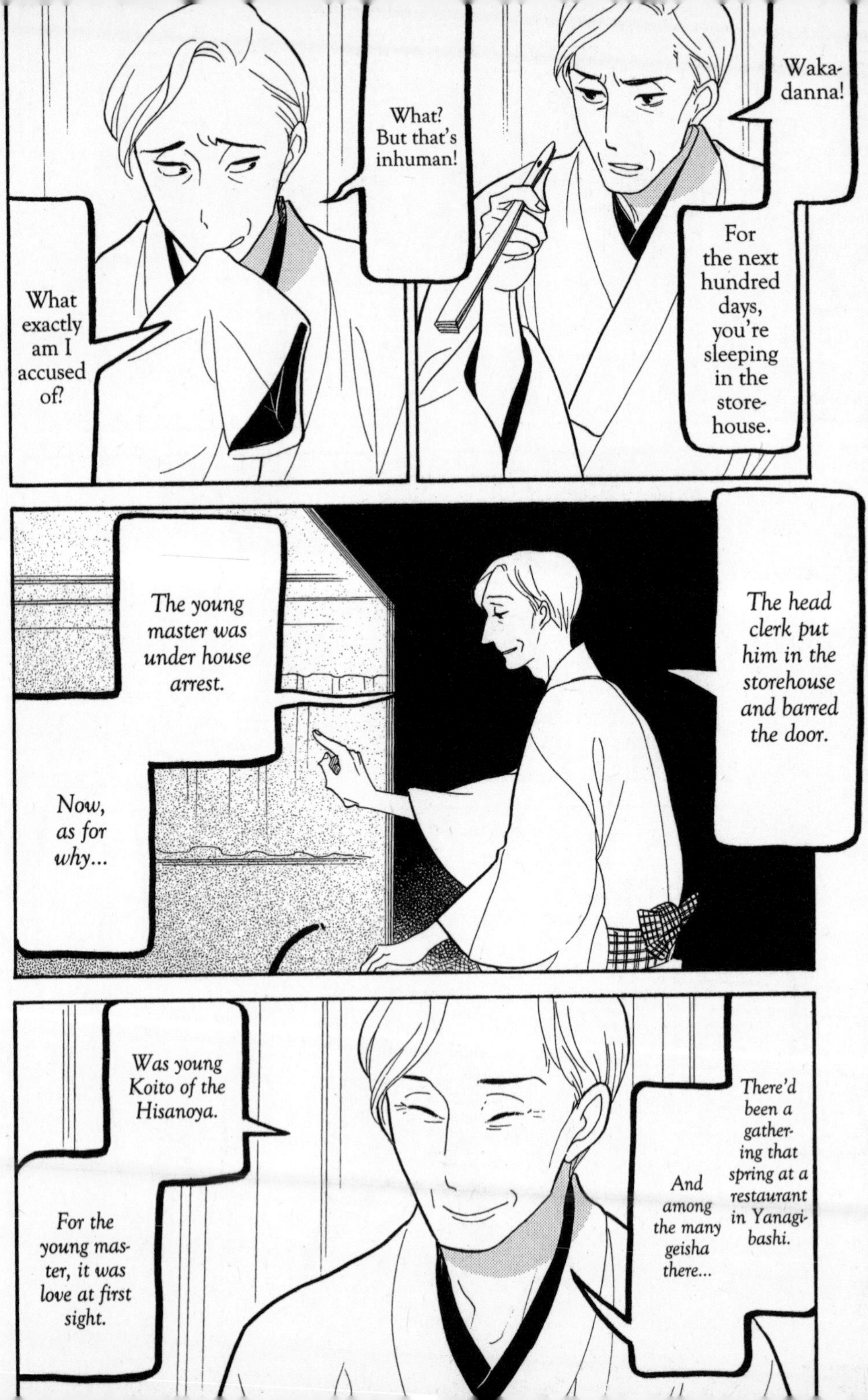
Waka-danna!
For the next hundred days, you're sleeping in the storehouse.
What? But that's inhuman!
What exactly am I accused of?
The head clerk put him in the storehouse and barred the door.
The young master was under house arrest.
Now, as for why...
There'd been a gathering that spring at a restaurant in Yanagibashi.
And among the many geisha there...
Was young Koito of the Hisanoya.
For the young master, it was love at first sight.

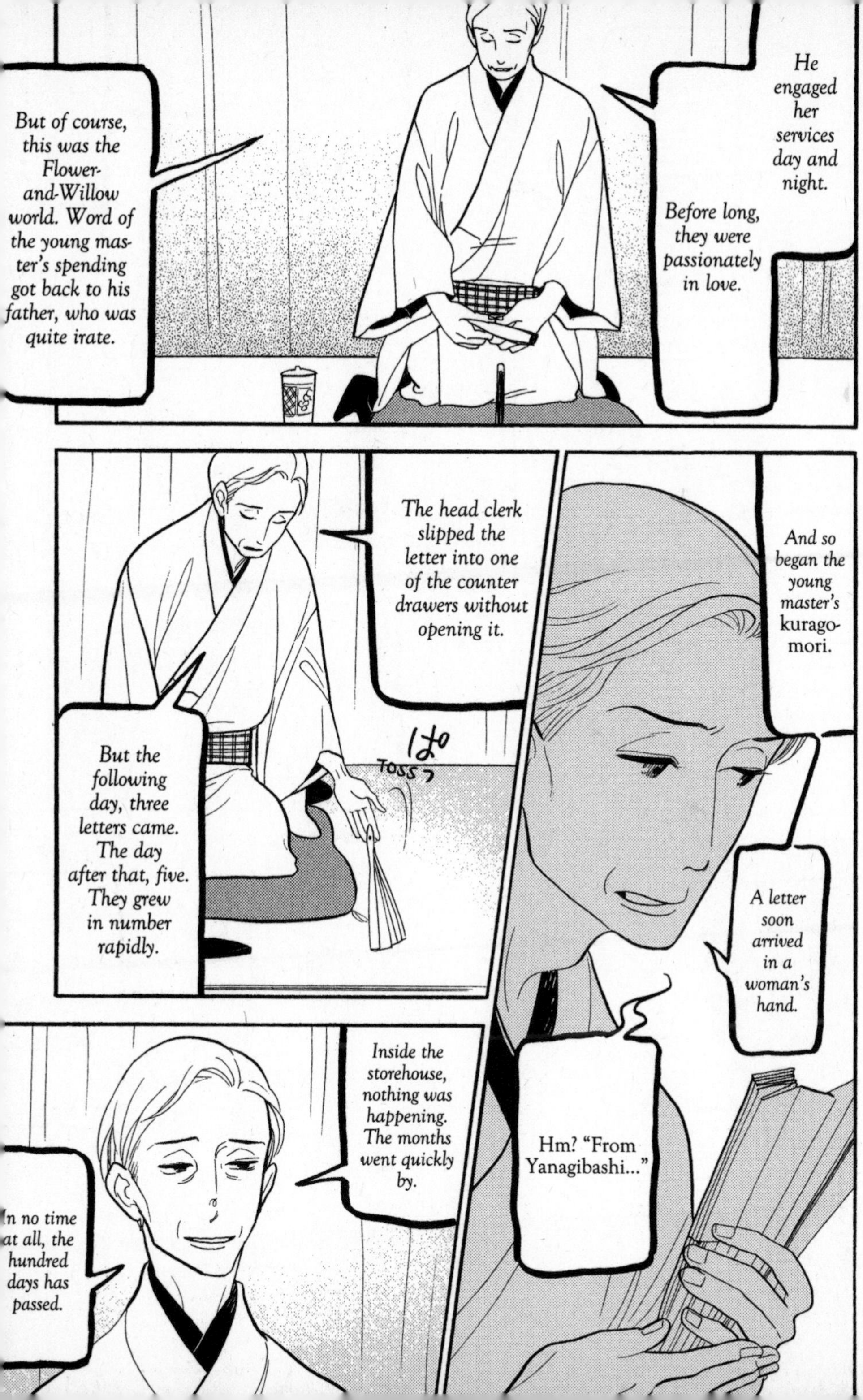

He engaged her services day and night.
Before long, they were passionately in love.
But of course, this was the Flower-and-Willow world. Word of the young master's spending got back to his father, who was quite irate.
And so began the young master's kurago-mori.
A letter soon arrived in a woman's hand.
Hm? "From Yanagibashi..."
The head clerk slipped the letter into one of the counter drawers without opening it.
But the following day, three letters came. The day after that, five. They grew in number rapidly.
TOSS
Inside the storehouse, nothing was happening. The months went quickly by.
In no time at all, the hundred days has passed.

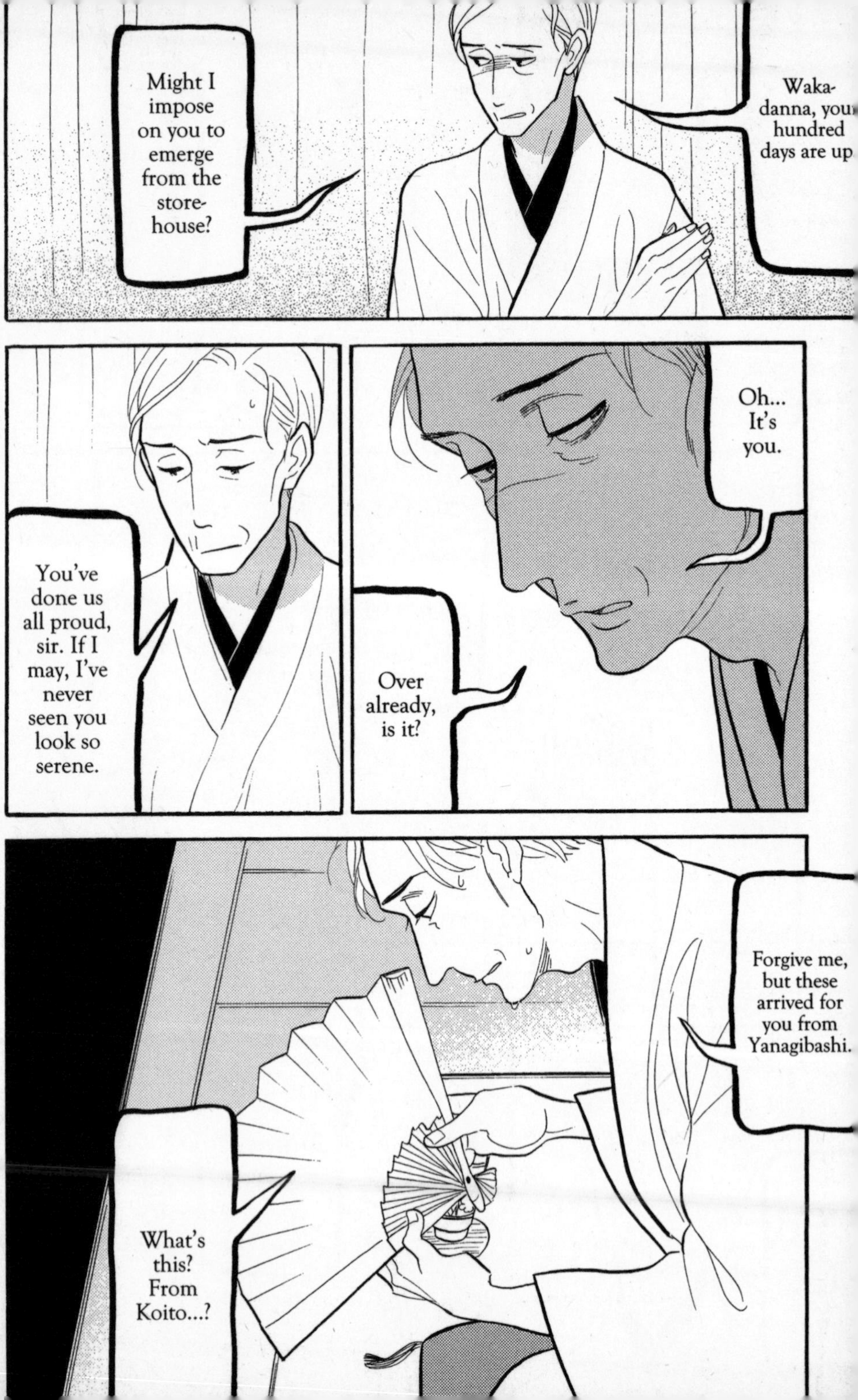
Waka-danna, you hundred days are up
Might I impose on you to emerge from the store-house?
Oh... It's you.
Over already, is it?
You've done us all proud, sir. If I may, I've never seen you look so serene.
Forgive me, but these arrived for you from Yanagibashi.
What's this? From Koito...?

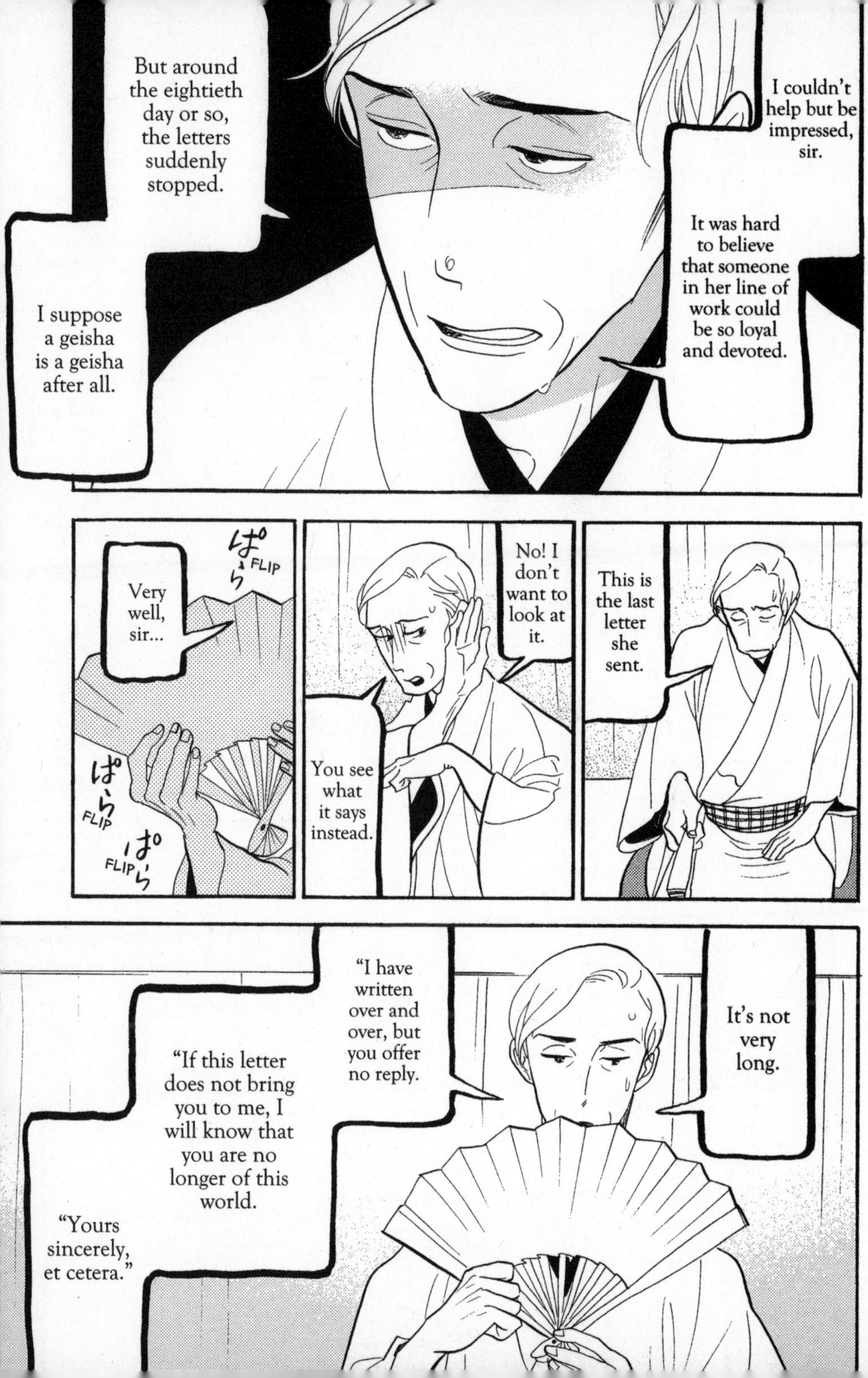
I couldn't help but be impressed, sir.
It was hard to believe that someone in her line of work could be so loyal and devoted.
But around the eightieth day or so, the letters suddenly stopped.
I suppose a geisha is a geisha after all.
This is the last letter she sent.
No! I don't want to look at it.
You see what it says instead.
ぱら FLIP
Very well, sir...
ぱら FLIP
ぱら FLIP
It's not very long.
"I have written over and over, but you offer no reply.
"If this letter does not bring you to me, I will know that you are no longer of this world.
"Yours sincerely, et cetera."

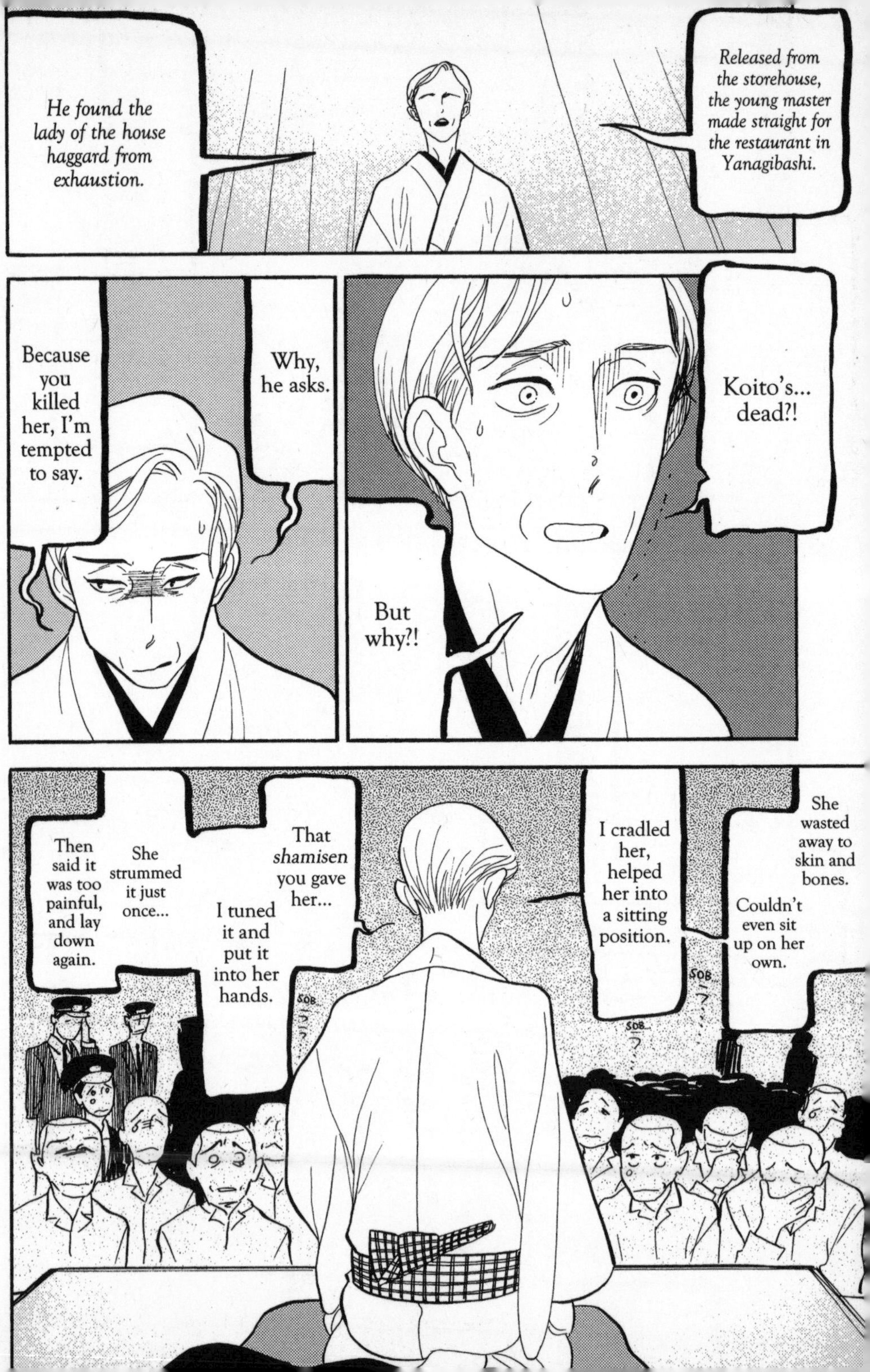
Released from the storehouse, the young master made straight for the restaurant in Yanagibashi.
He found the lady of the house haggard from exhaustion.
Koito's... dead?!
But why?!
Why, he asks.
Because you killed her, I'm tempted to say.
She wasted away to skin and bones.
Couldn't even sit up on her own.
SOB
I cradled her, helped her into a sitting position.
SOB...
That *shamisen* you gave her...
I tuned it and put it into her hands.
SOB
She strummed it just once...
Then said it was too painful, and lay down again.

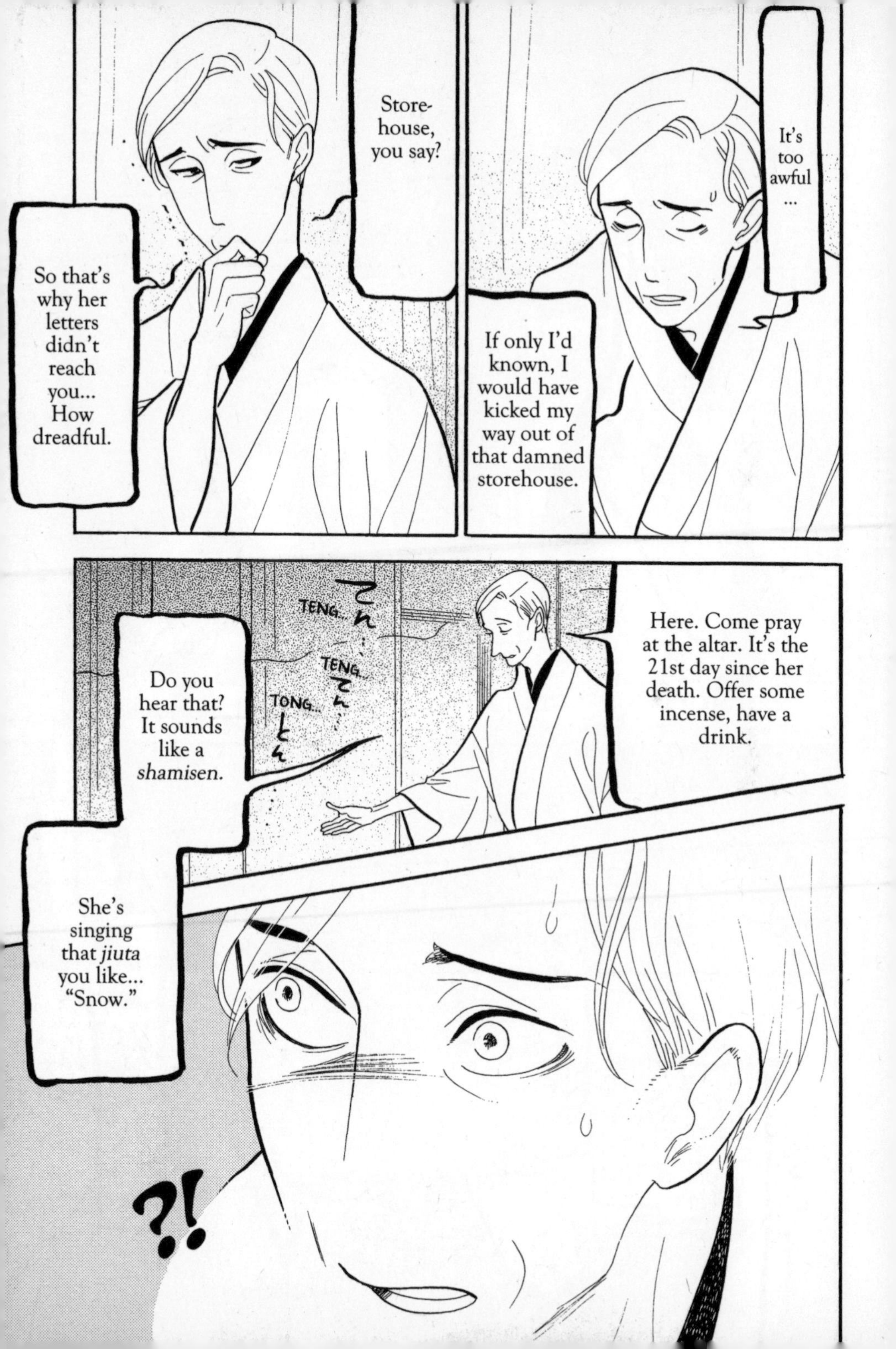
It's too awful...
If only I'd known, I would have kicked my way out of that damned storehouse.
Store-house, you say?
So that's why her letters didn't reach you... How dreadful.
Here. Come pray at the altar. It's the 21st day since her death. Offer some incense, have a drink.
TENG... てん
TENG... てん
TONG... とん
Do you hear that? It sounds like a *shamisen.*
She's singing that *jiuta* you like... "Snow."
?!

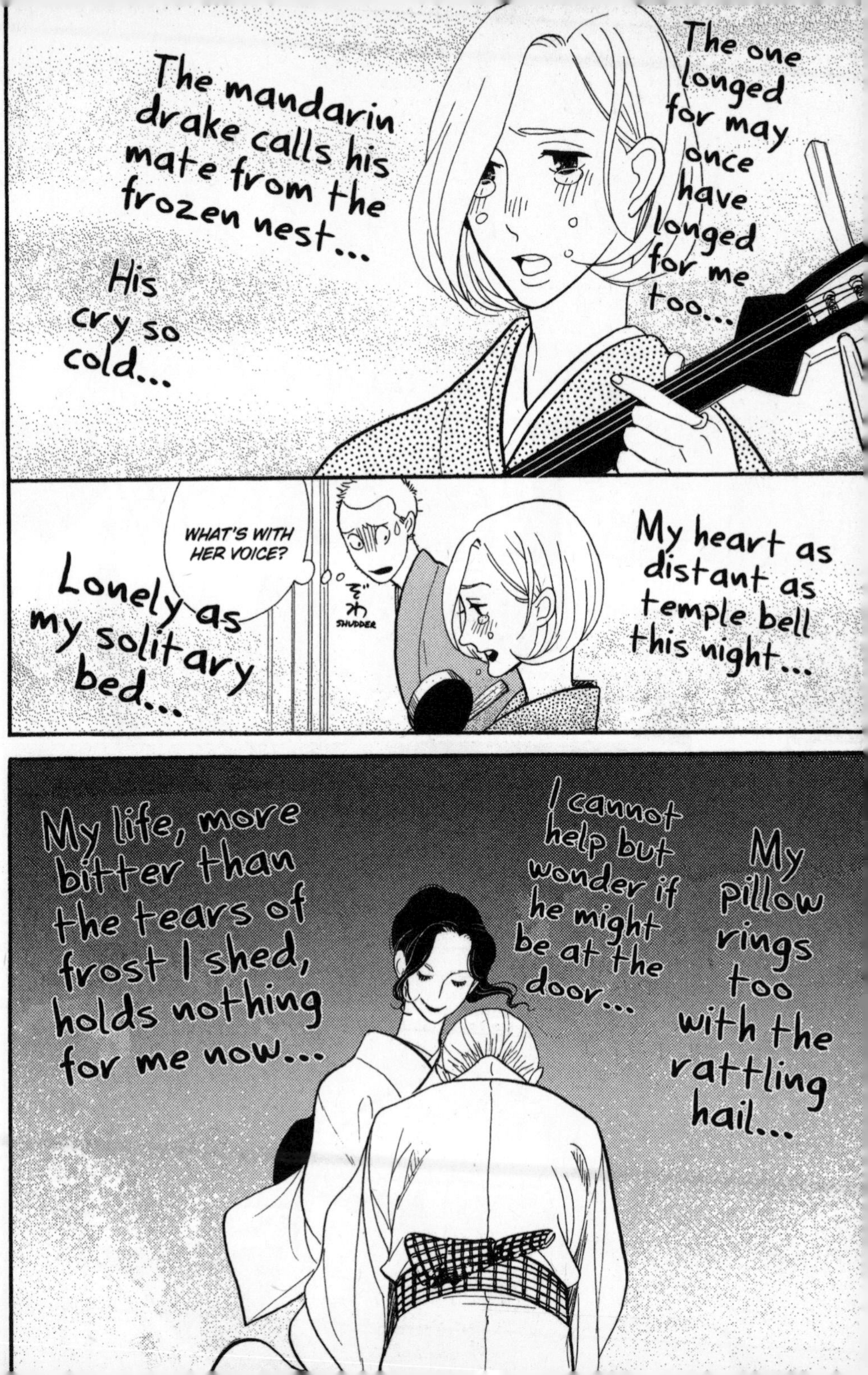
The one longed for may once have longed for me too...
The mandarin drake calls his mate from the frozen nest...
His cry so cold...
My heart as distant as temple bell this night...
WHAT'S WITH HER VOICE?
SHUDDER
Lonely as my solitary bed...
My pillow rings too with the rattling hail...
I cannot help but wonder if he might be at the door...
My life, more bitter than the tears of frost I shed, holds nothing for me now...

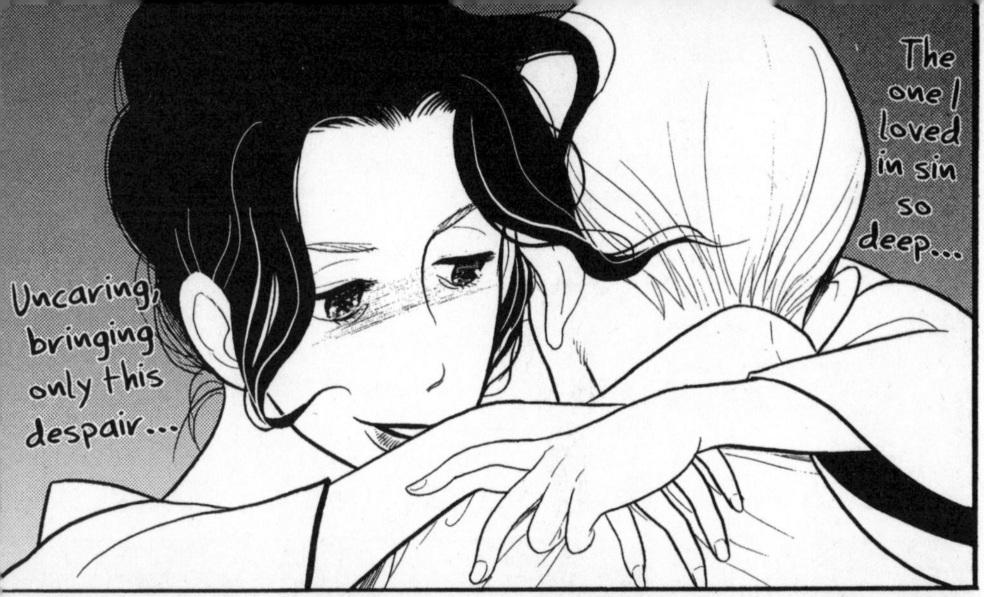
The one I loved in sin so deep...
Uncaring, bringing only this despair...

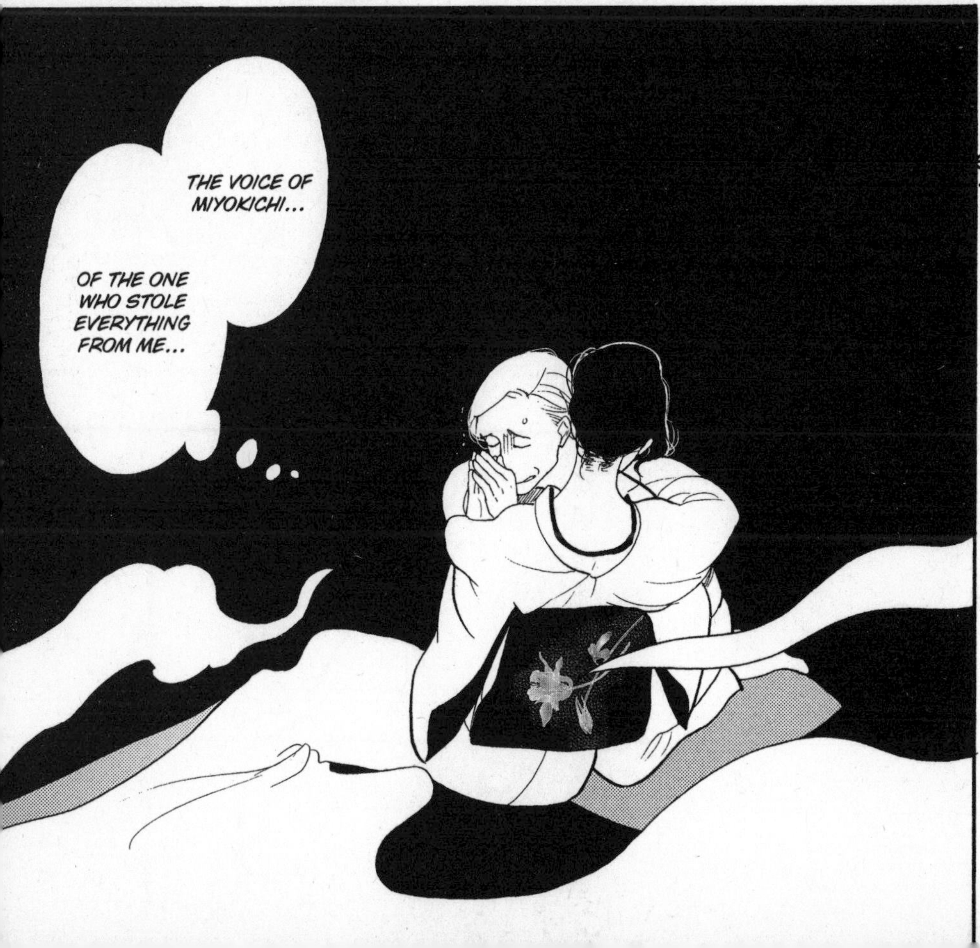
THE VOICE OF MIYOKICHI...
OF THE ONE WHO STOLE EVERYTHING FROM ME...

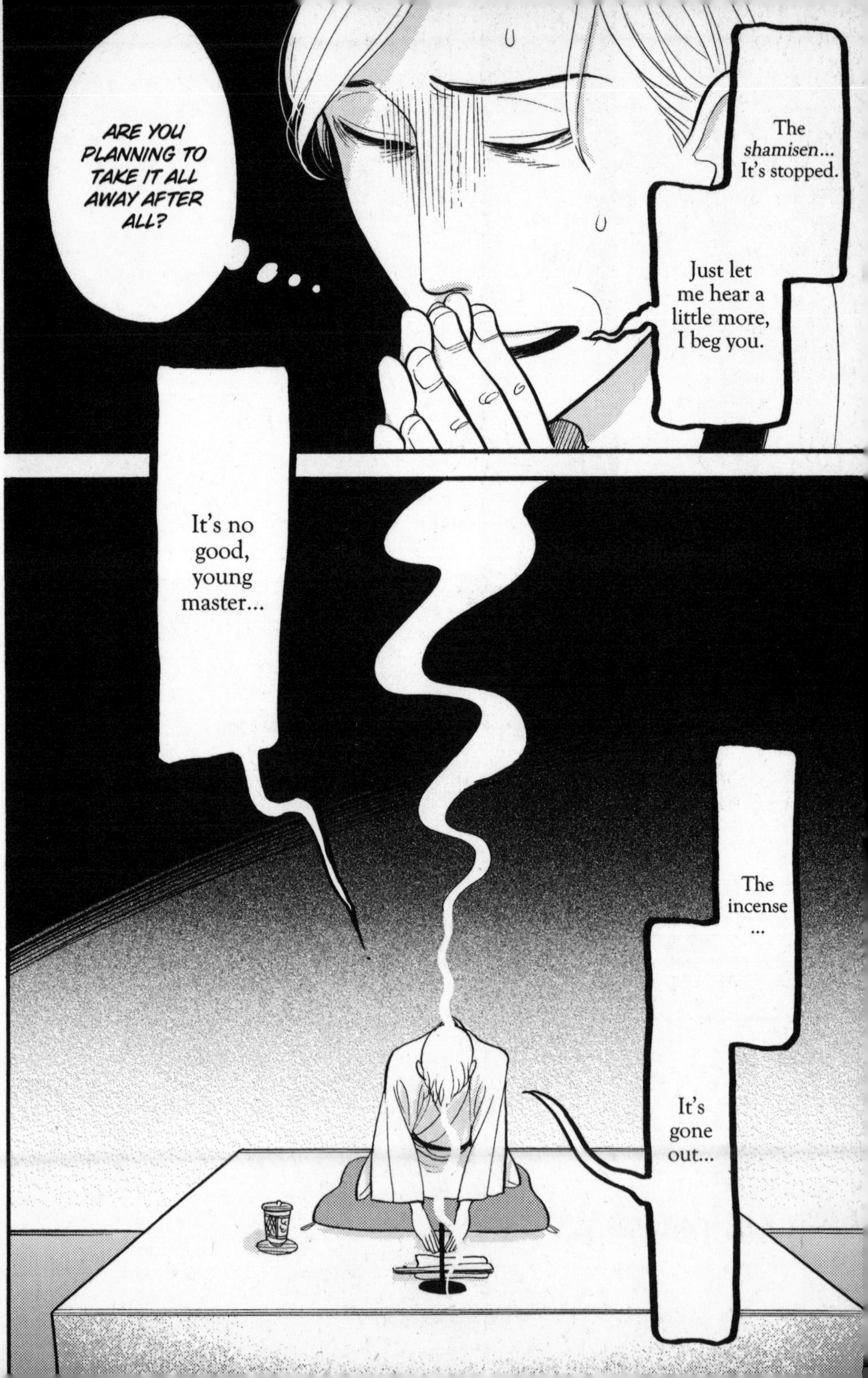
The *shamisen*... It's stopped.
Just let me hear a little more, I beg you.
ARE YOU PLANNING TO TAKE IT ALL AWAY AFTER ALL?
The incense ...
It's gone out...
It's no good, young master...

DESCENDING
STORIES
SHOWA
GENROKU
RAKUGO
SHINJU

HARUKO KUMOTA

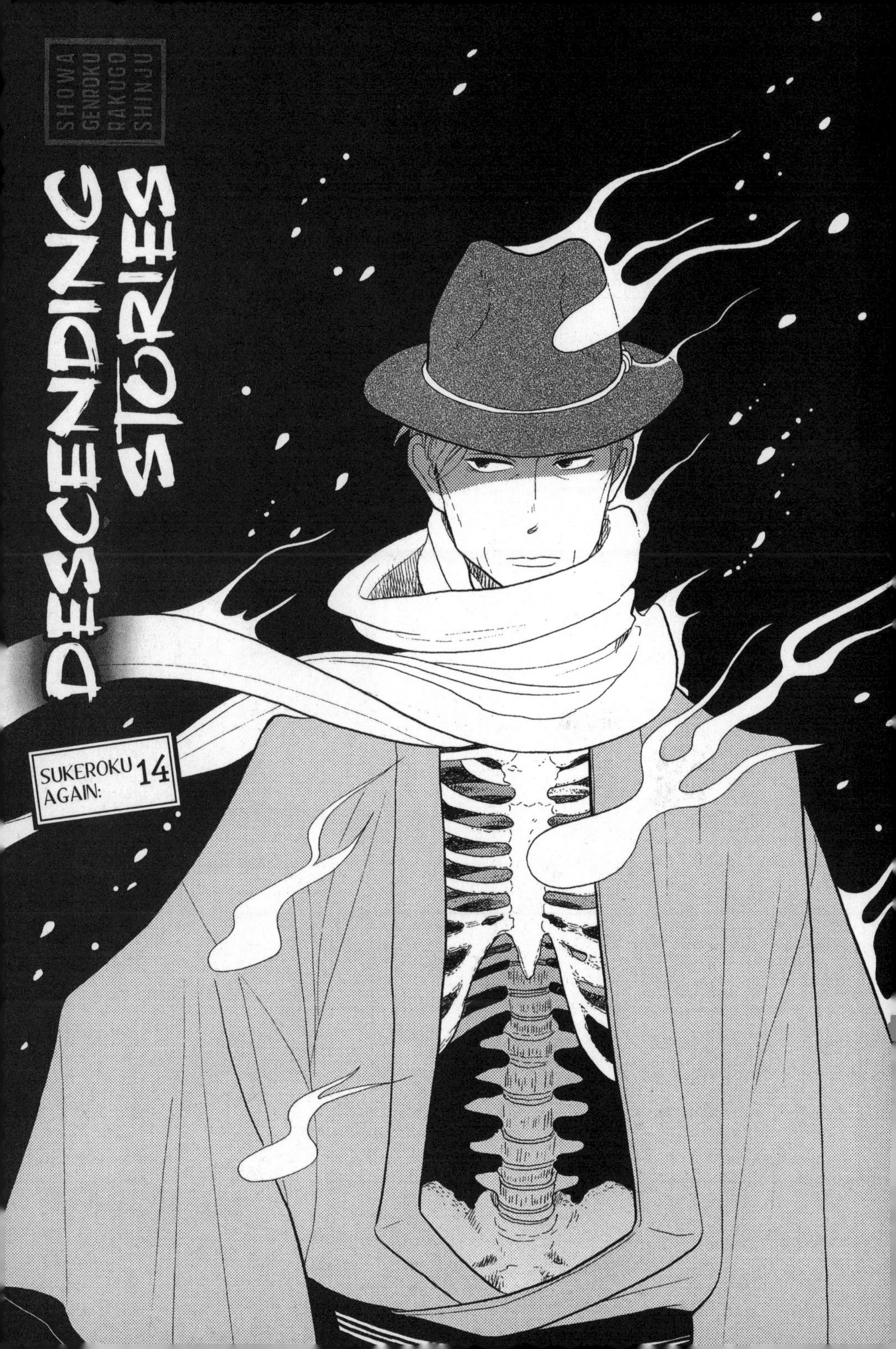
SHOWA GENROKU RAKUGO SHINJU
DESCENDING STORIES
SUKEROKU AGAIN: 14

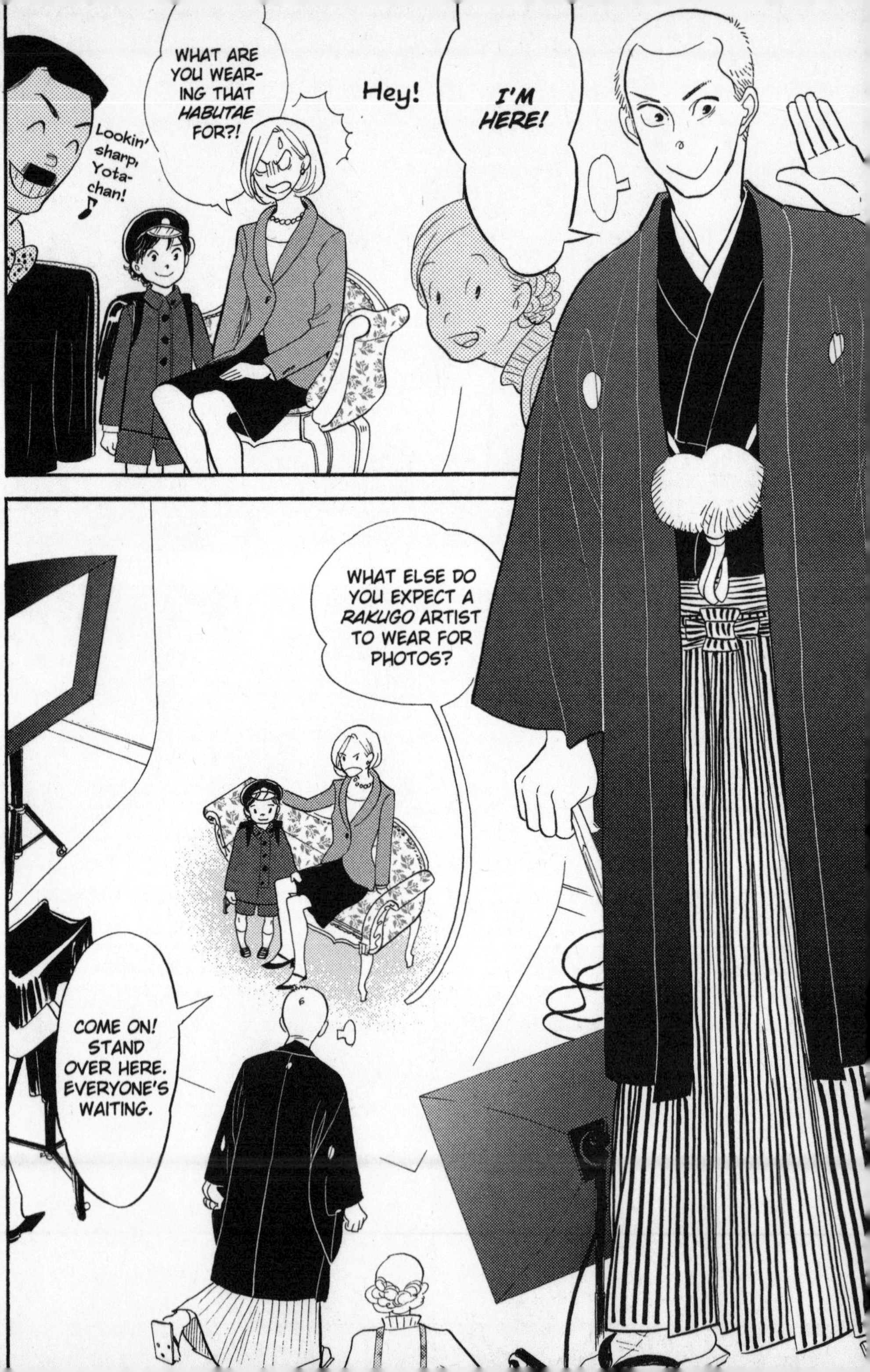
I'M HERE!
Hey!
WHAT ARE YOU WEAR-ING THAT HABUTAE FOR?!
Lookin' sharp, Yota-chan!
WHAT ELSE DO YOU EXPECT A RAKUGO ARTIST TO WEAR FOR PHOTOS?
COME ON! STAND OVER HERE. EVERYONE'S WAITING.

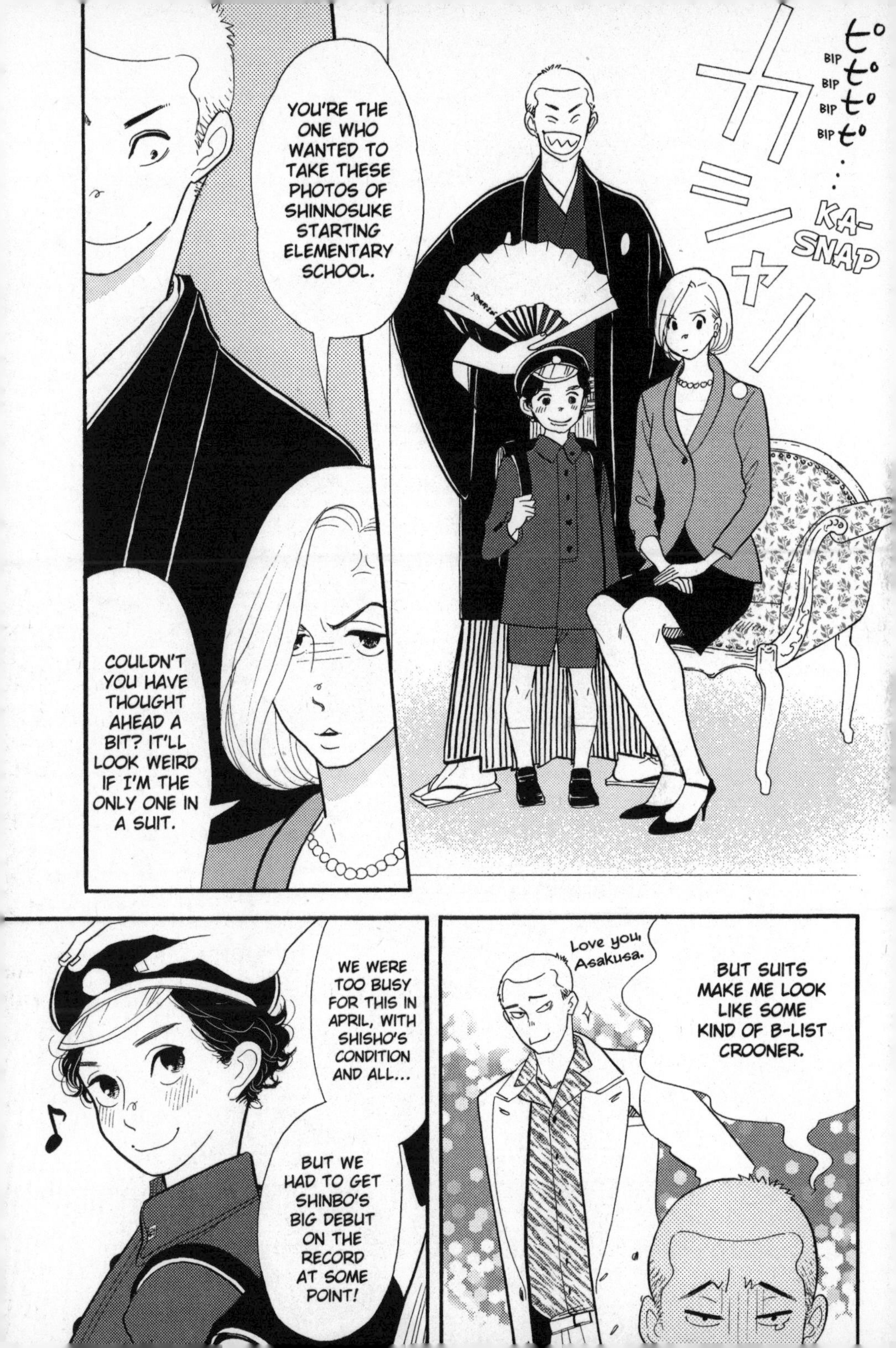
ピピピピピ…
BIP BIP BIP BIP
カシャン
KA-SNAP
YOU'RE THE ONE WHO WANTED TO TAKE THESE PHOTOS OF SHINNOSUKE STARTING ELEMENTARY SCHOOL.
COULDN'T YOU HAVE THOUGHT AHEAD A BIT? IT'LL LOOK WEIRD IF I'M THE ONLY ONE IN A SUIT.
Love you, Asakusa.
BUT SUITS MAKE ME LOOK LIKE SOME KIND OF B-LIST CROONER.
WE WERE TOO BUSY FOR THIS IN APRIL, WITH SHISHO'S CONDITION AND ALL...
BUT WE HAD TO GET SHINBO'S BIG DEBUT ON THE RECORD AT SOME POINT!

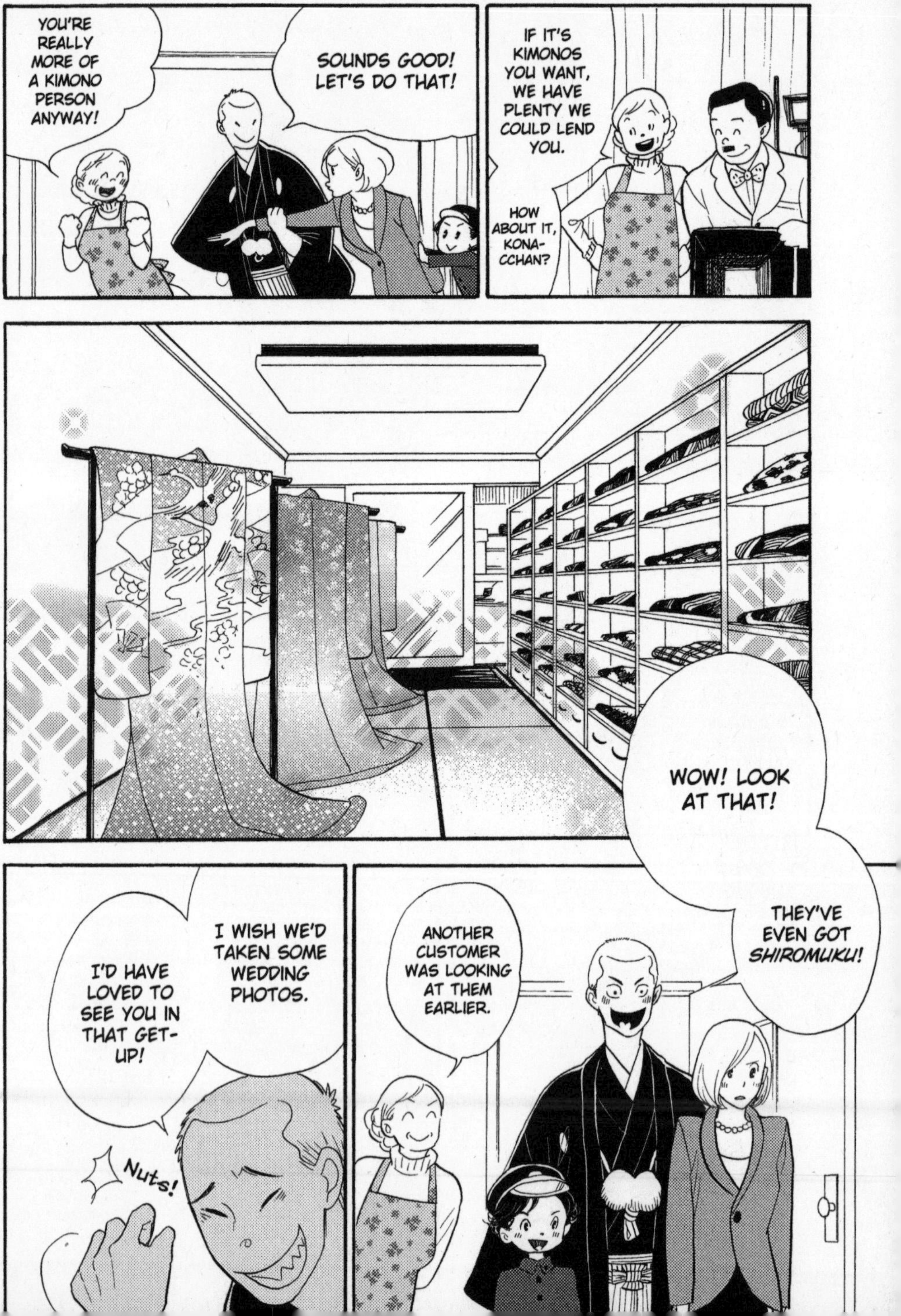
IF IT'S KIMONOS YOU WANT, WE HAVE PLENTY WE COULD LEND YOU.
HOW ABOUT IT, KONA-CCHAN?
SOUNDS GOOD! LET'S DO THAT!
YOU'RE REALLY MORE OF A KIMONO PERSON ANYWAY!
WOW! LOOK AT THAT!
THEY'VE EVEN GOT *SHIROMUKU*!
ANOTHER CUSTOMER WAS LOOKING AT THEM EARLIER.
I WISH WE'D TAKEN SOME WEDDING PHOTOS.
I'D HAVE LOVED TO SEE YOU IN THAT GET-UP!
Nuts!

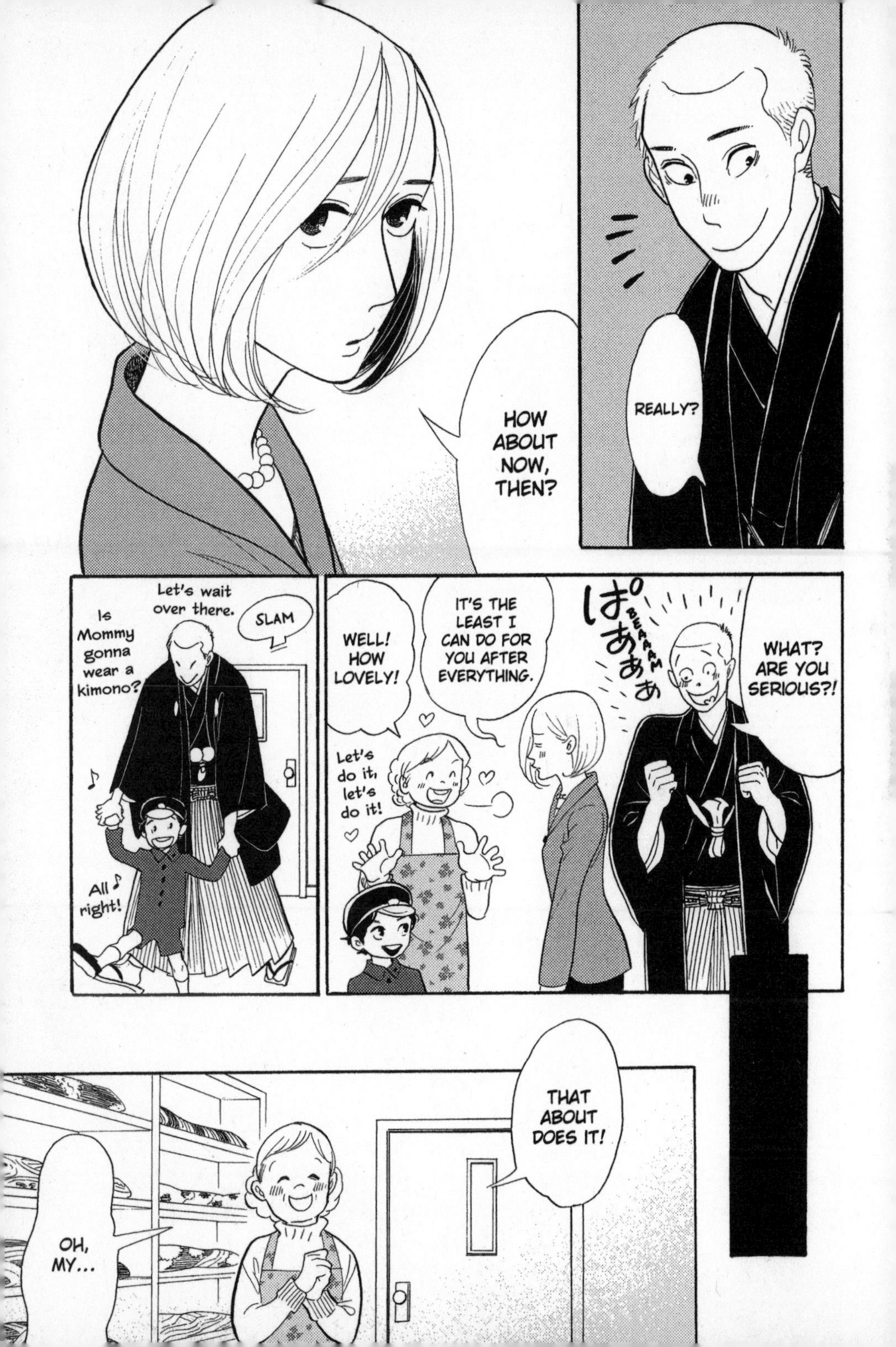
REALLY?
HOW ABOUT NOW, THEN?
WHAT? ARE YOU SERIOUS?!
ぱあああ
BEAAAM
IT'S THE LEAST I CAN DO FOR YOU AFTER EVERYTHING.
WELL! HOW LOVELY!
Let's do it, let's do it!
SLAM
Let's wait over there.
Is Mommy gonna wear a kimono?
All right!
THAT ABOUT DOES IT!
OH, MY...

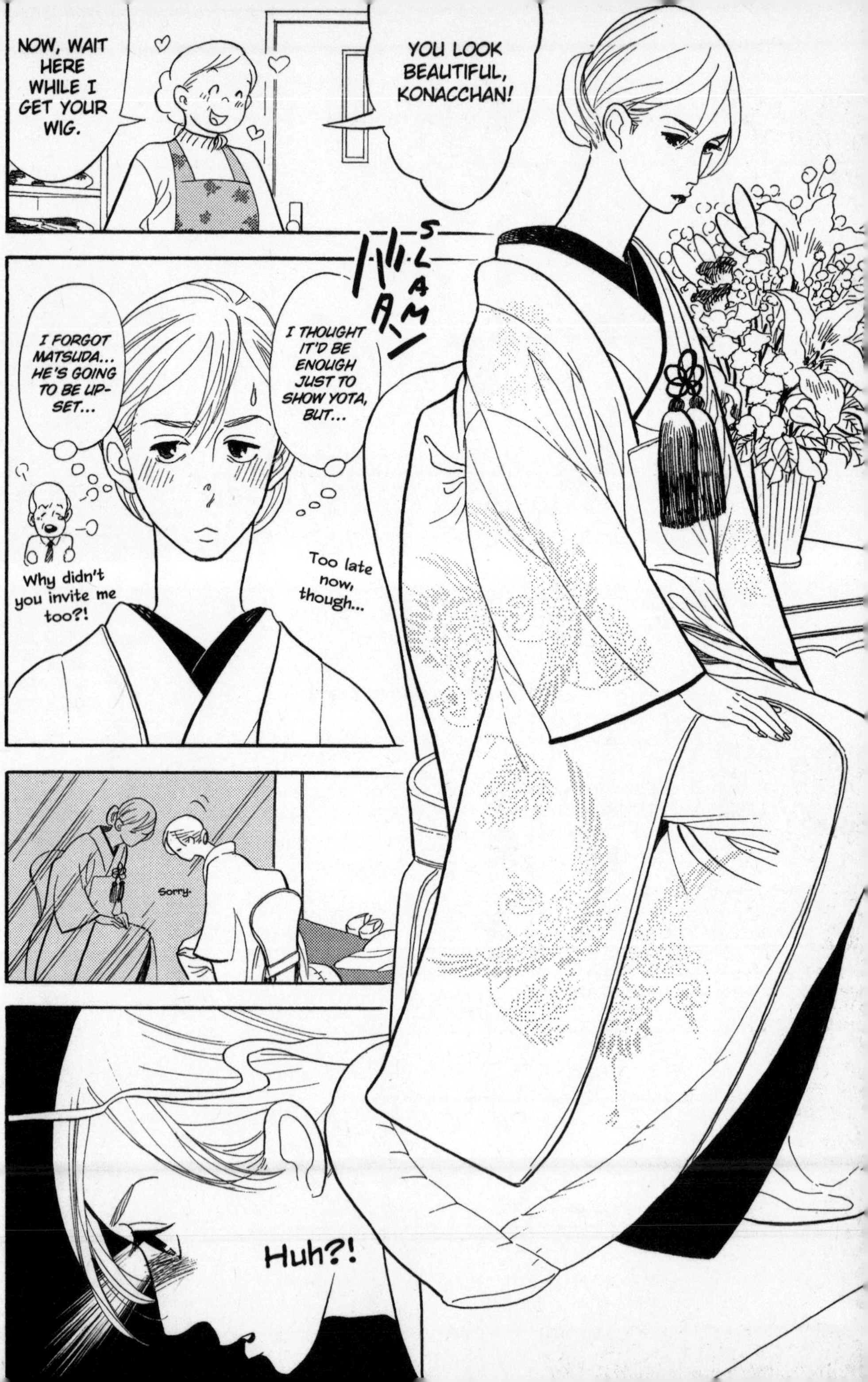
YOU LOOK BEAUTIFUL, KONACCHAN!
NOW, WAIT HERE WHILE I GET YOUR WIG.
SLAM
I THOUGHT IT'D BE ENOUGH JUST TO SHOW YOTA, BUT...
I FORGOT MATSUDA... HE'S GOING TO BE UP-SET...
Why didn't you invite me too?!
Too late now, though...
Sorry.
Huh?!

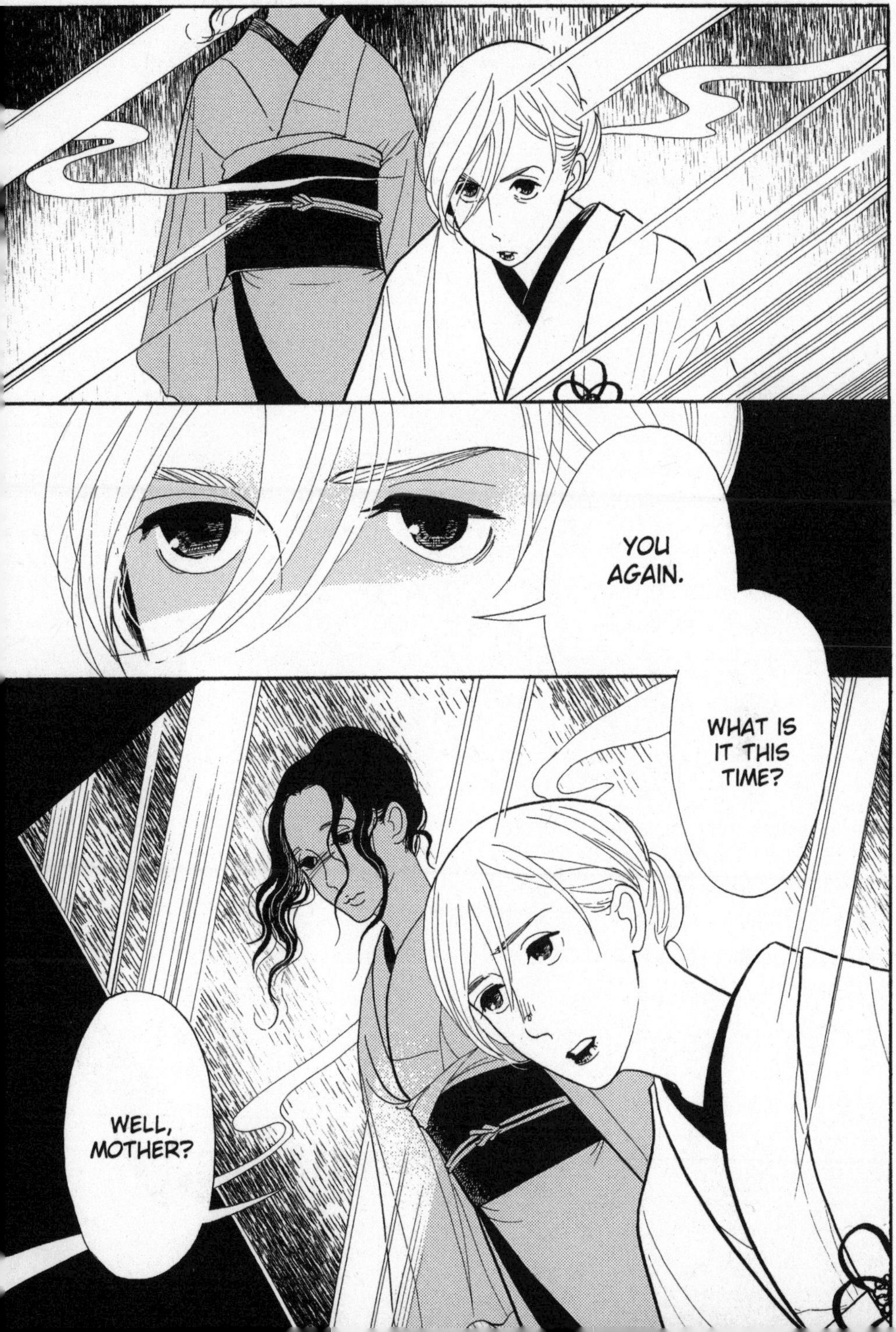
YOU AGAIN.
WHAT IS IT THIS TIME?
WELL, MOTHER?

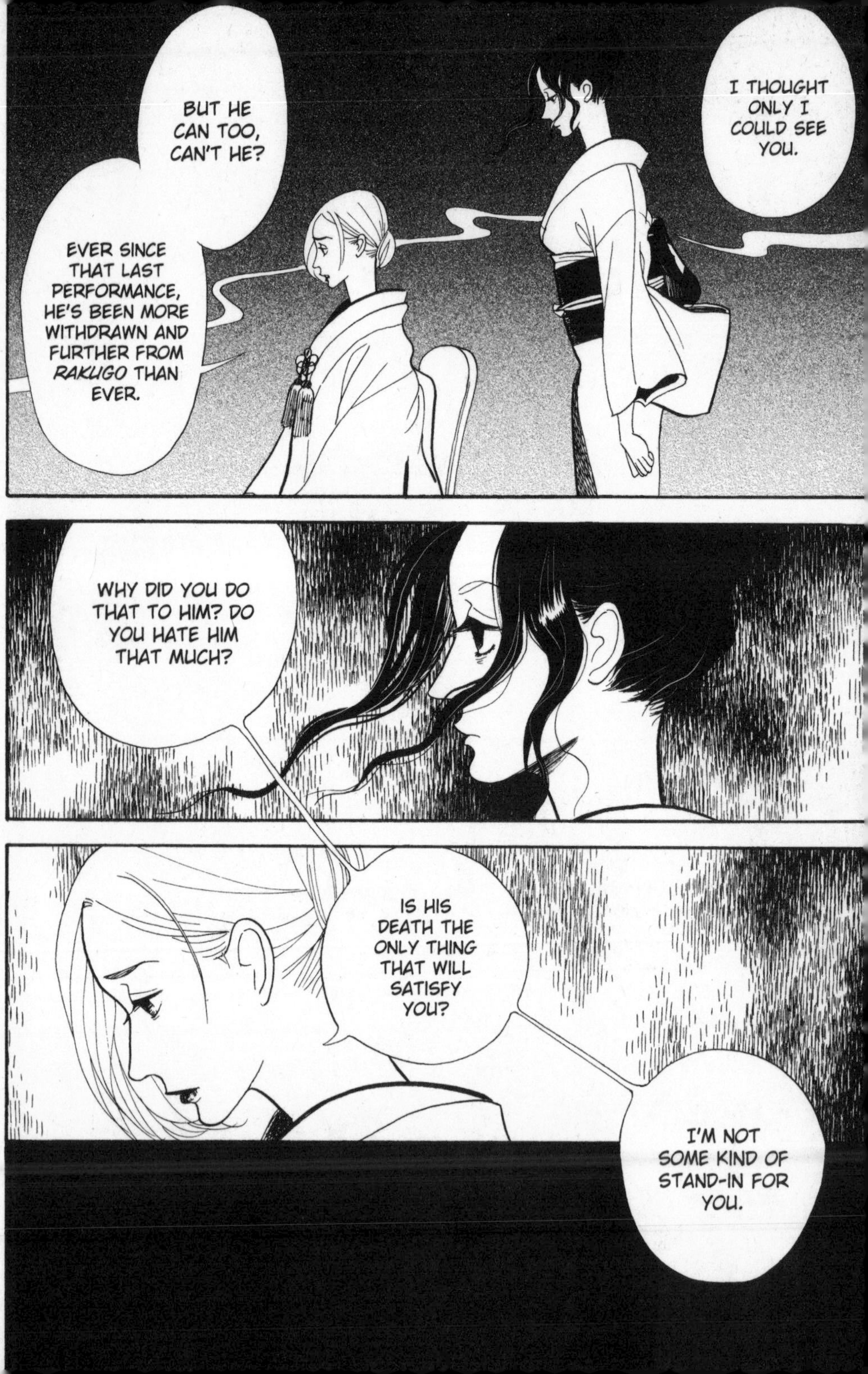
I THOUGHT ONLY I COULD SEE YOU.
BUT HE CAN TOO, CAN'T HE?
EVER SINCE THAT LAST PERFORMANCE, HE'S BEEN MORE WITHDRAWN AND FURTHER FROM *RAKUGO* THAN EVER.
WHY DID YOU DO THAT TO HIM? DO YOU HATE HIM THAT MUCH?
IS HIS DEATH THE ONLY THING THAT WILL SATISFY YOU?
I'M NOT SOME KIND OF STAND-IN FOR YOU.

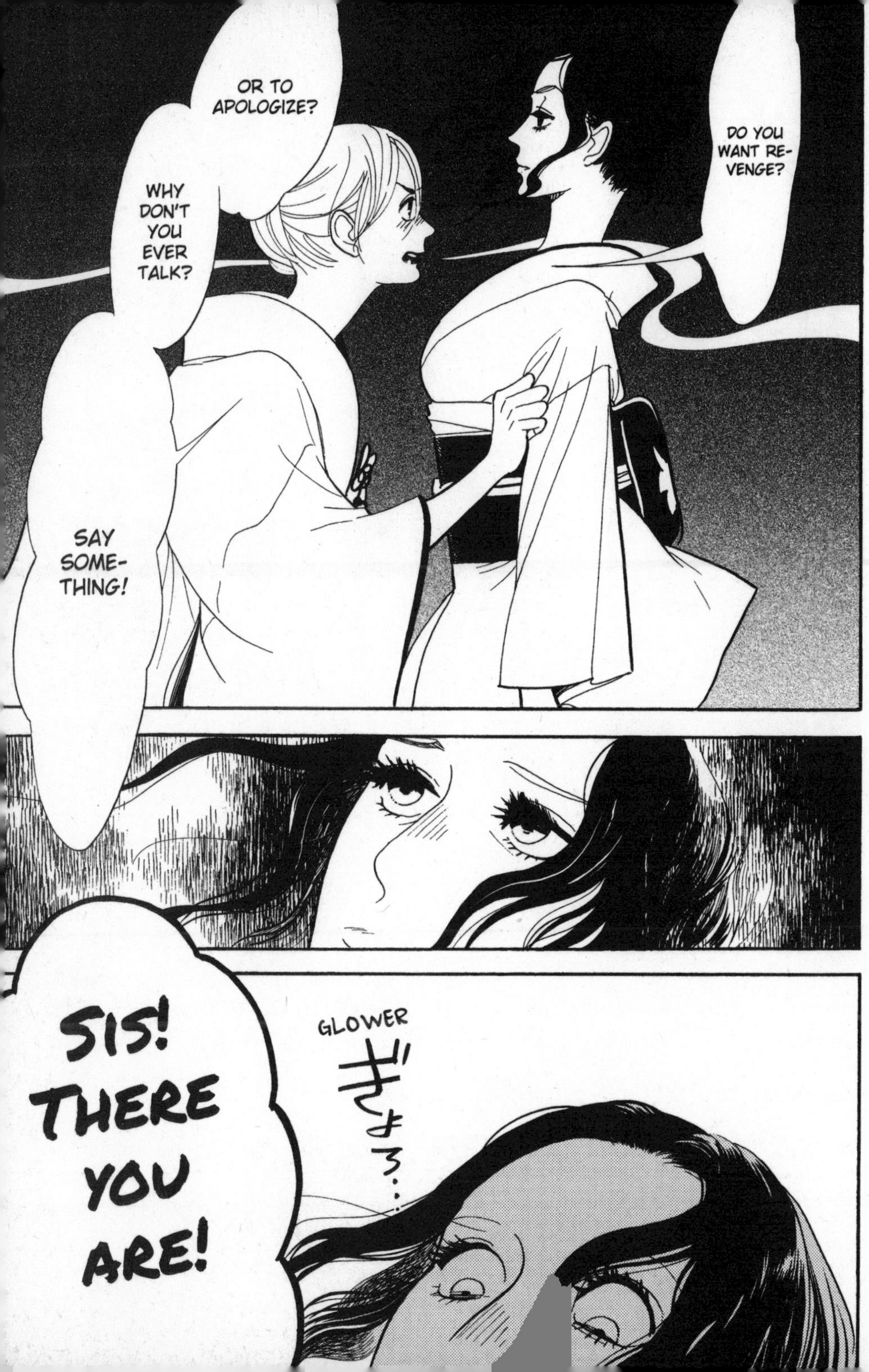
DO YOU WANT RE-VENGE?
OR TO APOLOGIZE?
WHY DON'T YOU EVER TALK?
SAY SOME-THING!
GLOWER
ぎょろ…
SIS! THERE YOU ARE!

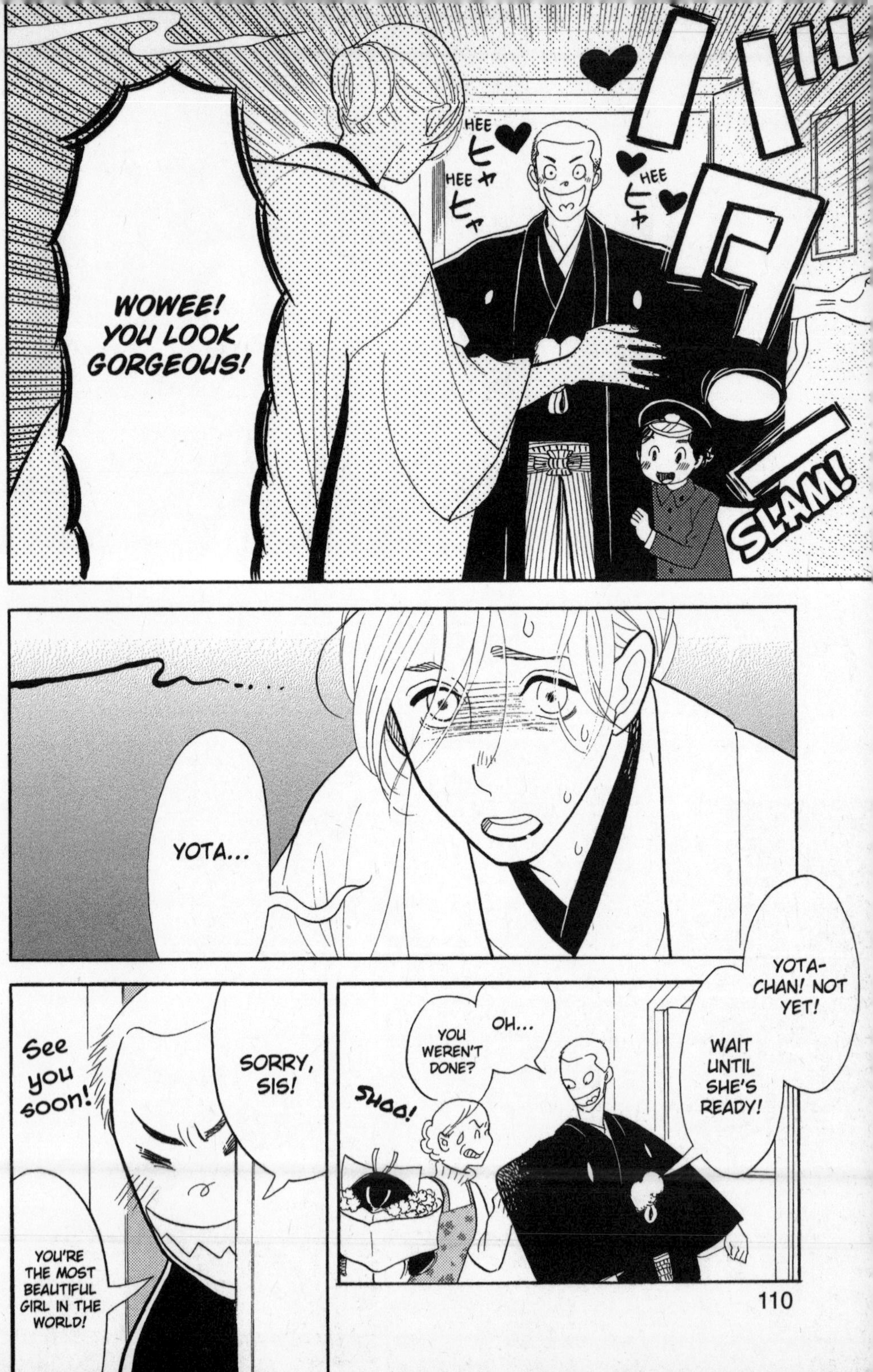
SLAM!
HEE
ヒャ
HEE
ヒャ
HEE
ヒャ
WOWEE! YOU LOOK GORGEOUS!
YOTA...
YOTA-CHAN! NOT YET!
WAIT UNTIL SHE'S READY!
OH...
YOU WEREN'T DONE?
SHOO!
SORRY, SIS!
See you soon!
YOU'RE THE MOST BEAUTIFUL GIRL IN THE WORLD!

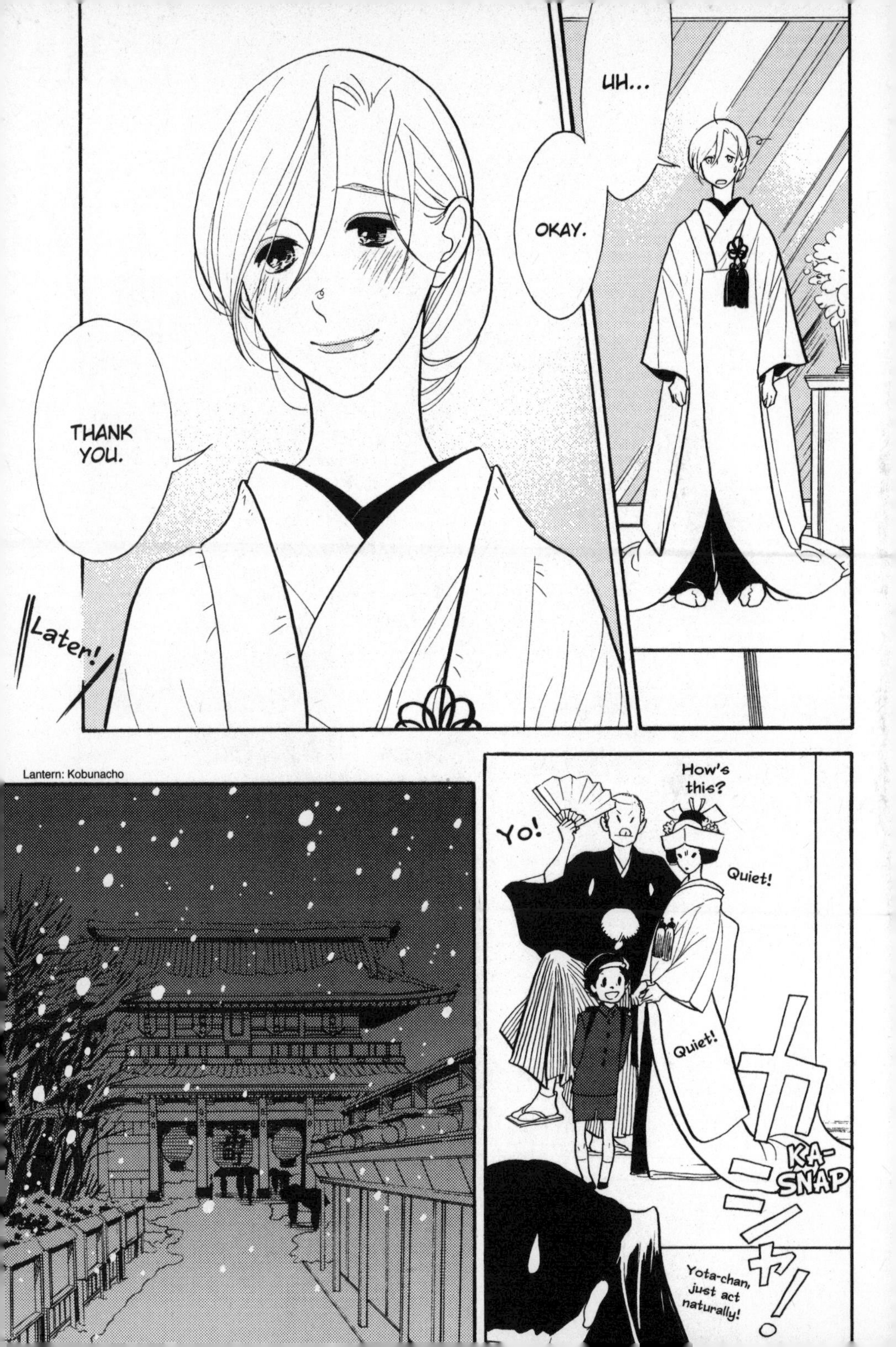
UH...
OKAY.
THANK YOU.
Later!
How's this?
Yo!
Quiet!
Quiet!
KA-SNAP
Yota-chan, just act naturally!
Lantern: Kobunacho

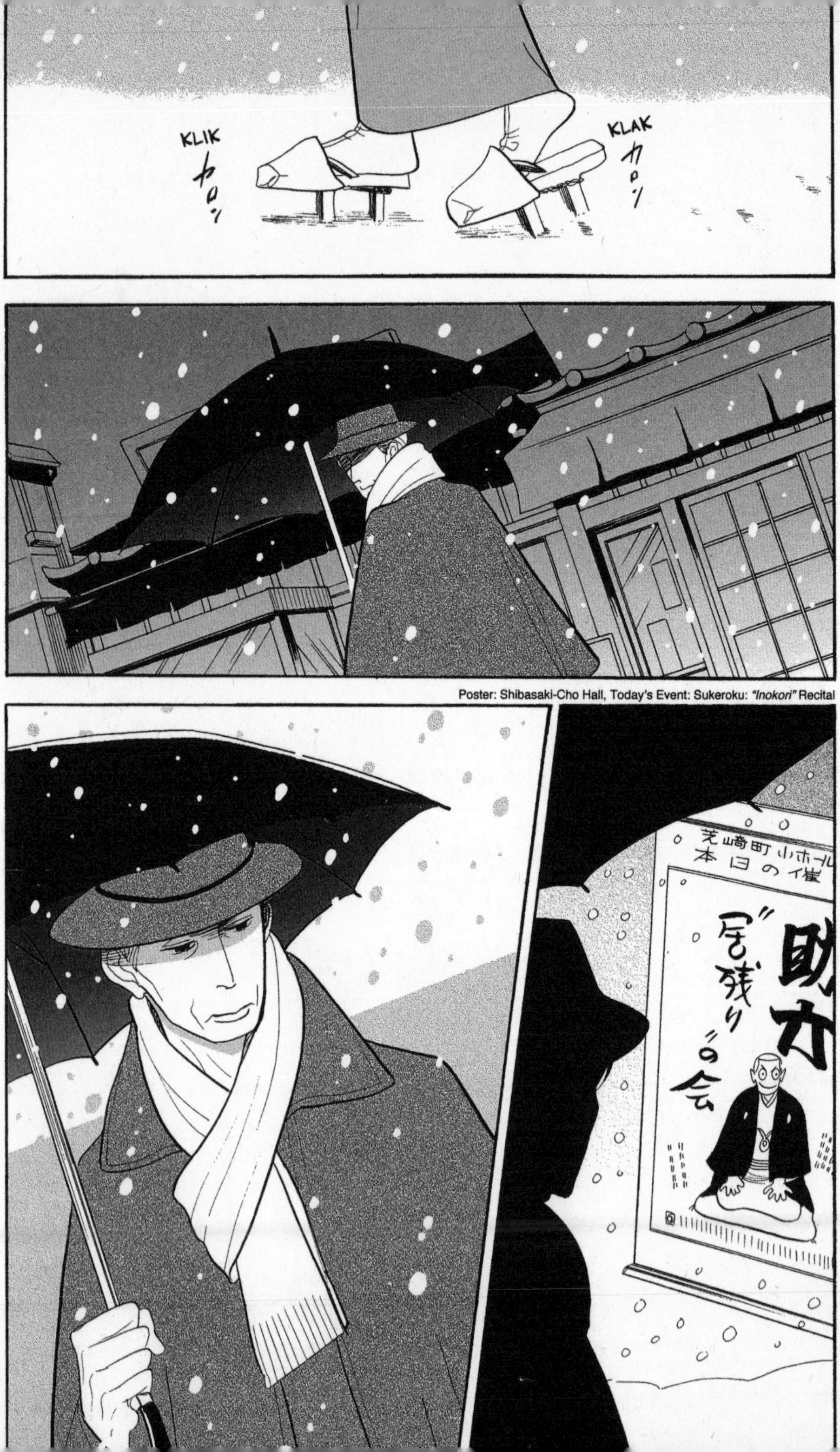
KLAK
カロン
KLIK
カロン
芝崎町小ホール
本日の催
助六
"居残り"の会

Poster: Shibasaki-Cho Hall, Today's Event: Sukeroku: *"Inokori"* Recital

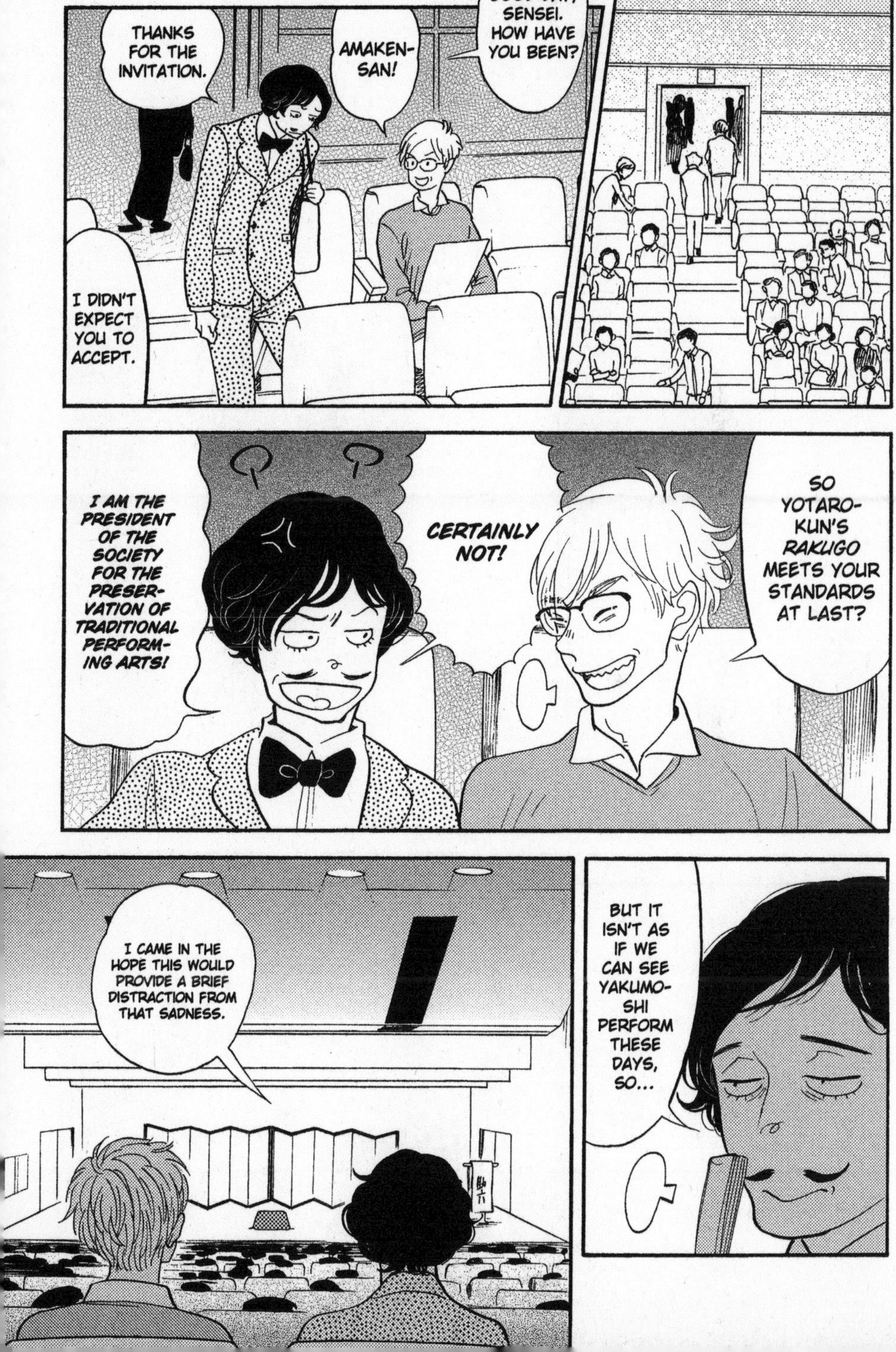
GOOD DAY, SENSEI. HOW HAVE YOU BEEN?
AMAKEN-SAN!
THANKS FOR THE INVITATION.
I DIDN'T EXPECT YOU TO ACCEPT.
SO YOTARO-KUN'S *RAKUGO* MEETS YOUR STANDARDS AT LAST?
CERTAINLY NOT!
I AM THE PRESIDENT OF THE SOCIETY FOR THE PRESERVATION OF TRADITIONAL PERFORMING ARTS!
BUT IT ISN'T AS IF WE CAN SEE YAKUMO-SHI PERFORM THESE DAYS, SO...
I CAME IN THE HOPE THIS WOULD PROVIDE A BRIEF DISTRACTION FROM THAT SADNESS.

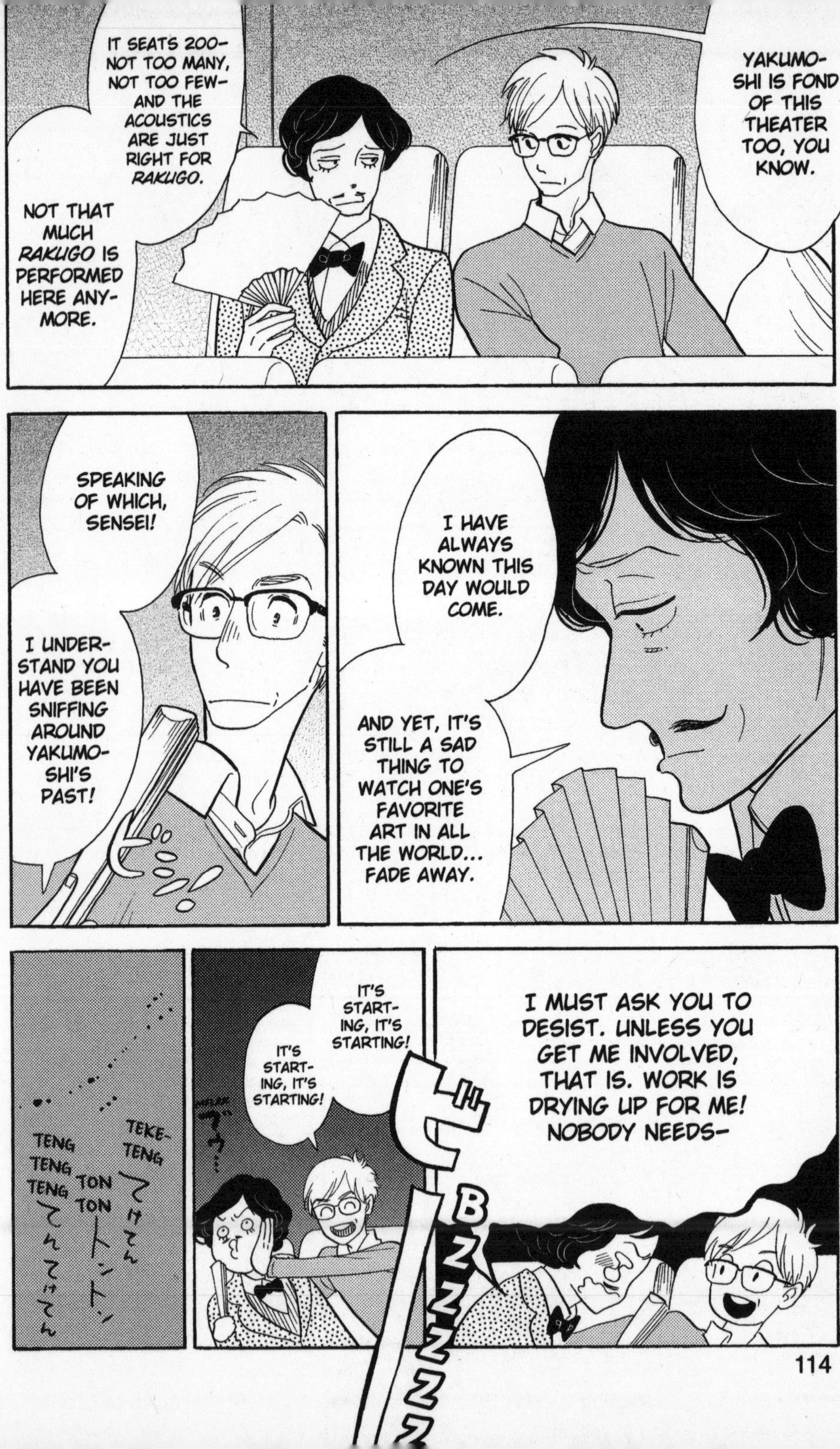
YAKUMO-SHI IS FOND OF THIS THEATER TOO, YOU KNOW.
IT SEATS 200—NOT TOO MANY, NOT TOO FEW—AND THE ACOUSTICS ARE JUST RIGHT FOR *RAKUGO.*
NOT THAT MUCH *RAKUGO* IS PERFORMED HERE ANY-MORE.
I HAVE ALWAYS KNOWN THIS DAY WOULD COME.
AND YET, IT'S STILL A SAD THING TO WATCH ONE'S FAVORITE ART IN ALL THE WORLD... FADE AWAY.
SPEAKING OF WHICH, SENSEI!
I UNDER-STAND YOU HAVE BEEN SNIFFING AROUND YAKUMO-SHI'S PAST!
I MUST ASK YOU TO DESIST. UNLESS YOU GET ME INVOLVED, THAT IS. WORK IS DRYING UP FOR ME! NOBODY NEEDS—
BZZZZZ
IT'S START-ING, IT'S STARTING!
IT'S START-ING, IT'S STARTING!
TEKE-TENG
TENG TENG TENG
TON TON

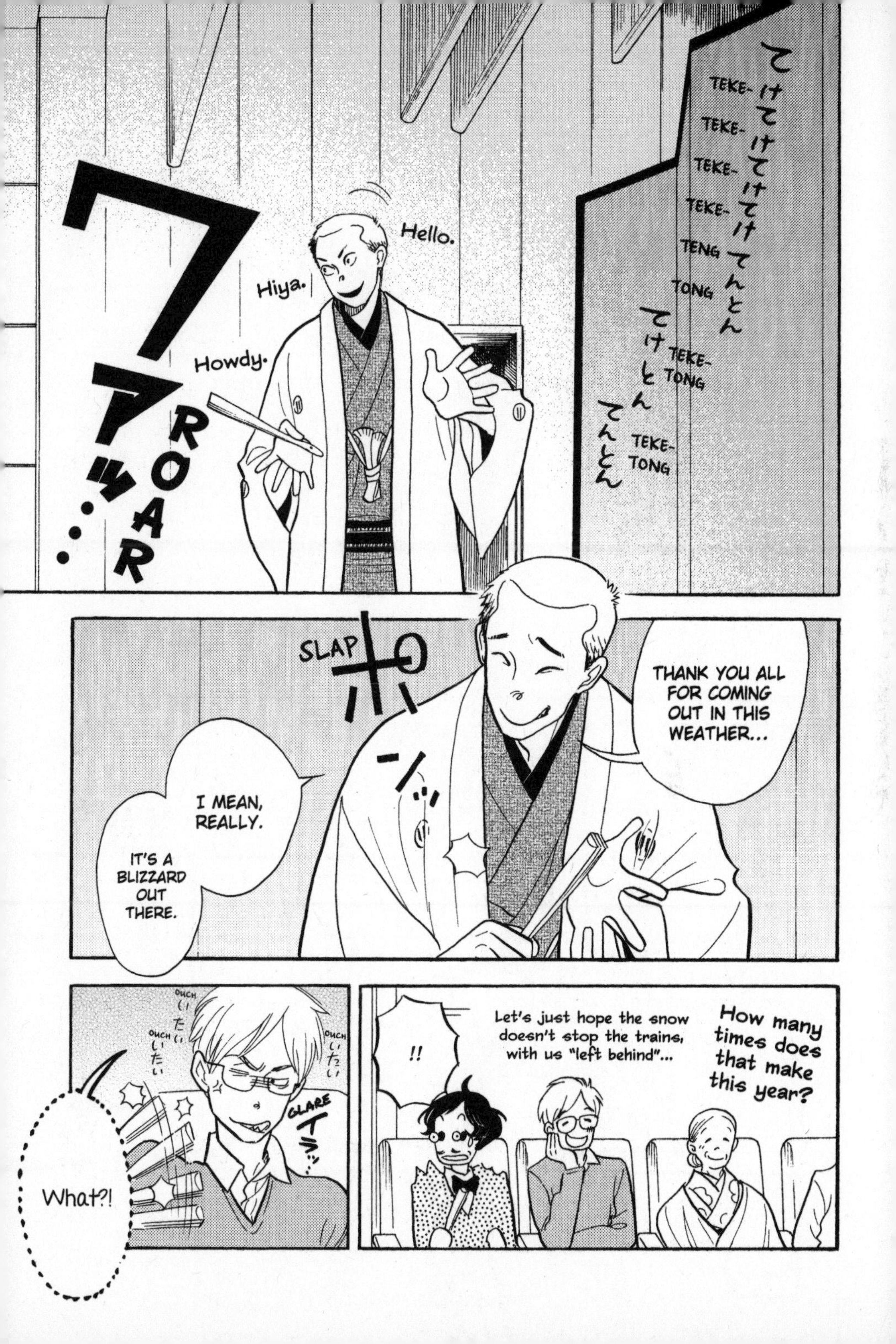
てけてけてけてけてんとん
TEKE- TEKE- TEKE- TEKE- TENG TONG
てけとん
TEKE-TONG
てんとん
TEKE-TONG
Hello.
Hiya.
Howdy.
ワァッ…
ROAR
THANK YOU ALL FOR COMING OUT IN THIS WEATHER...
ポン
SLAP
I MEAN, REALLY.
IT'S A BLIZZARD OUT THERE.
How many times does that make this year?
Let's just hope the snow doesn't stop the trains, with us "left behind"...
!!
いたい
OUCH
いたい
OUCH
いたい
OUCH
イラッ
GLARE
What?!

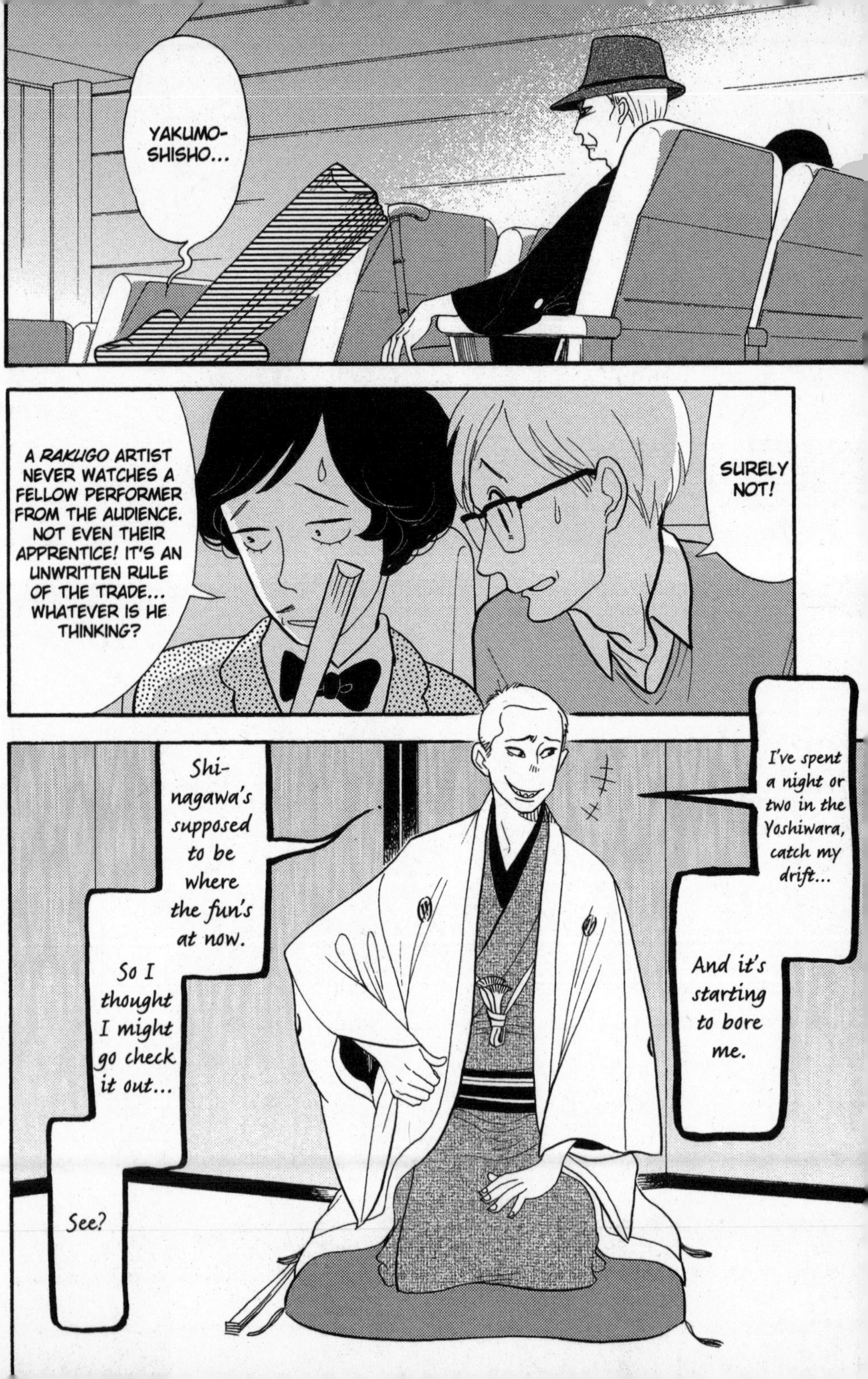
YAKUMO-SHISHO...
SURELY NOT!
A *RAKUGO* ARTIST NEVER WATCHES A FELLOW PERFORMER FROM THE AUDIENCE. NOT EVEN THEIR APPRENTICE! IT'S AN UNWRITTEN RULE OF THE TRADE... WHATEVER IS HE THINKING?
I've spent a night or two in the Yoshiwara, catch my drift...
And it's starting to bore me.
Shinagawa's supposed to be where the fun's at now.
So I thought I might go check it out...
See?

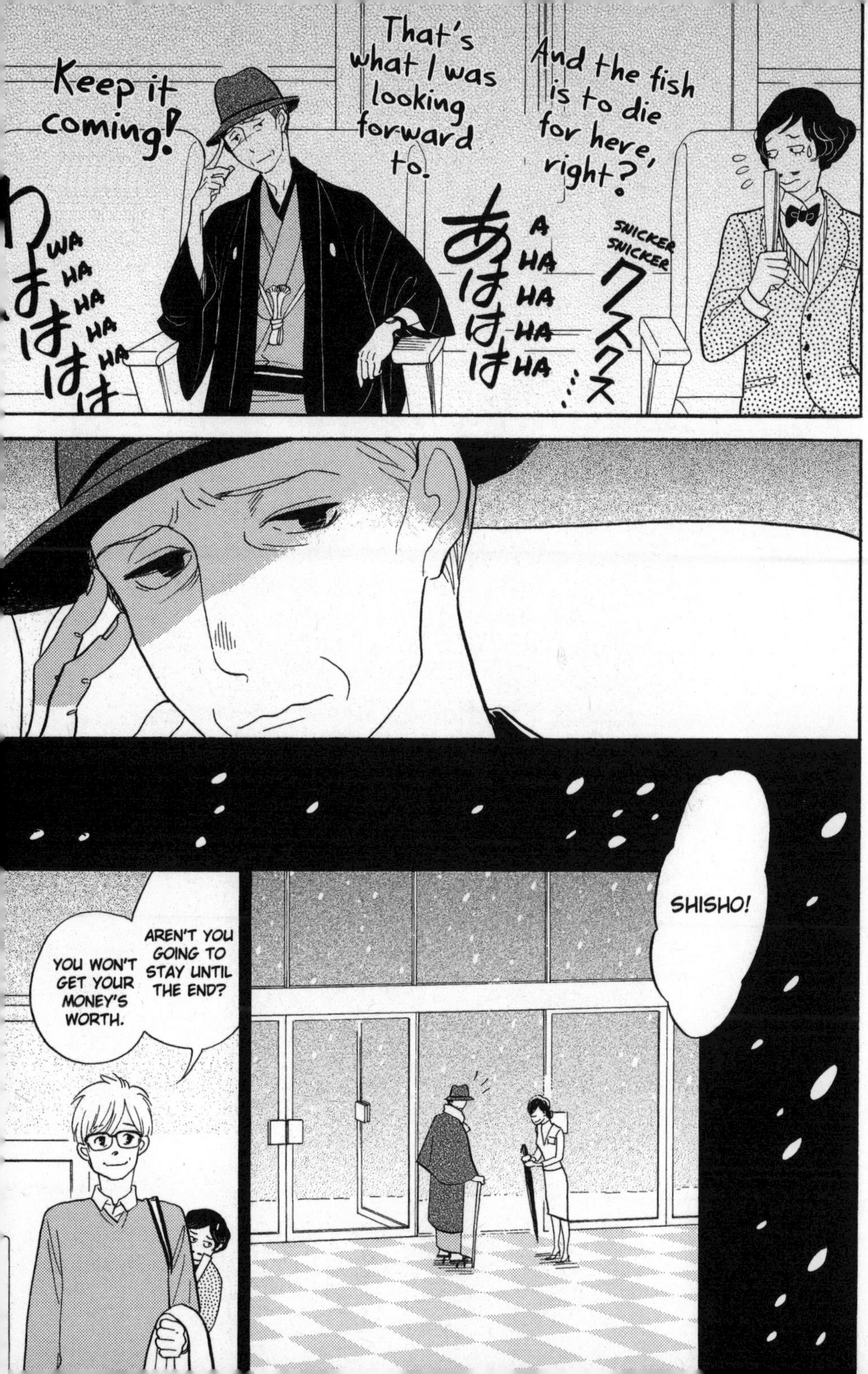
And the fish is to die for here, right?
SNICKER SNICKER
クスクス…
That's what I was looking forward to.
A HA HA HA HA
あははは
Keep it coming!
WA HA HA HA HA
わははは
SHISHO!
AREN'T YOU GOING TO STAY UNTIL THE END?
YOU WON'T GET YOUR MONEY'S WORTH.

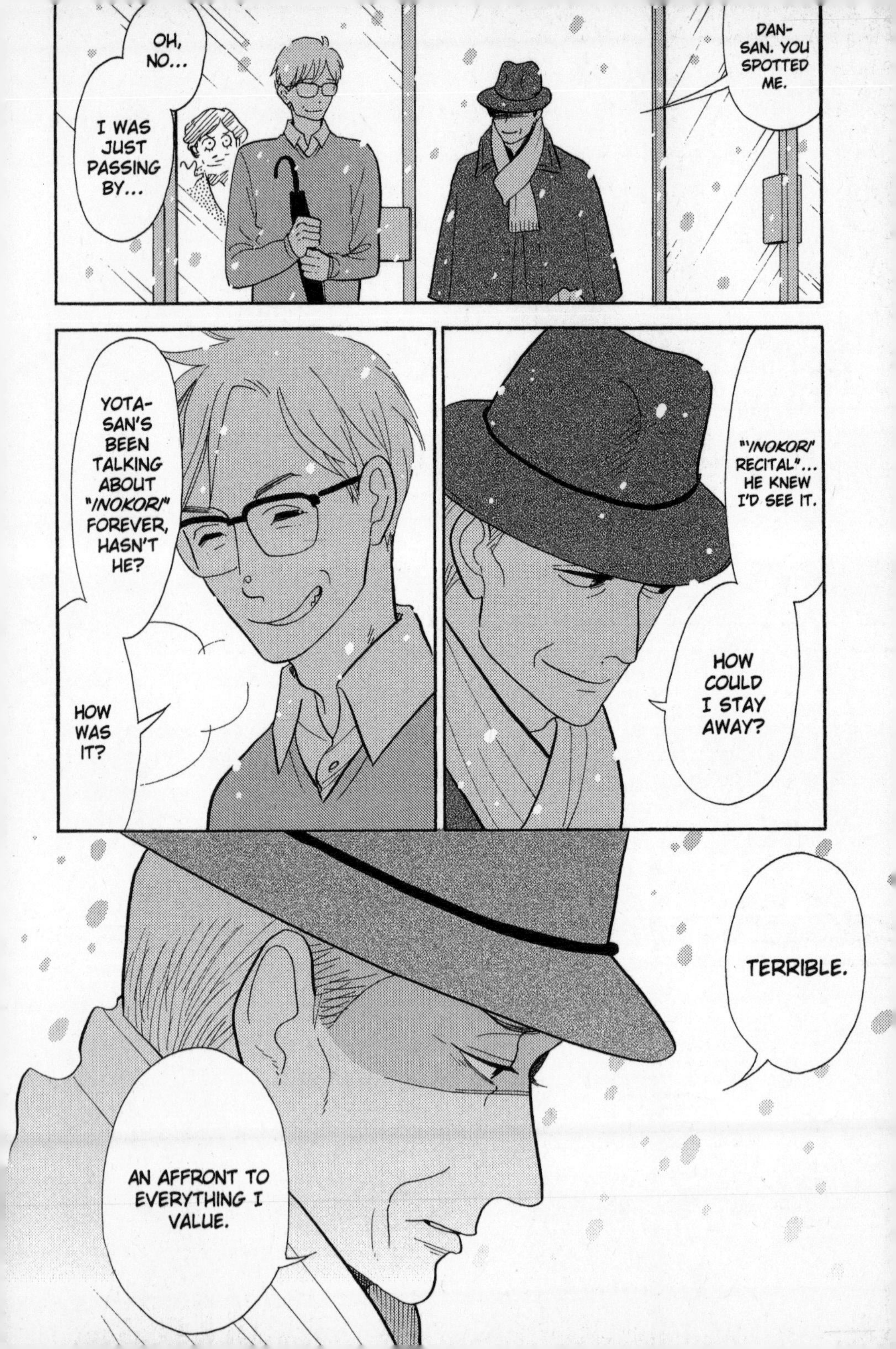
DAN-SAN. YOU SPOTTED ME.
OH, NO... I WAS JUST PASSING BY...
"*INOKORI*" RECITAL"... HE KNEW I'D SEE IT.
HOW COULD I STAY AWAY?
YOTA-SAN'S BEEN TALKING ABOUT "*INOKORI*" FOREVER, HASN'T HE?
HOW WAS IT?
TERRIBLE.
AN AFFRONT TO EVERYTHING I VALUE.

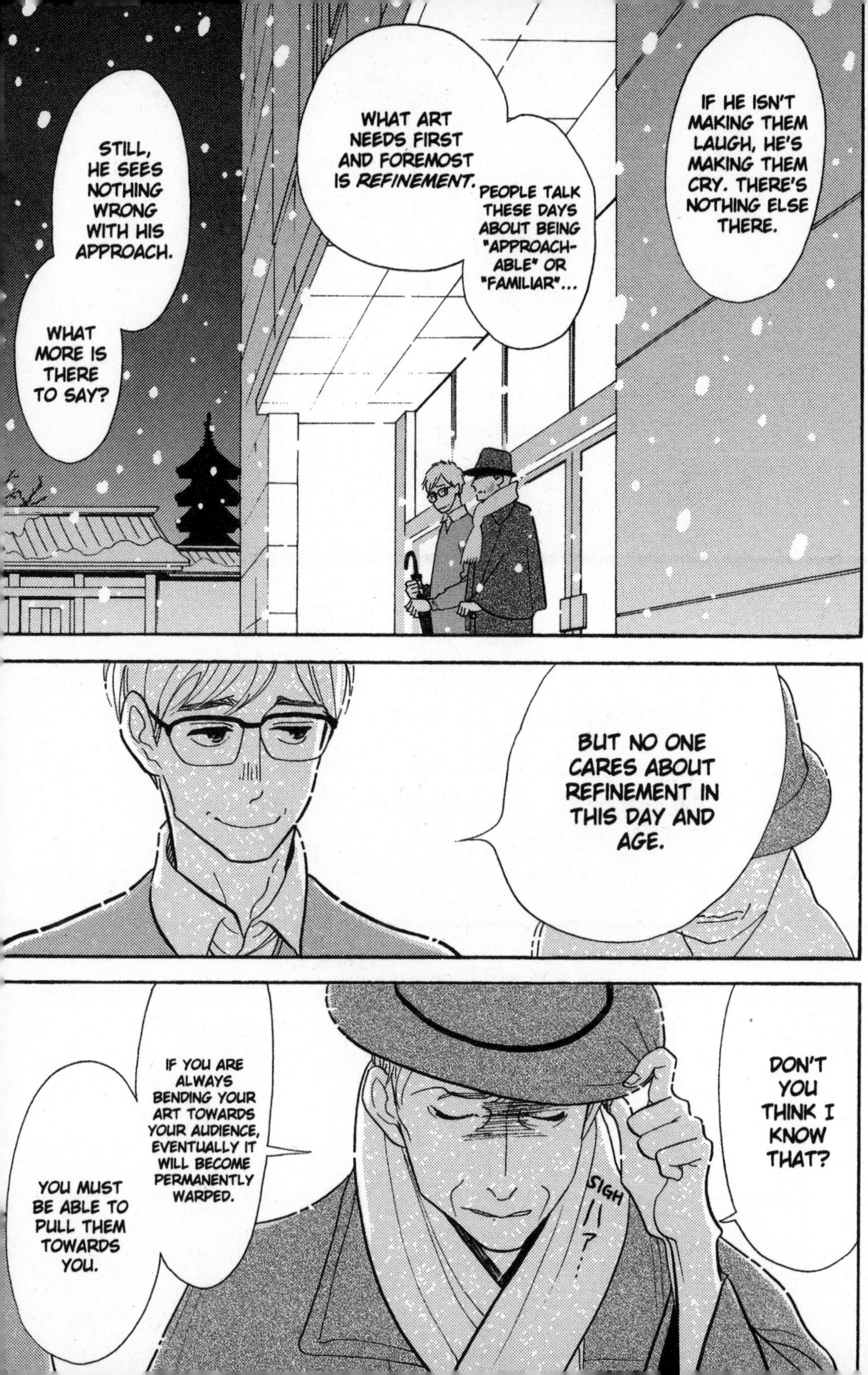
IF HE ISN'T MAKING THEM LAUGH, HE'S MAKING THEM CRY. THERE'S NOTHING ELSE THERE.
WHAT ART NEEDS FIRST AND FOREMOST IS *REFINEMENT*.
PEOPLE TALK THESE DAYS ABOUT BEING "APPROACH-ABLE" OR "FAMILIAR"...
STILL, HE SEES NOTHING WRONG WITH HIS APPROACH.
WHAT MORE IS THERE TO SAY?
BUT NO ONE CARES ABOUT REFINEMENT IN THIS DAY AND AGE.
DON'T YOU THINK I KNOW THAT?
SIGH
IF YOU ARE ALWAYS BENDING YOUR ART TOWARDS YOUR AUDIENCE, EVENTUALLY IT WILL BECOME PERMANENTLY WARPED.
YOU MUST BE ABLE TO PULL THEM TOWARDS YOU.

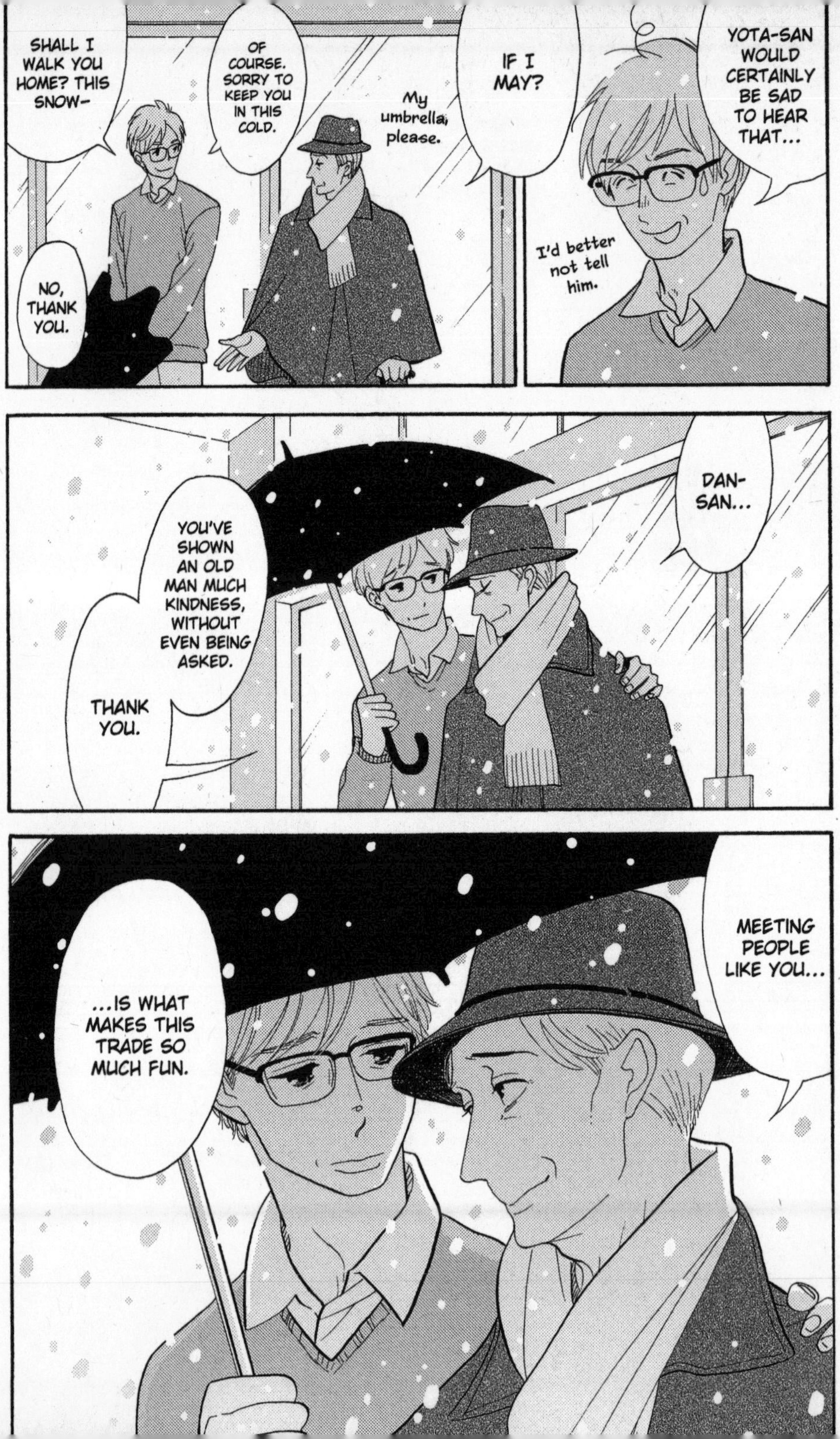
YOTA-SAN WOULD CERTAINLY BE SAD TO HEAR THAT…
I'd better not tell him.
IF I MAY?
My umbrella, please.
OF COURSE. SORRY TO KEEP YOU IN THIS COLD.
SHALL I WALK YOU HOME? THIS SNOW-
NO, THANK YOU.
DAN-SAN…
YOU'VE SHOWN AN OLD MAN MUCH KINDNESS, WITHOUT EVEN BEING ASKED.
THANK YOU.
MEETING PEOPLE LIKE YOU…
…IS WHAT MAKES THIS TRADE SO MUCH FUN.

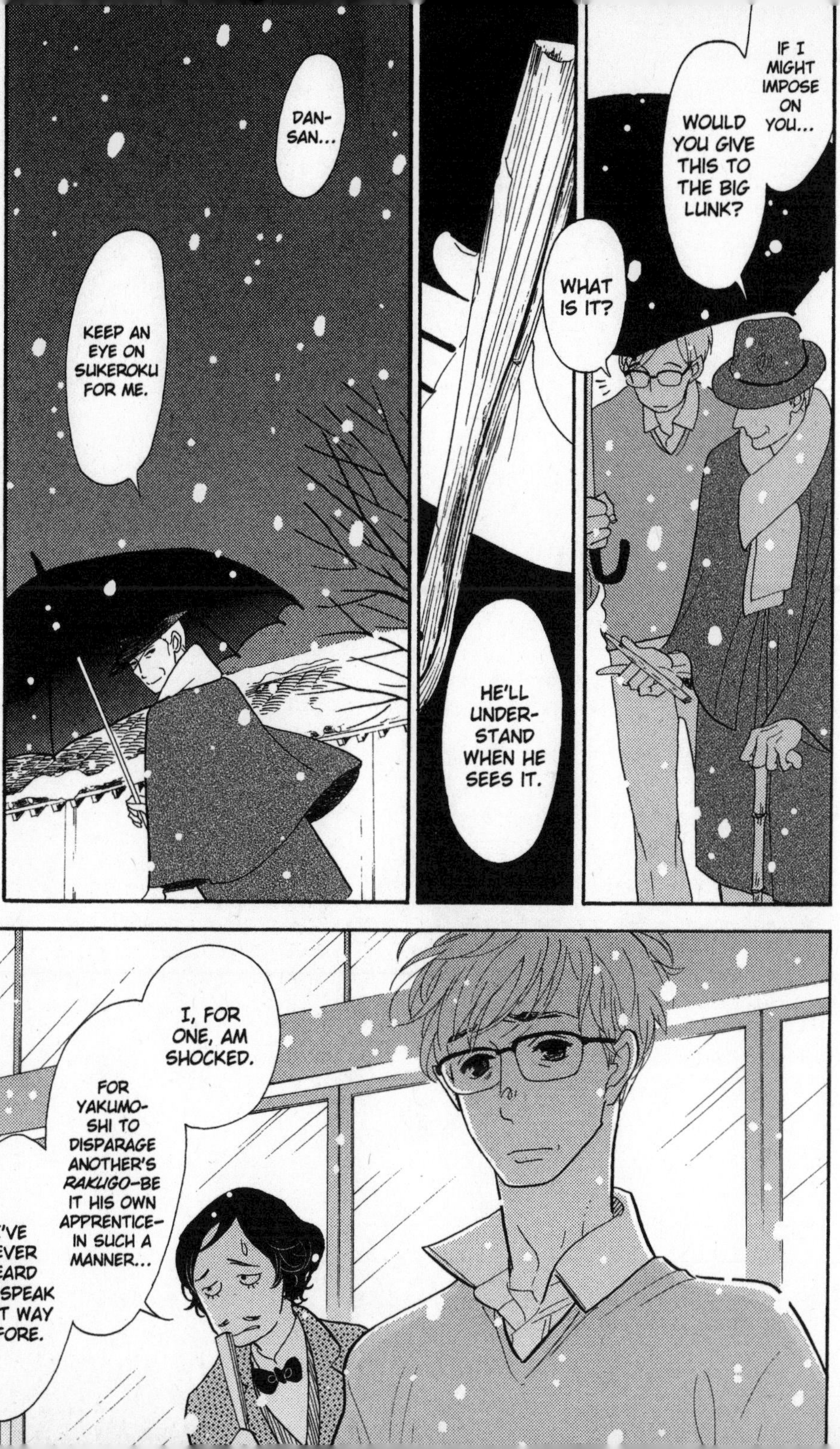
IF I MIGHT IMPOSE ON YOU...
WOULD YOU GIVE THIS TO THE BIG LUNK?
WHAT IS IT?
HE'LL UNDERSTAND WHEN HE SEES IT.
DAN-SAN...
KEEP AN EYE ON SUKEROKU FOR ME.
I, FOR ONE, AM SHOCKED.
FOR YAKUMO-SHI TO DISPARAGE ANOTHER'S *RAKUGO*—BE IT HIS OWN APPRENTICE—IN SUCH A MANNER...
I'VE NEVER HEARD HIM SPEAK THAT WAY BEFORE.

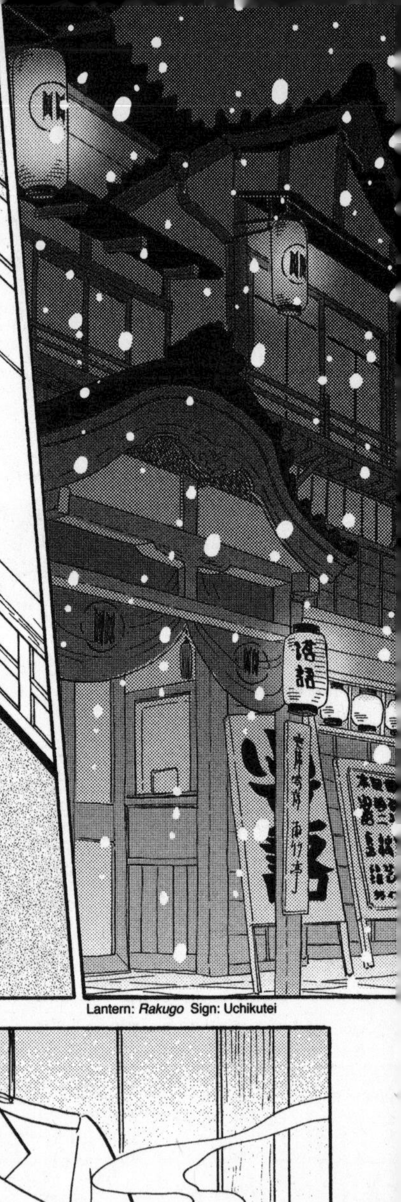

Lantern: *Rakugo* Sign: Uchikutei

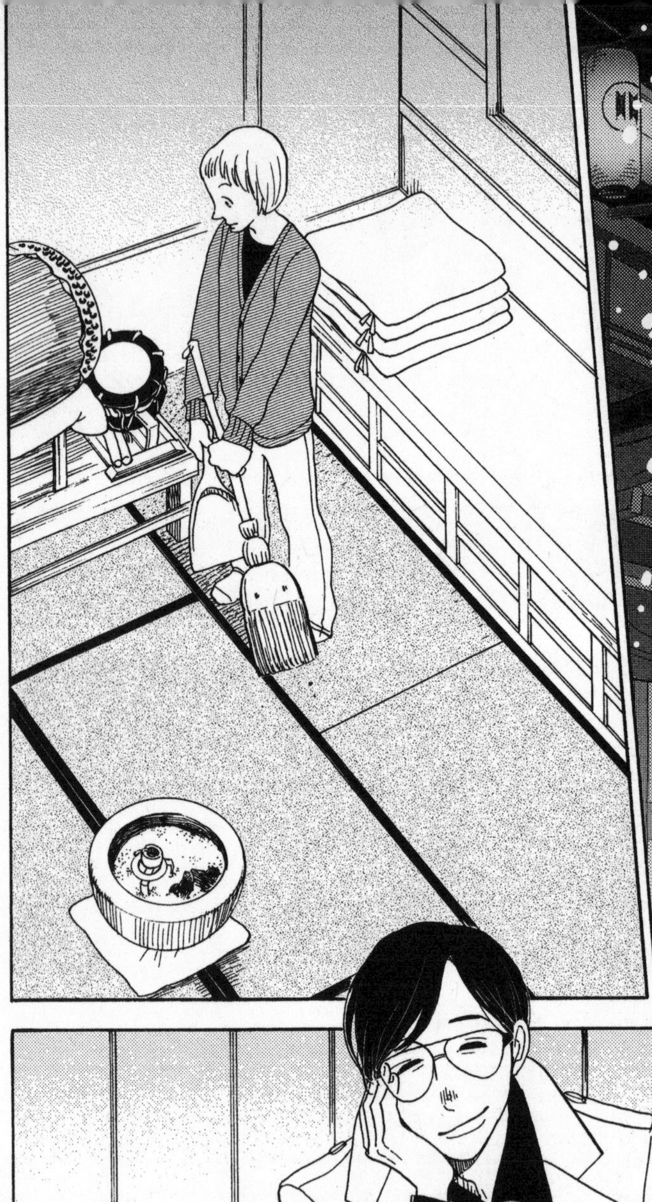

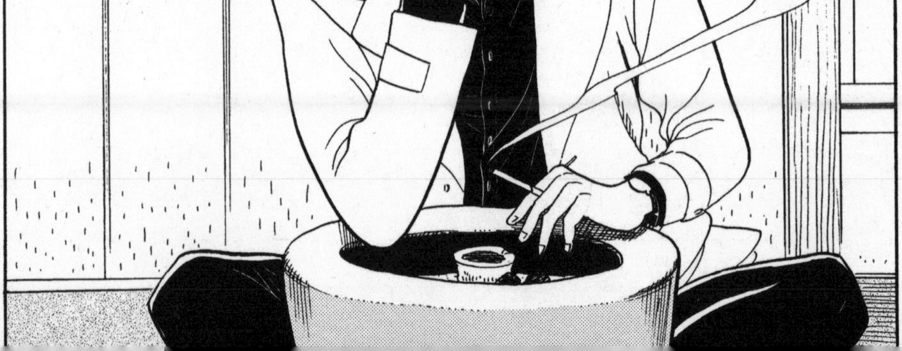

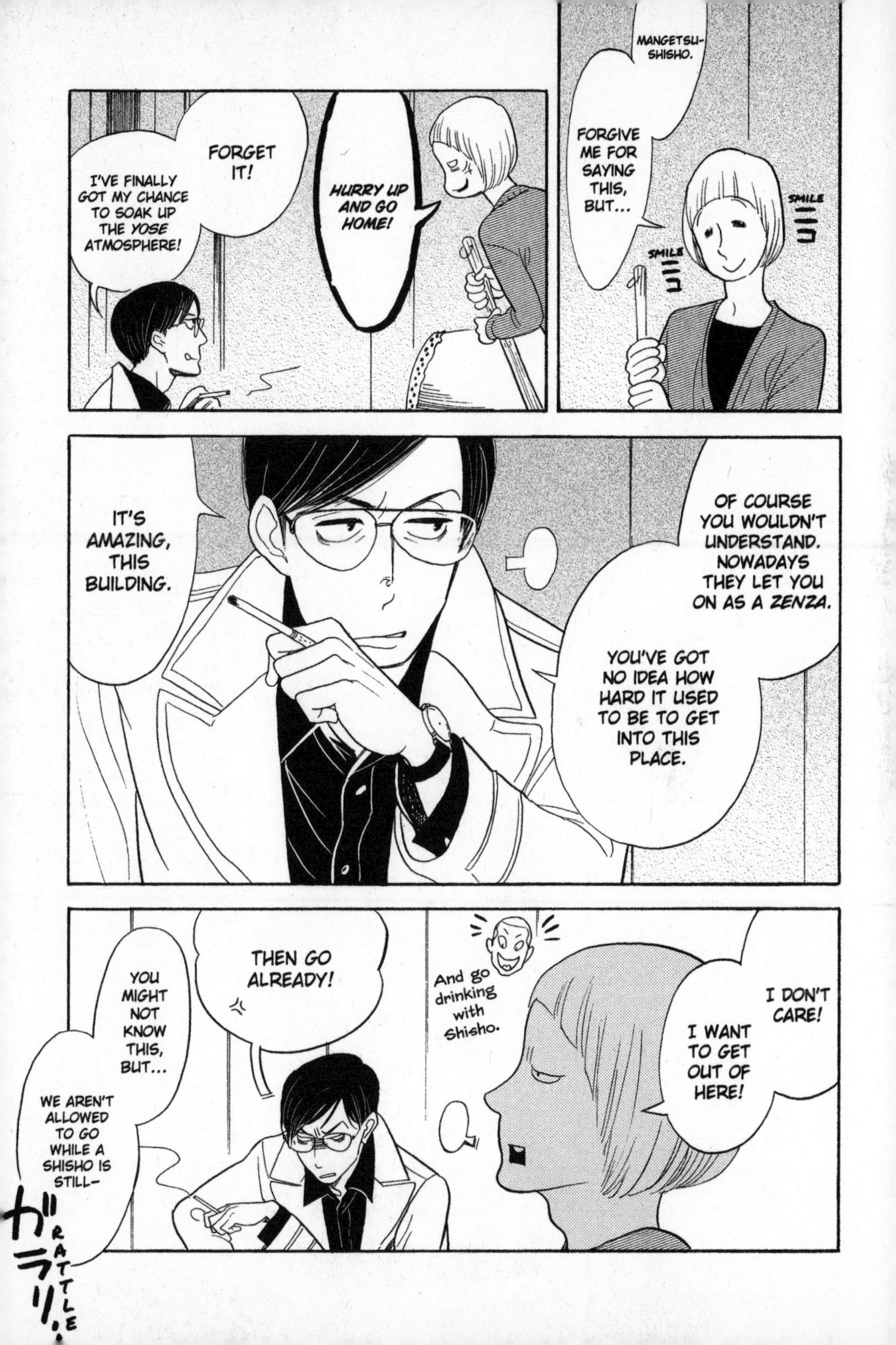
MANGETSU-SHISHO.
FORGIVE ME FOR SAYING THIS, BUT...
SMILE
SMILE
HURRY UP AND GO HOME!
FORGET IT!
I'VE FINALLY GOT MY CHANCE TO SOAK UP THE YOSE ATMOSPHERE!
OF COURSE YOU WOULDN'T UNDERSTAND. NOWADAYS THEY LET YOU ON AS A ZENZA.
YOU'VE GOT NO IDEA HOW HARD IT USED TO BE TO GET INTO THIS PLACE.
IT'S AMAZING, THIS BUILDING.
I DON'T CARE!
I WANT TO GET OUT OF HERE!
And go drinking with Shisho.
THEN GO ALREADY!
YOU MIGHT NOT KNOW THIS, BUT...
WE AREN'T ALLOWED TO GO WHILE A SHISHO IS STILL-
ガラリ
RATTLE

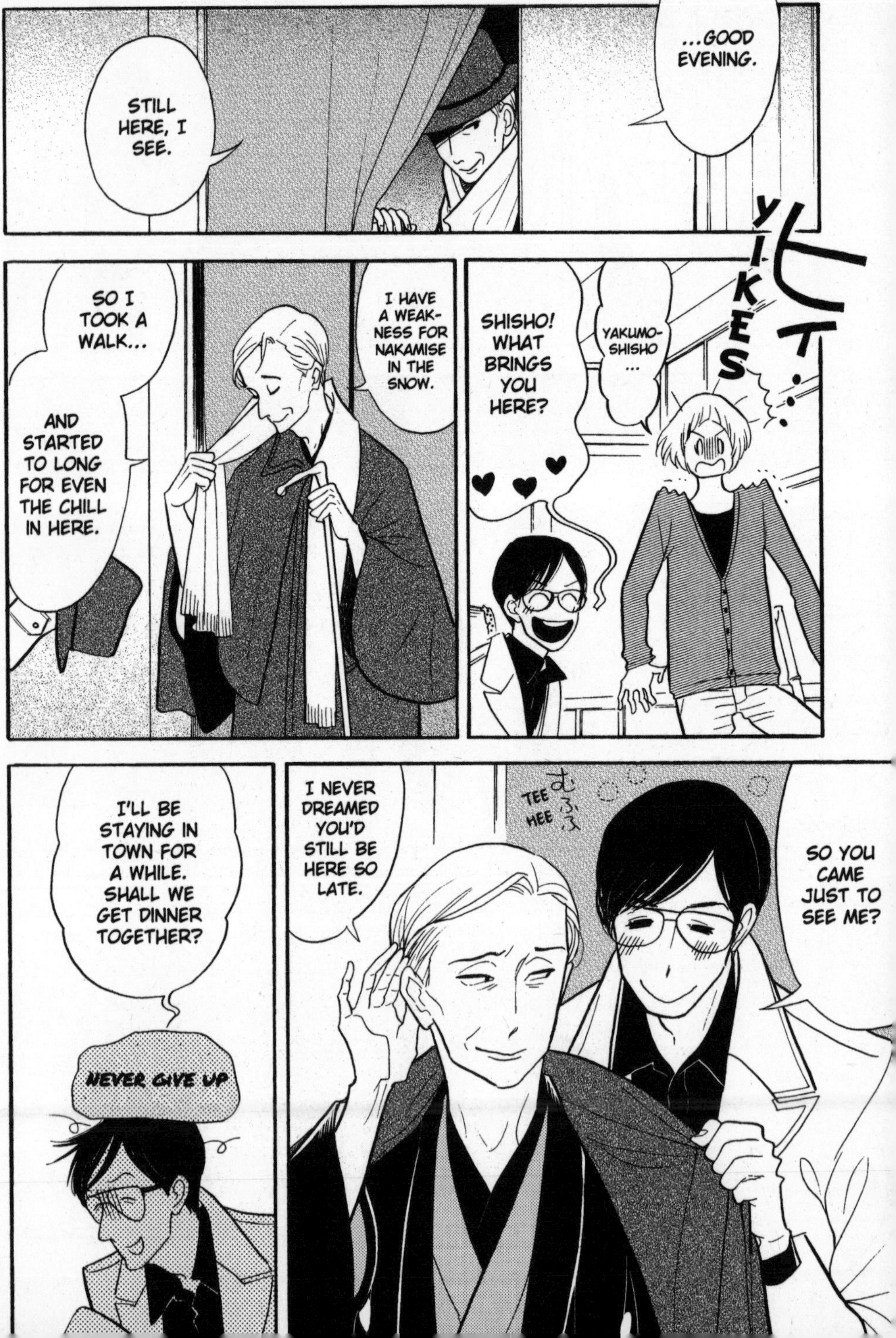
...GOOD EVENING.
STILL HERE, I SEE.
YIKES
YAKUMO-SHISHO...
SHISHO! WHAT BRINGS YOU HERE?
I HAVE A WEAKNESS FOR NAKAMISE IN THE SNOW.
SO I TOOK A WALK...
AND STARTED TO LONG FOR EVEN THE CHILL IN HERE.
SO YOU CAME JUST TO SEE ME?
むふふ
TEE HEE
I NEVER DREAMED YOU'D STILL BE HERE SO LATE.
I'LL BE STAYING IN TOWN FOR A WHILE. SHALL WE GET DINNER TOGETHER?
NEVER GIVE UP

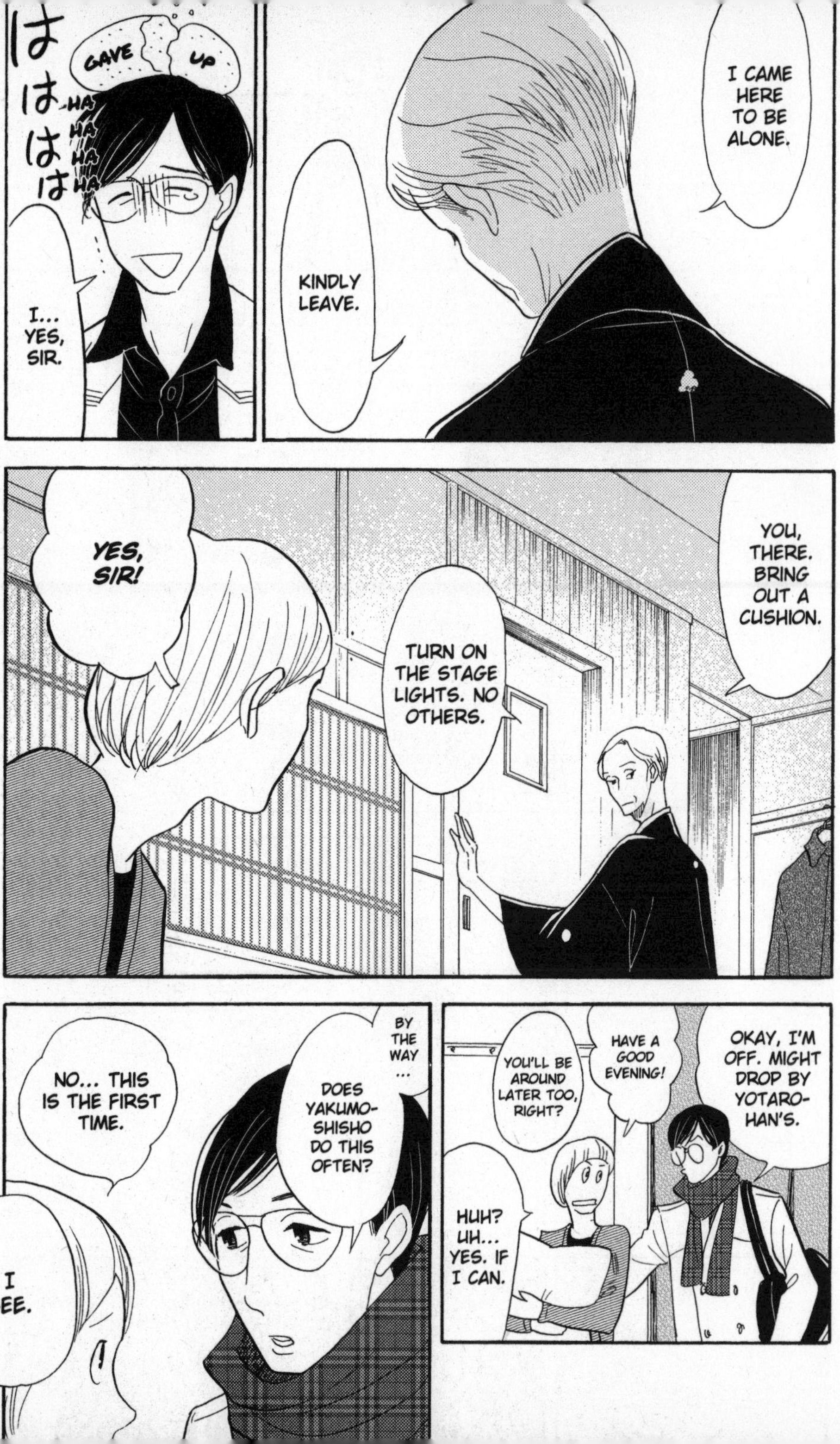
I CAME HERE TO BE ALONE.
KINDLY LEAVE.
GAVE UP
ははははは
HA HA HA HA
I... YES, SIR.
YOU, THERE. BRING OUT A CUSHION.
TURN ON THE STAGE LIGHTS. NO OTHERS.
YES, SIR!
OKAY, I'M OFF. MIGHT DROP BY YOTARO-HAN'S.
HAVE A GOOD EVENING!
YOU'LL BE AROUND LATER TOO, RIGHT?
HUH? UH... YES. IF I CAN.
BY THE WAY...
DOES YAKUMO-SHISHO DO THIS OFTEN?
NO... THIS IS THE FIRST TIME.
I SEE.

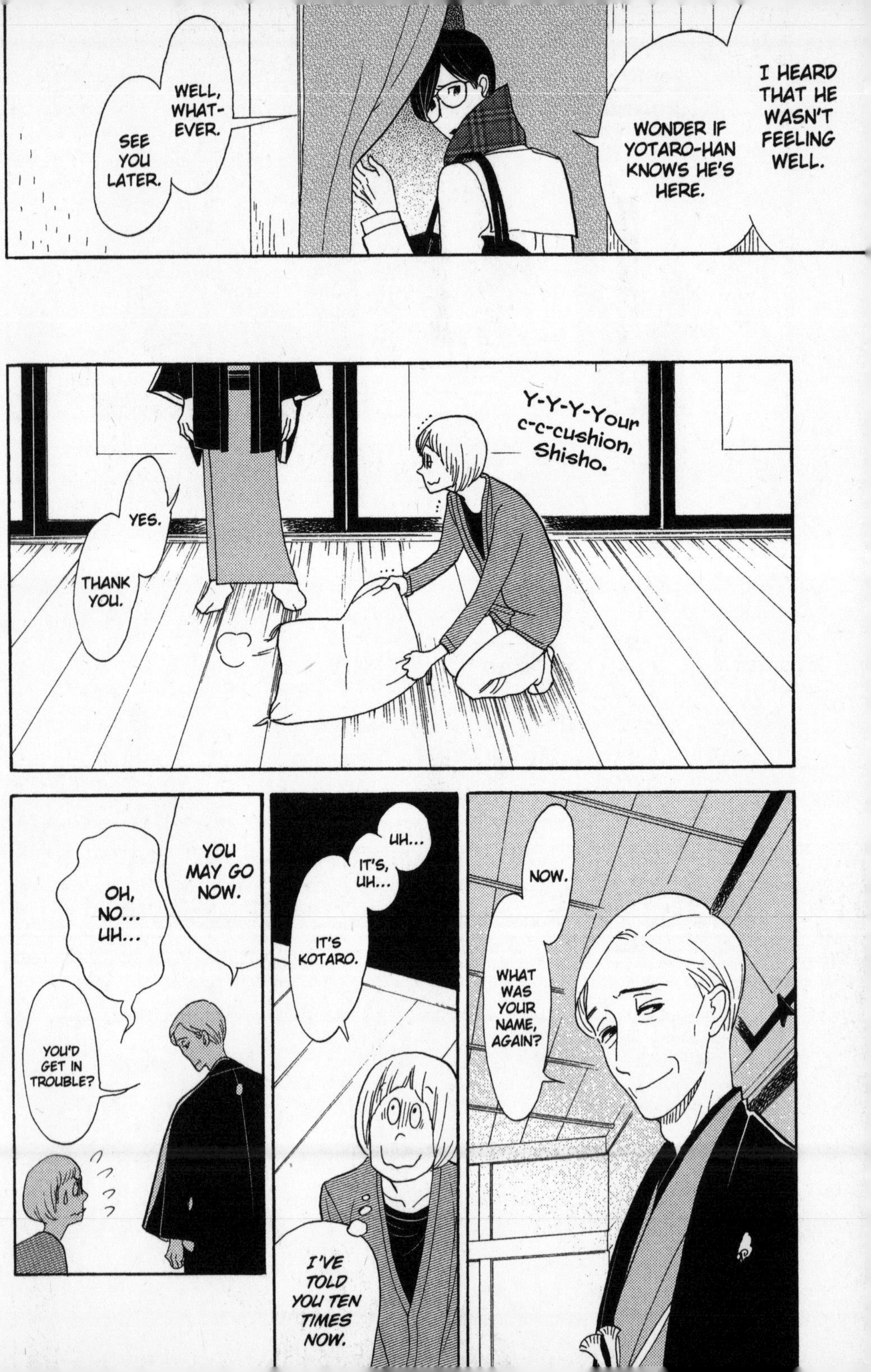
I HEARD THAT HE WASN'T FEELING WELL.
WONDER IF YOTARO-HAN KNOWS HE'S HERE.
WELL, WHAT-EVER.
SEE YOU LATER.
Y-Y-Y-Your c-c-cushion, Shisho.
YES.
THANK YOU.
NOW.
WHAT WAS YOUR NAME, AGAIN?
UH...
IT'S, UH...
IT'S KOTARO.
I'VE TOLD YOU TEN TIMES NOW.
YOU MAY GO NOW.
OH, NO... UH...
YOU'D GET IN TROUBLE?

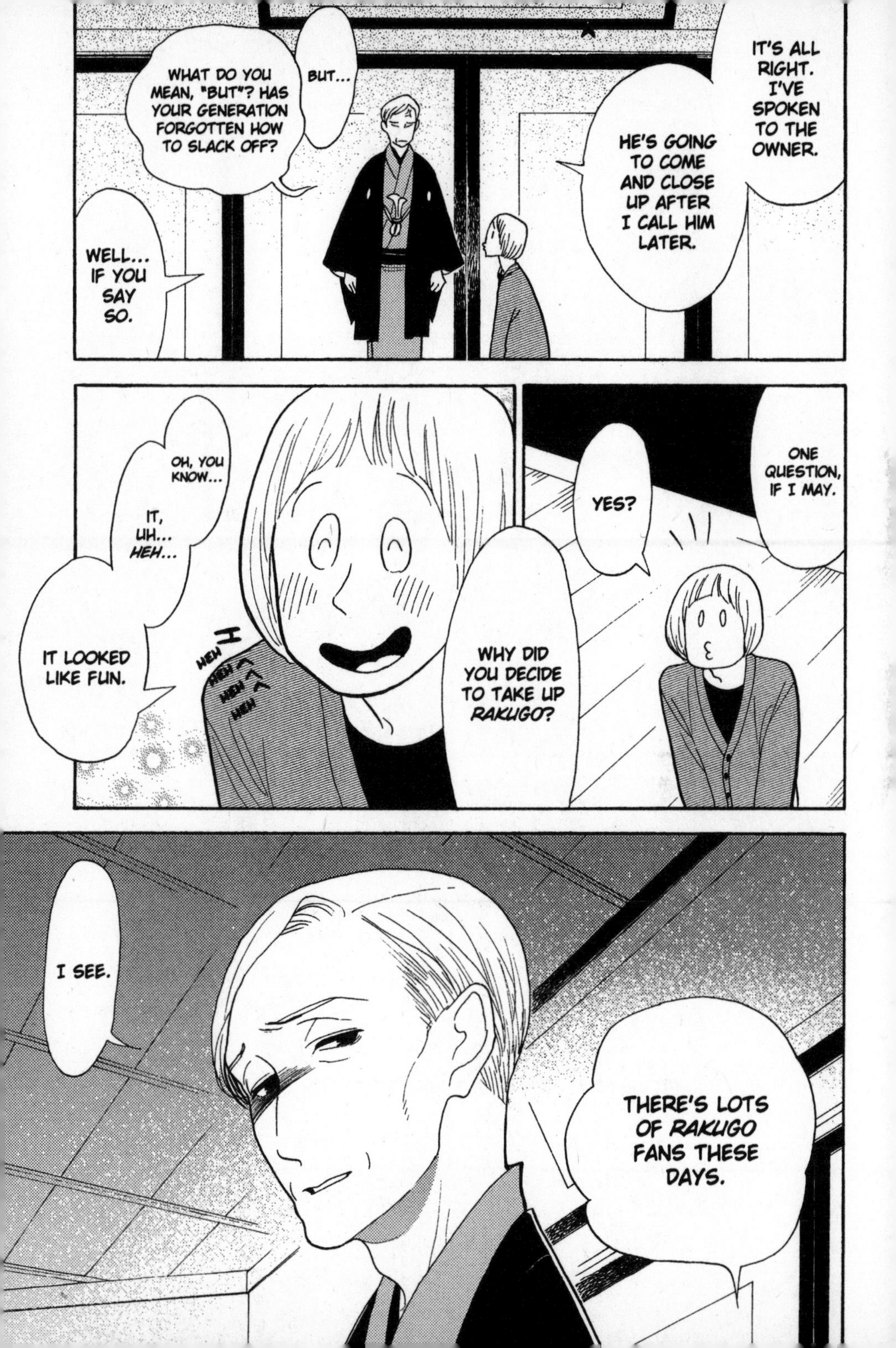
IT'S ALL RIGHT. I'VE SPOKEN TO THE OWNER.
HE'S GOING TO COME AND CLOSE UP AFTER I CALL HIM LATER.
BUT...
WHAT DO YOU MEAN, "BUT"? HAS YOUR GENERATION FORGOTTEN HOW TO SLACK OFF?
WELL... IF YOU SAY SO.
ONE QUESTION, IF I MAY.
YES?
WHY DID YOU DECIDE TO TAKE UP RAKUGO?
OH, YOU KNOW...
IT, UH... HEH...
H HEH HEH HEH HEH
IT LOOKED LIKE FUN.
I SEE.
THERE'S LOTS OF RAKUGO FANS THESE DAYS.

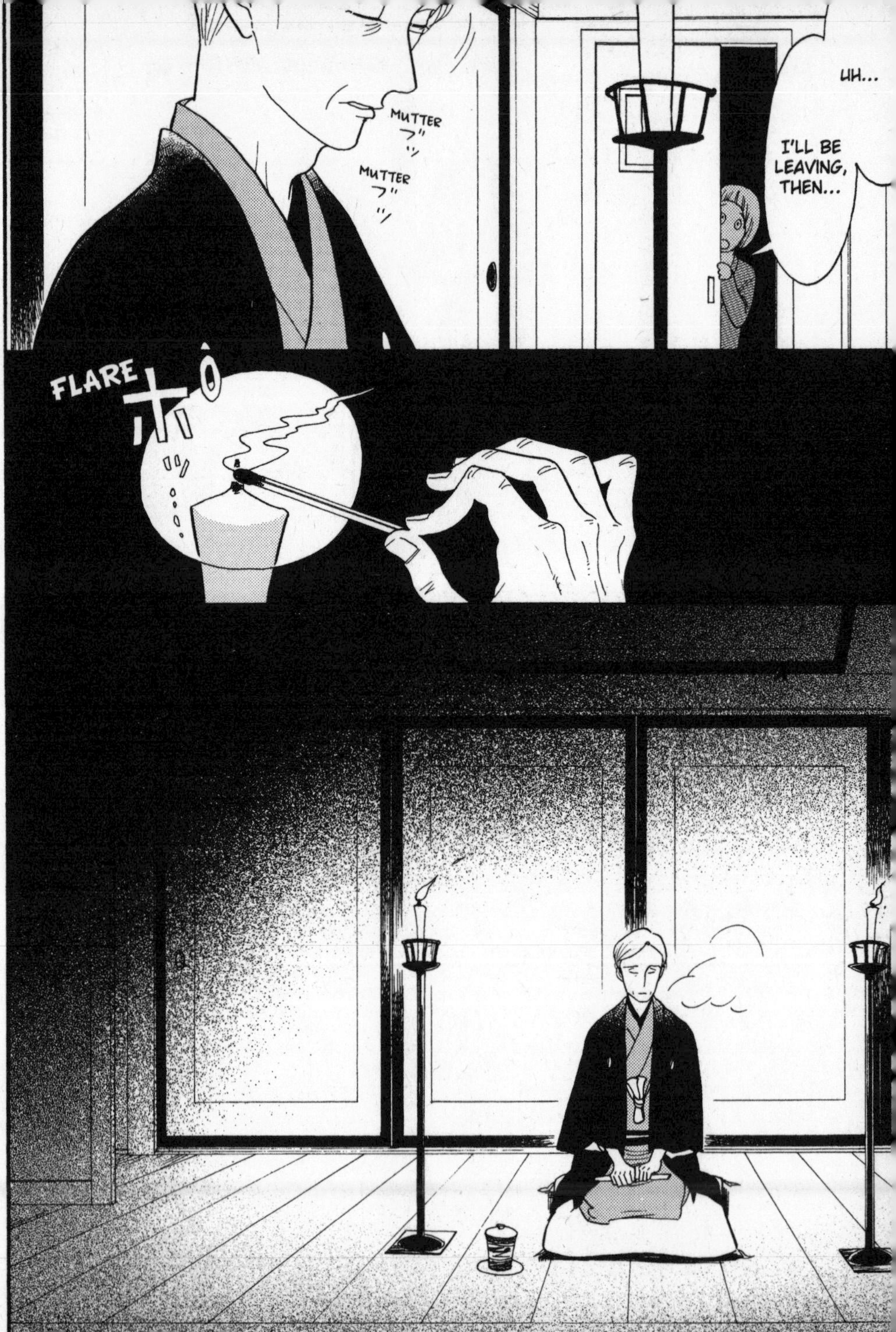
UH...
I'LL BE LEAVING, THEN...
MUTTER
MUTTER
FLARE

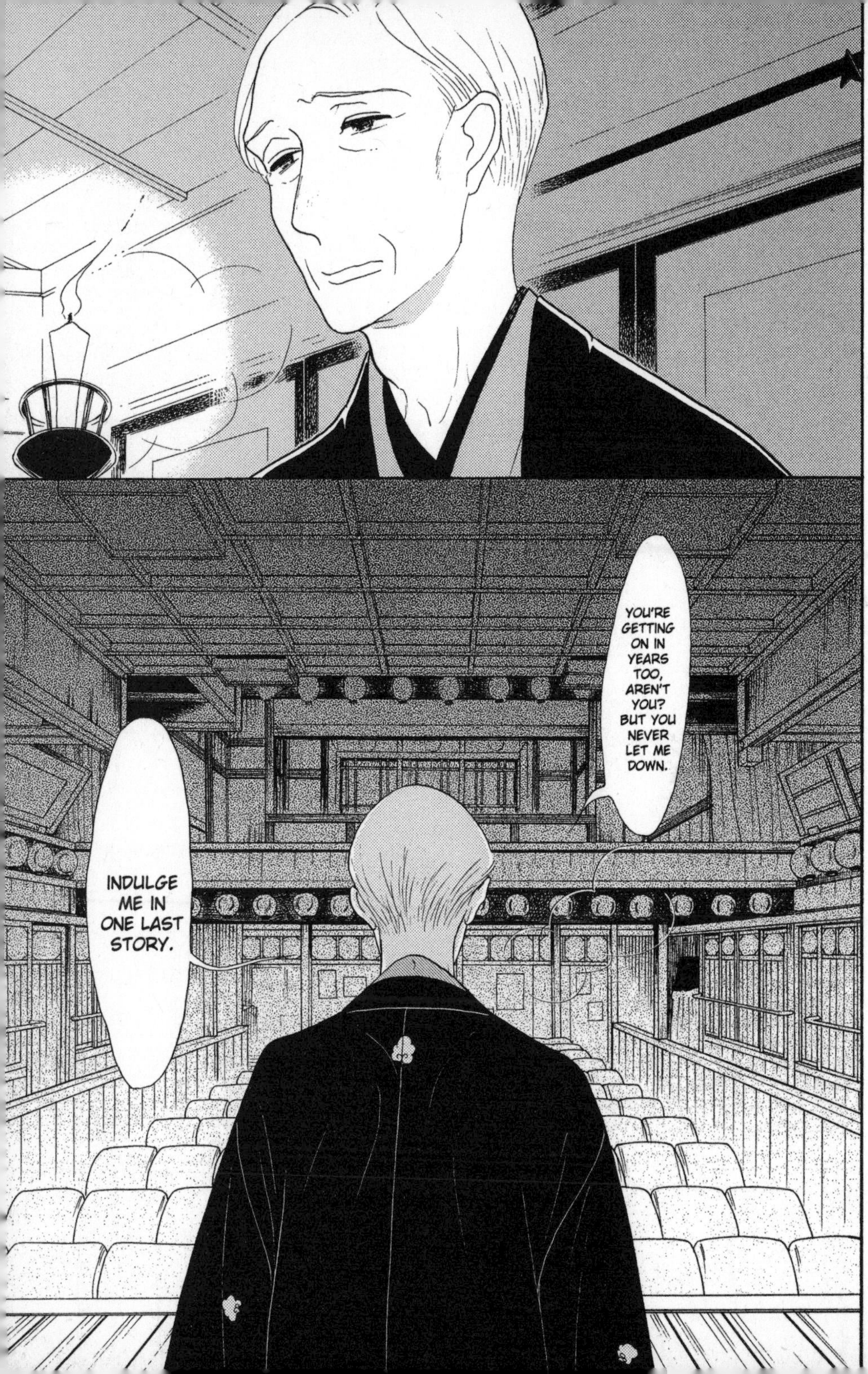
YOU'RE GETTING ON IN YEARS TOO, AREN'T YOU? BUT YOU NEVER LET ME DOWN.
INDULGE ME IN ONE LAST STORY.

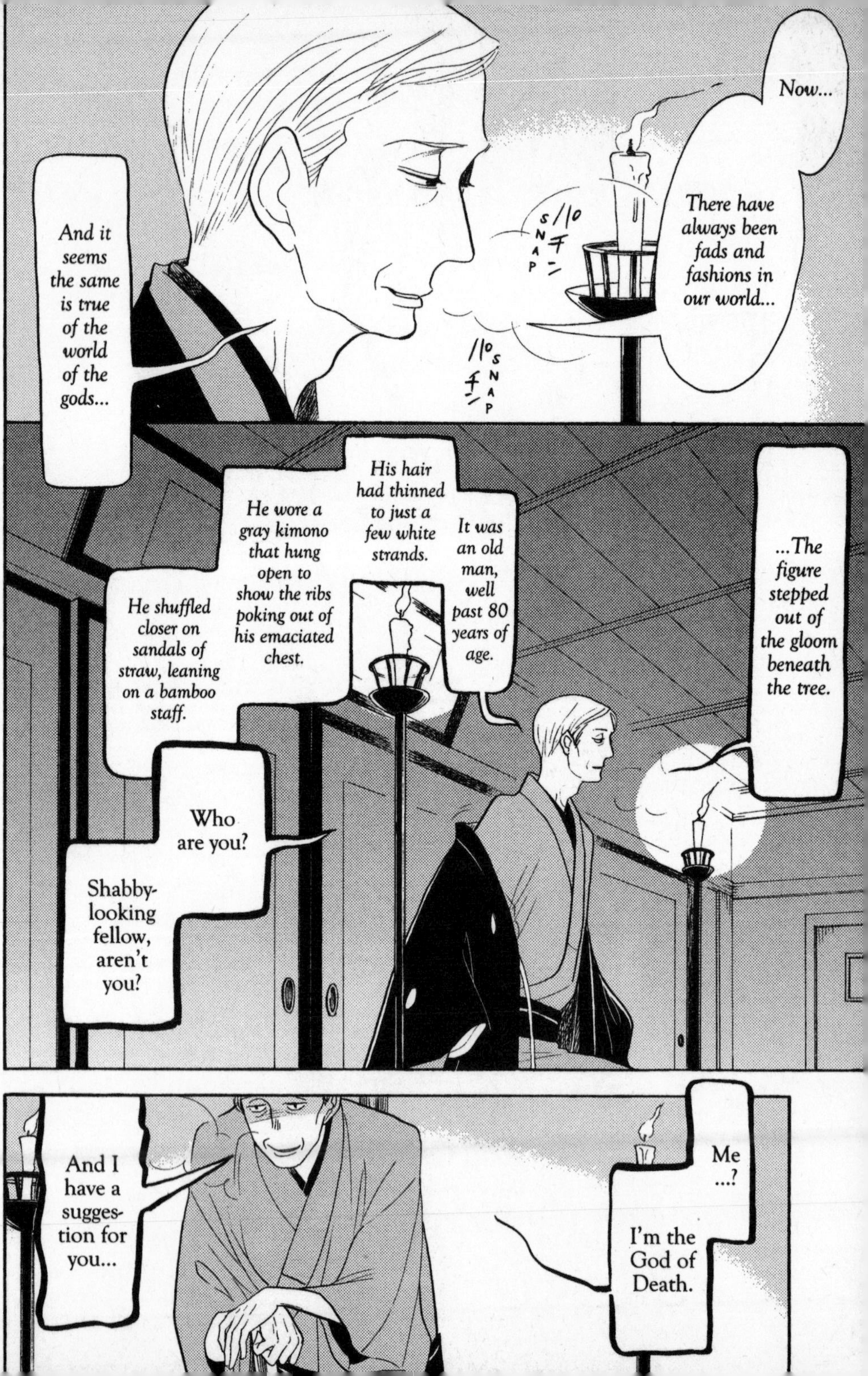
Now...
There have always been fads and fashions in our world...
SNAP
SNAP
And it seems the same is true of the world of the gods...
...The figure stepped out of the gloom beneath the tree.
It was an old man, well past 80 years of age.
His hair had thinned to just a few white strands.
He wore a gray kimono that hung open to show the ribs poking out of his emaciated chest.
He shuffled closer on sandals of straw, leaning on a bamboo staff.
Who are you?
Shabby-looking fellow, aren't you?
Me ...?
I'm the God of Death.
And I have a suggestion for you...

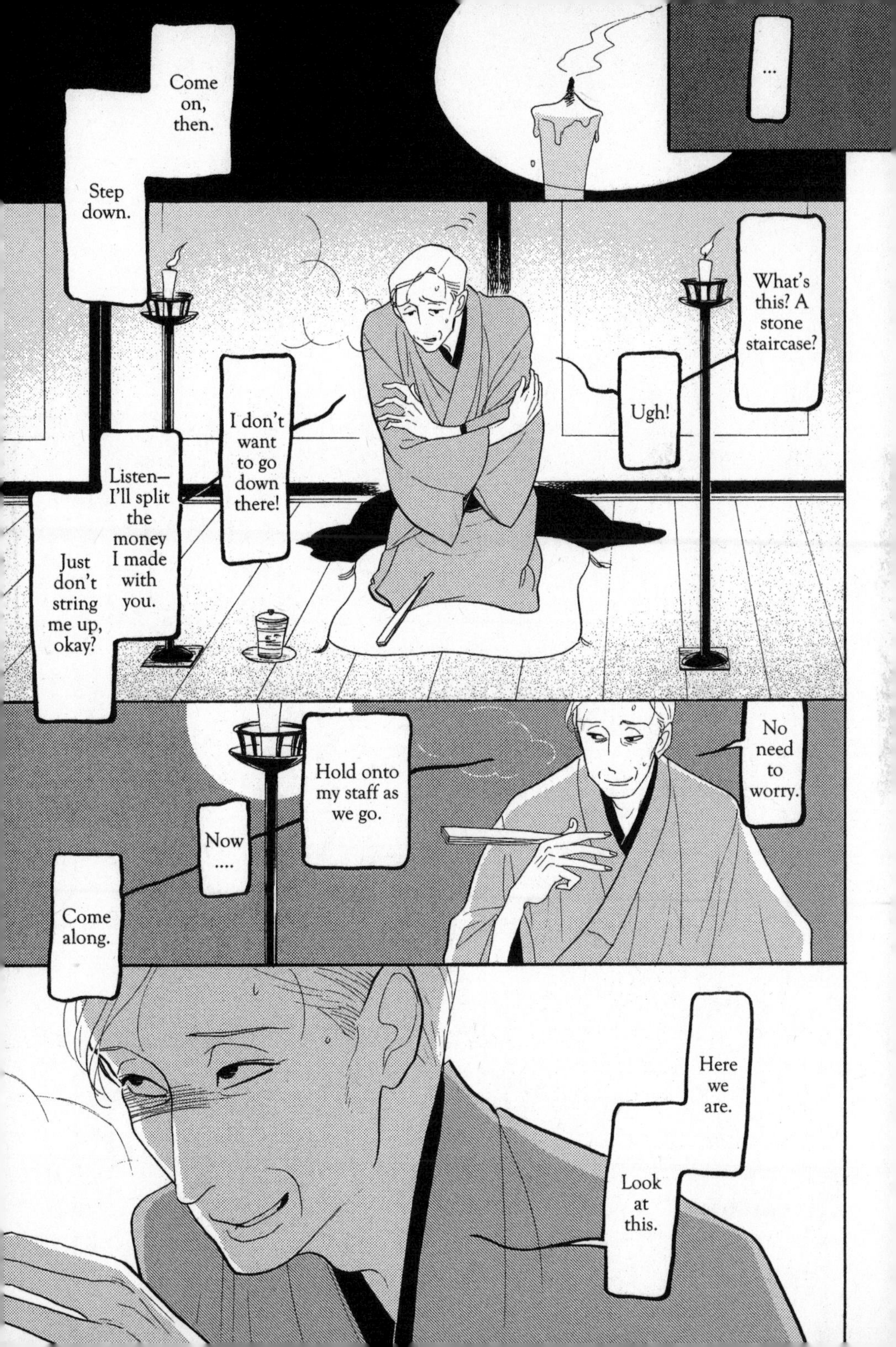

...
Come on, then.
Step down.
What's this? A stone staircase?
Ugh!
I don't want to go down there!
Listen— I'll split the money I made with you.
Just don't string me up, okay?
No need to worry.
Hold onto my staff as we go.
Now ....
Come along.
Here we are.
Look at this.

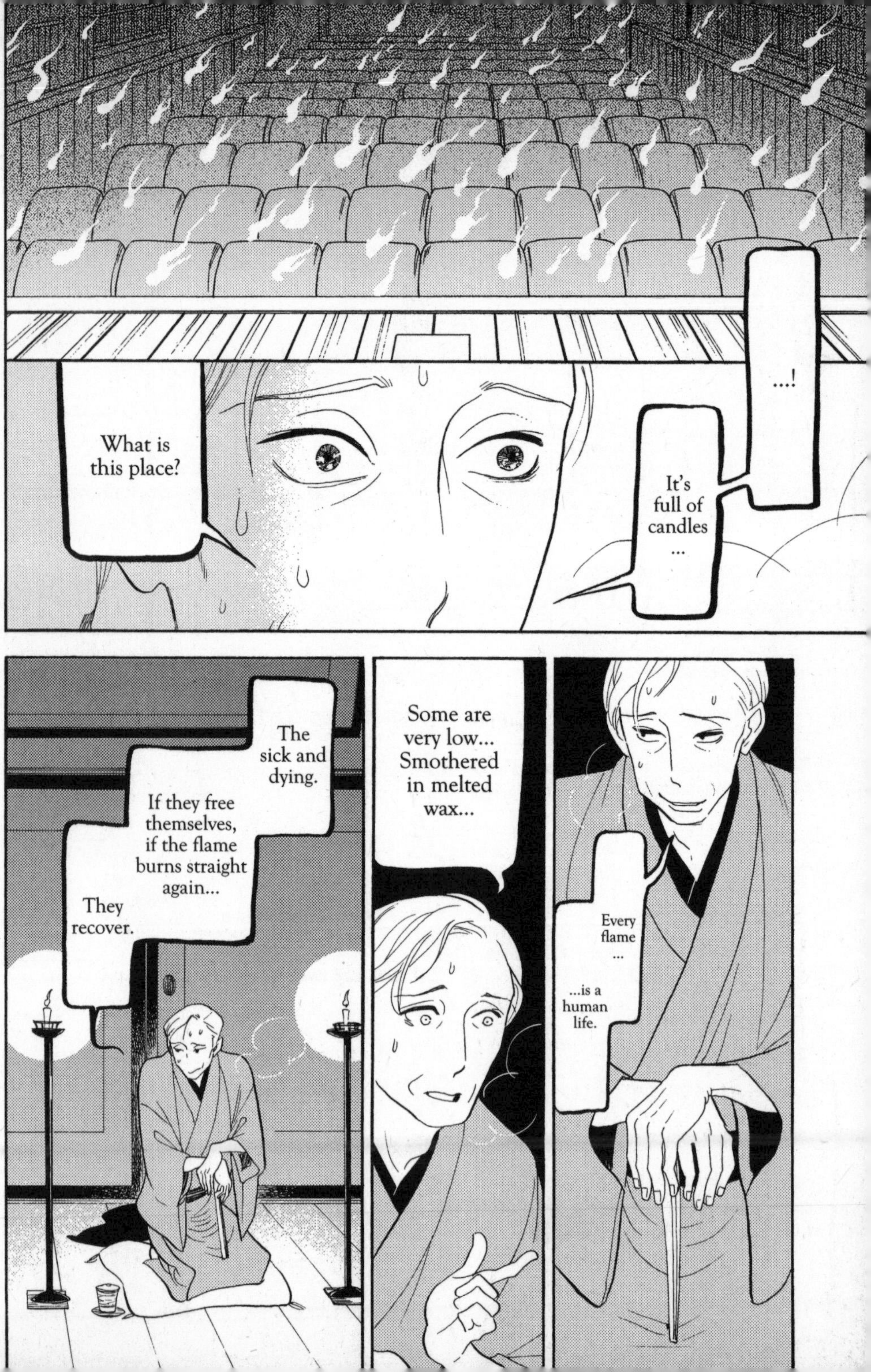
...!
It's full of candles ...
What is this place?
Every flame ...
...is a human life.
Some are very low... Smothered in melted wax...
The sick and dying.
If they free themselves, if the flame burns straight again...
They recover.

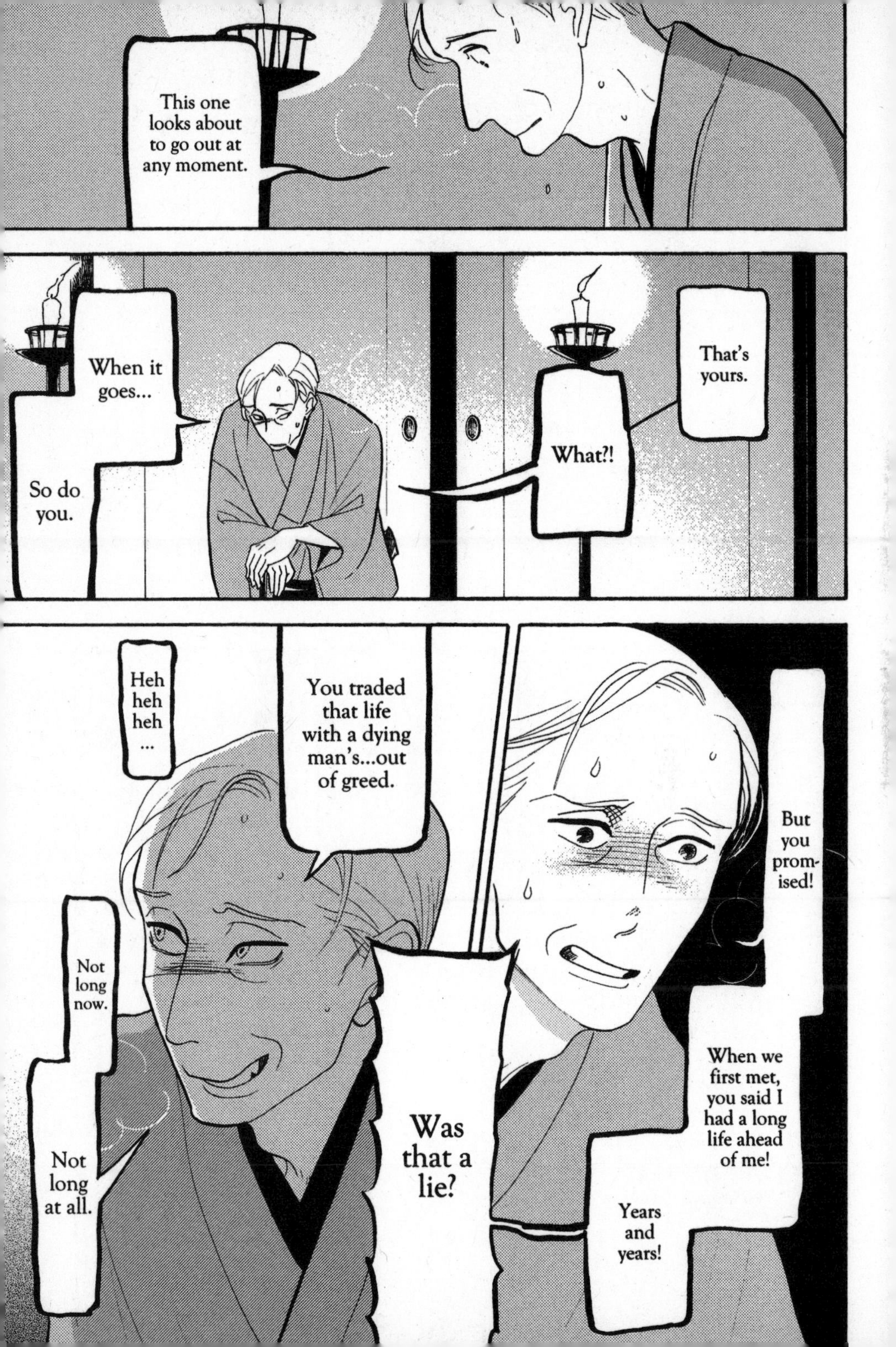
This one looks about to go out at any moment.
That's yours.
What?!
When it goes...
So do you.
But you promised!
When we first met, you said I had a long life ahead of me!
Years and years!
Was that a lie?
Heh heh heh...
You traded that life with a dying man's...out of greed.
Not long now.
Not long at all.

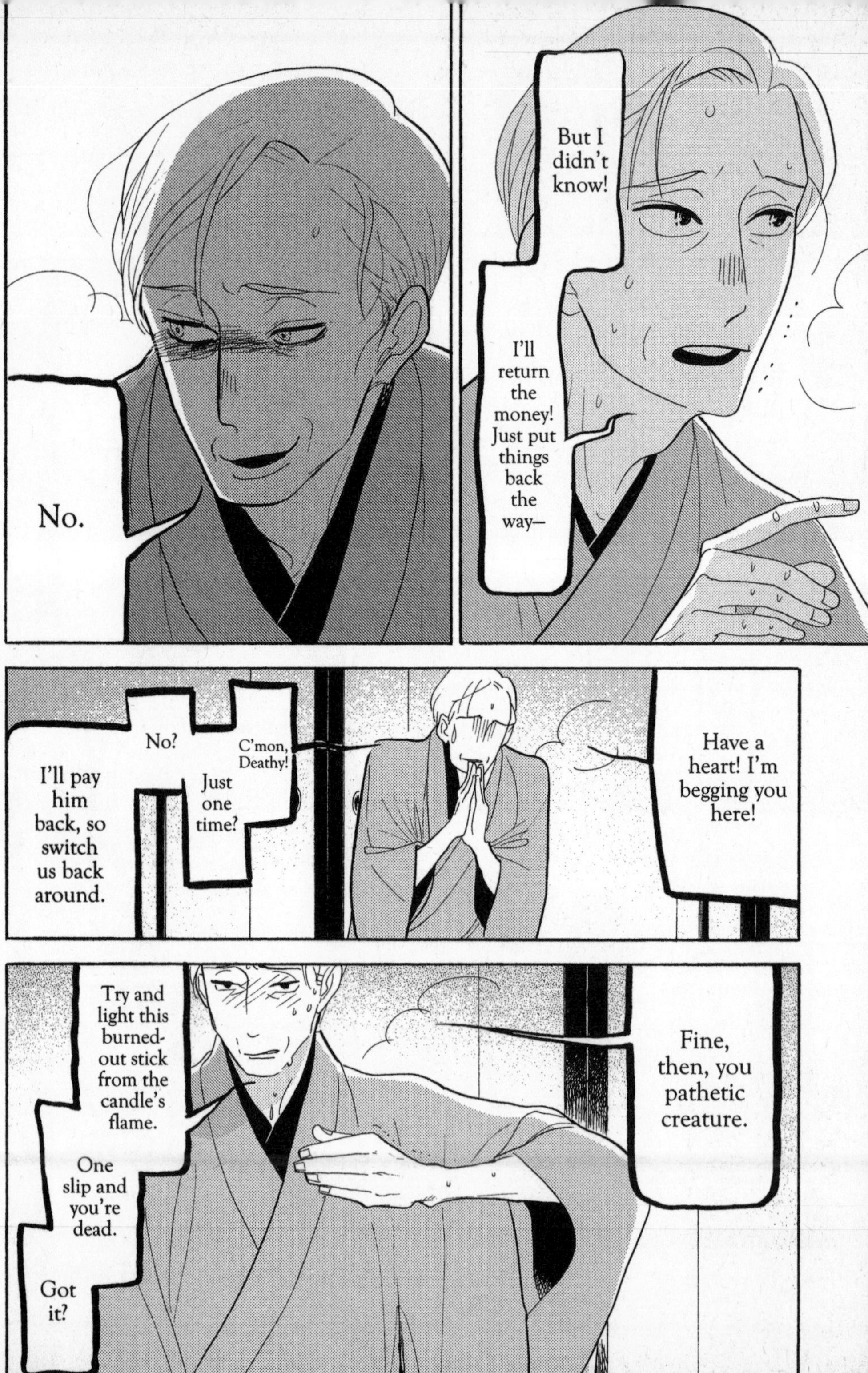
But I didn't know!
I'll return the money! Just put things back the way—
No.
Have a heart! I'm begging you here!
C'mon, Deathy!
Just one time?
No?
I'll pay him back, so switch us back around.
Fine, then, you pathetic creature.
Try and light this burned-out stick from the candle's flame.
One slip and you're dead.
Got it?

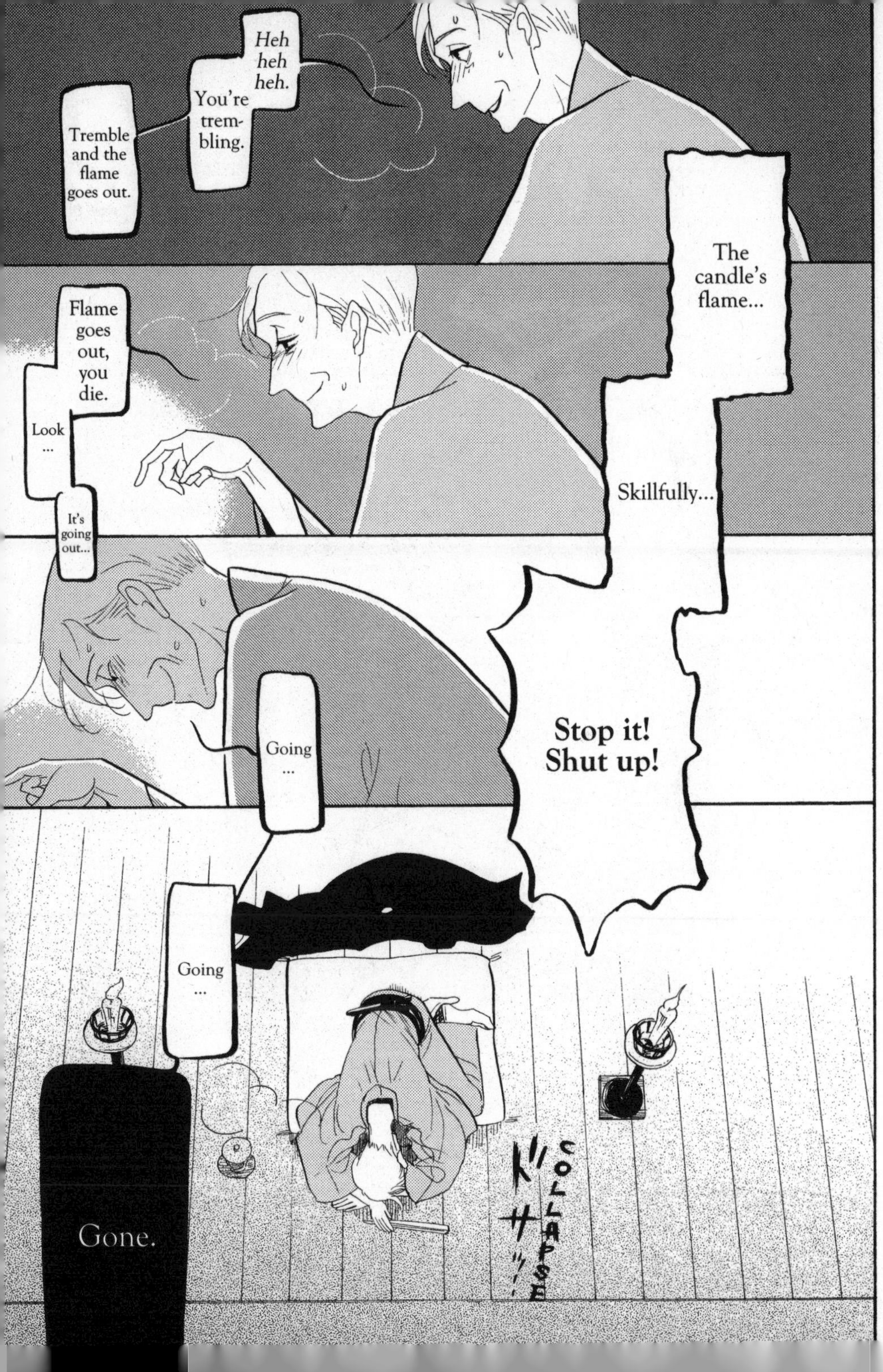
The candle's flame...
Heh heh heh.
You're trembling.
Tremble and the flame goes out.
Skillfully...
Flame goes out, you die.
Look ...
It's going out...
Stop it! Shut up!
Going ...
Going ...
COLLAPSE
Gone.

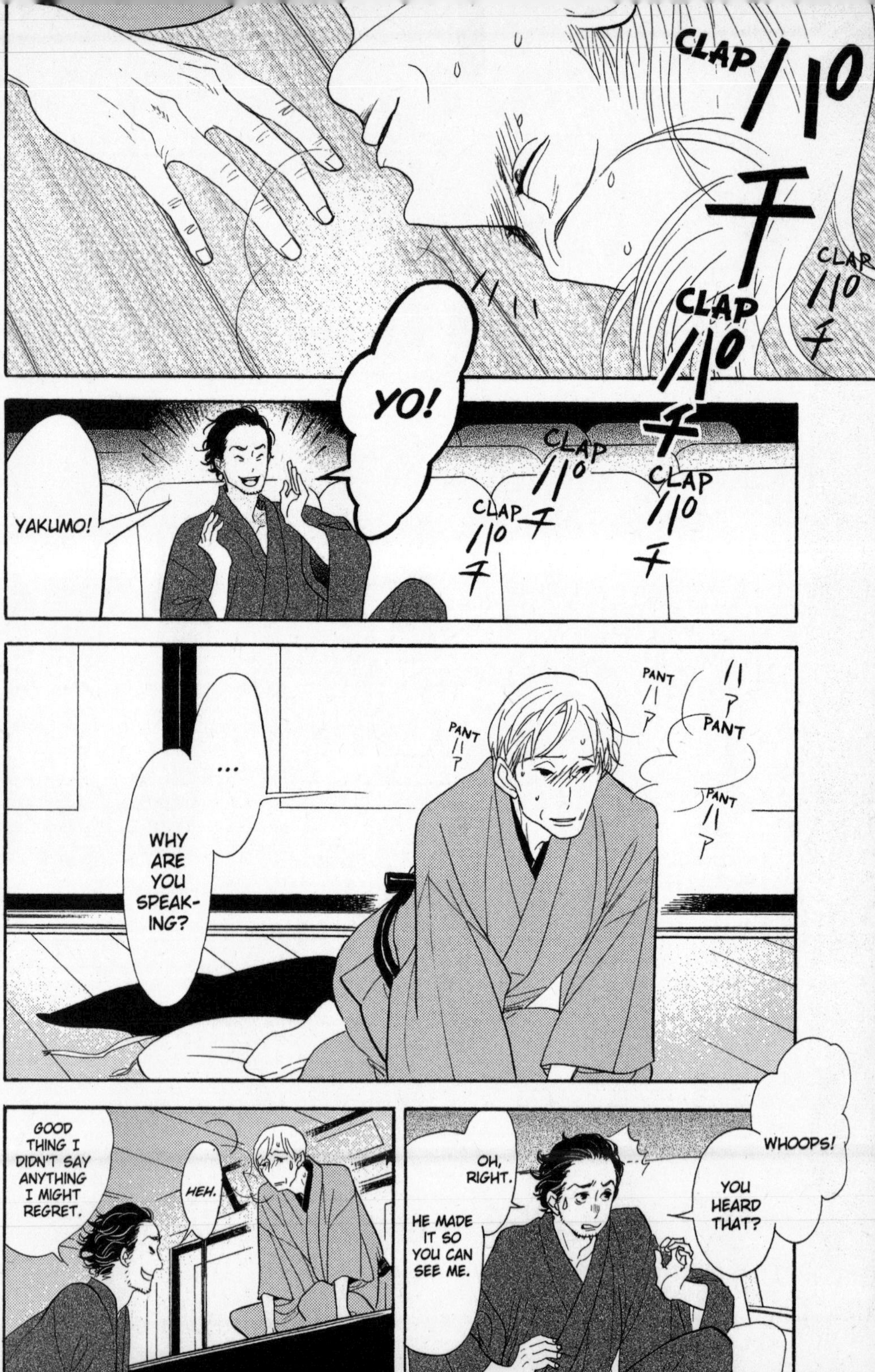
CLAP パチ
CLAP パチ
CLAP パチ
YO!
YAKUMO!
CLAP パチ
CLAP パチ
CLAP パチ
PANT ハァ
PANT ハァ
PANT ハァ
PANT ハァ
...
WHY ARE YOU SPEAKING?
WHOOPS!
YOU HEARD THAT?
OH, RIGHT.
HE MADE IT SO YOU CAN SEE ME.
HEH.
GOOD THING I DIDN'T SAY ANYTHING I MIGHT REGRET.

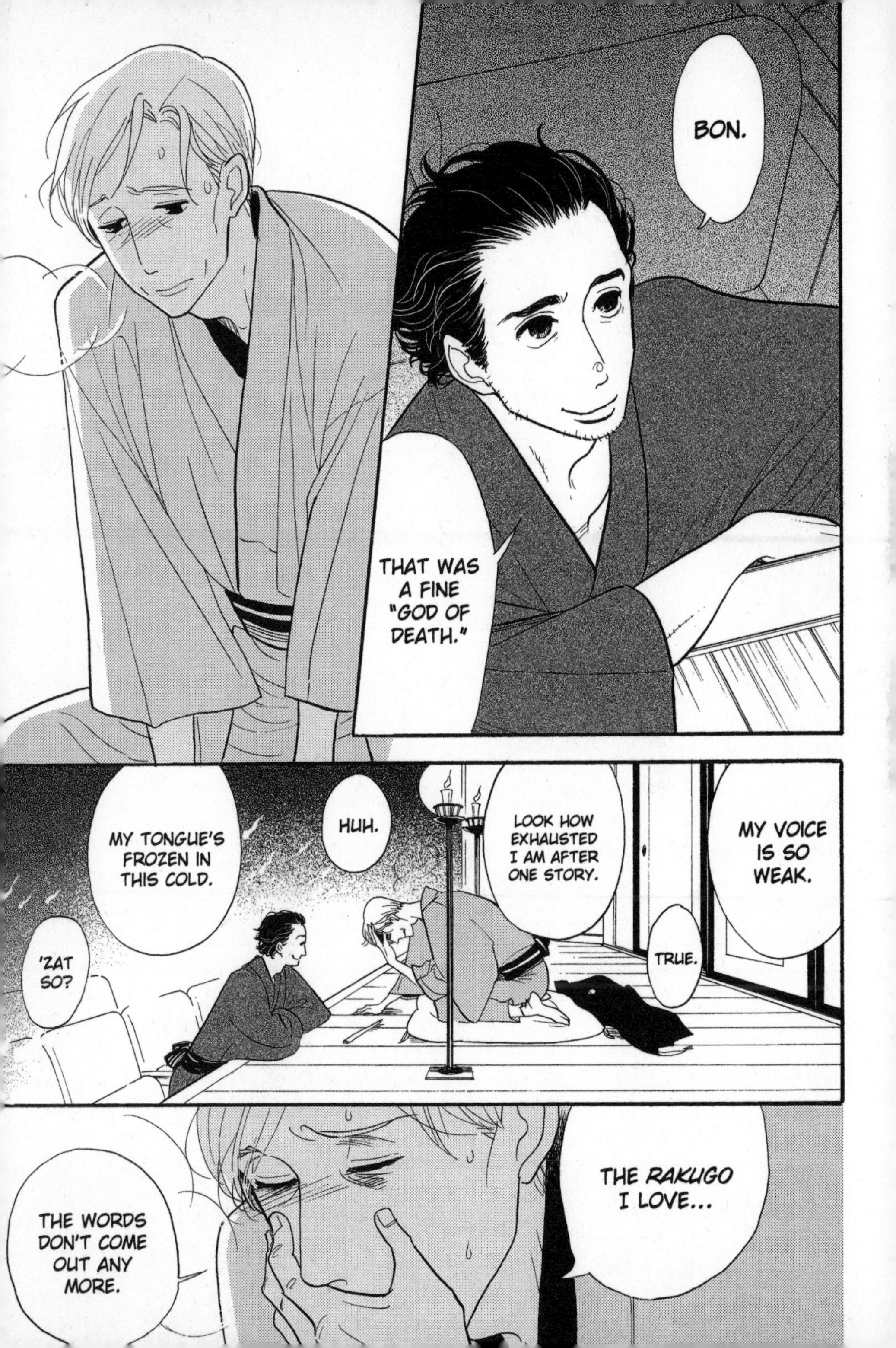
BON.
THAT WAS A FINE "GOD OF DEATH."
MY VOICE IS SO WEAK.
LOOK HOW EXHAUSTED I AM AFTER ONE STORY.
TRUE.
HUH.
MY TONGUE'S FROZEN IN THIS COLD.
'ZAT SO?
THE *RAKUGO* I LOVE...
THE WORDS DON'T COME OUT ANY MORE.

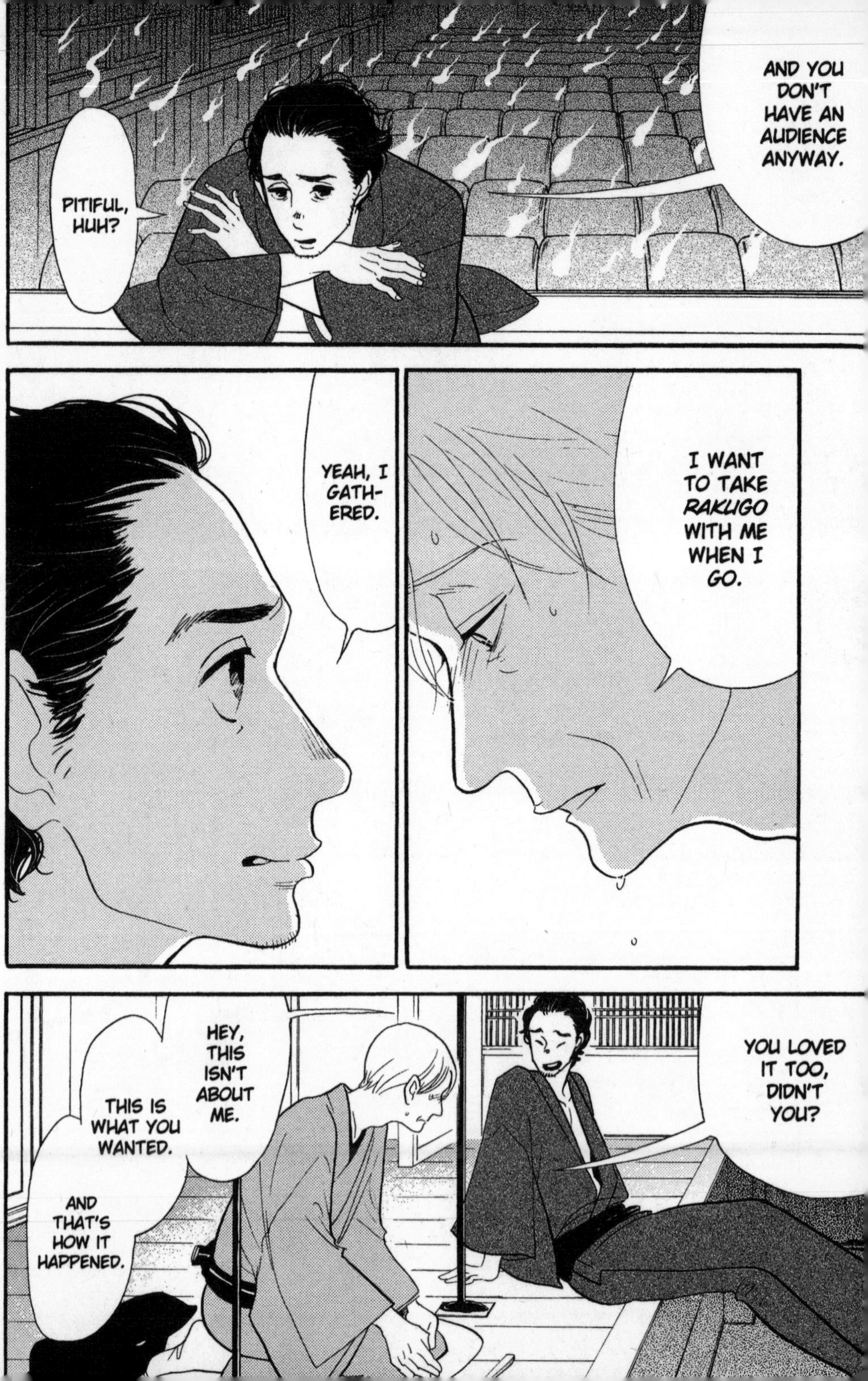
AND YOU DON'T HAVE AN AUDIENCE ANYWAY.
PITIFUL, HUH?
I WANT TO TAKE *RAKUGO* WITH ME WHEN I GO.
YEAH, I GATHERED.
YOU LOVED IT TOO, DIDN'T YOU?
HEY, THIS ISN'T ABOUT ME.
THIS IS WHAT YOU WANTED.
AND THAT'S HOW IT HAPPENED.

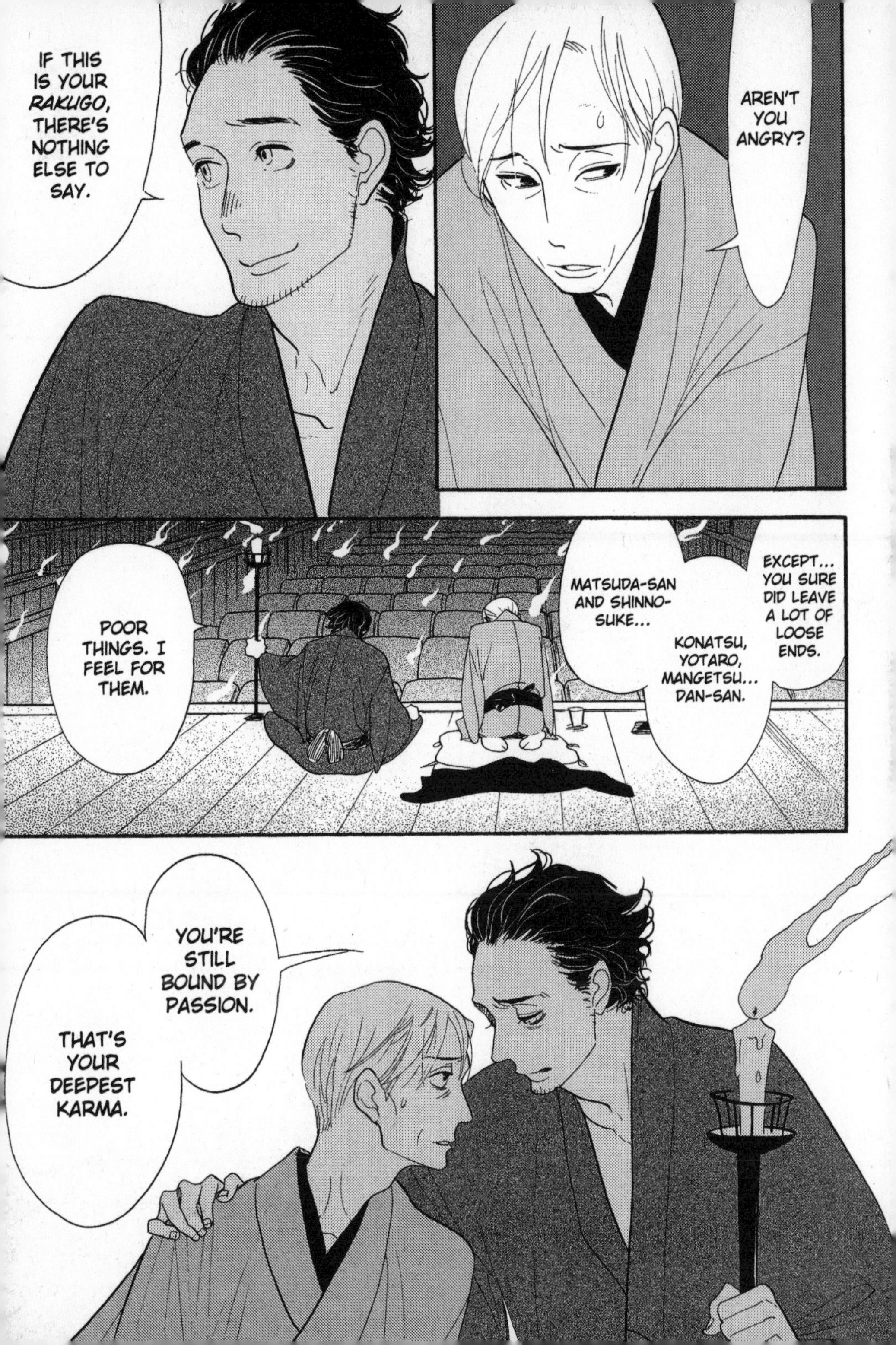
AREN'T YOU ANGRY?
IF THIS IS YOUR *RAKUGO*, THERE'S NOTHING ELSE TO SAY.
EXCEPT... YOU SURE DID LEAVE A LOT OF LOOSE ENDS.
MATSUDA-SAN AND SHINNOSUKE...
KONATSU, YOTARO, MANGETSU... DAN-SAN.
POOR THINGS. I FEEL FOR THEM.
YOU'RE STILL BOUND BY PASSION.
THAT'S YOUR DEEPEST KARMA.

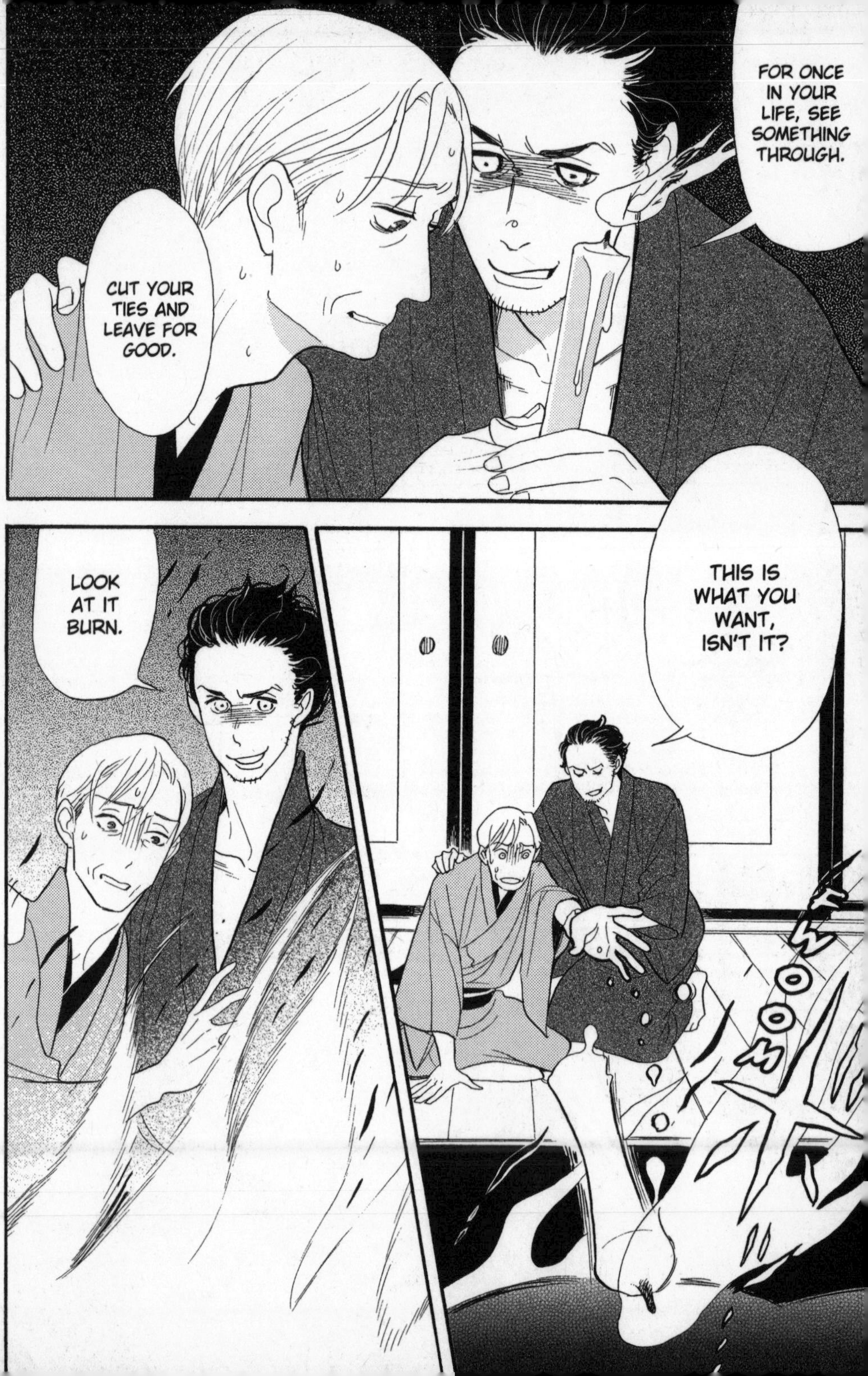
FOR ONCE IN YOUR LIFE, SEE SOMETHING THROUGH.
CUT YOUR TIES AND LEAVE FOR GOOD.
THIS IS WHAT YOU WANT, ISN'T IT?
FWOOOM
LOOK AT IT BURN.

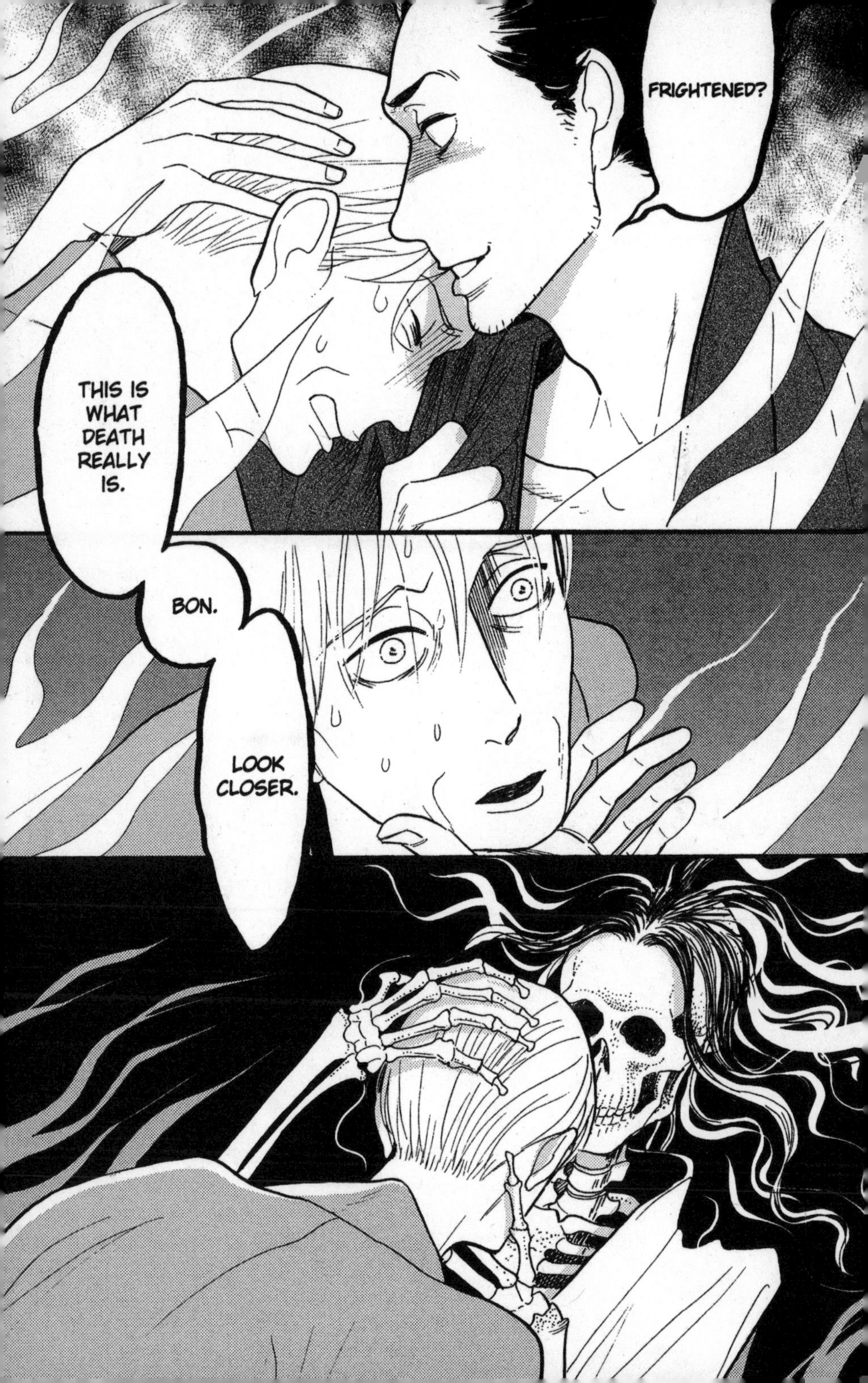
FRIGHTENED?
THIS IS WHAT DEATH REALLY IS.
BON.
LOOK CLOSER.

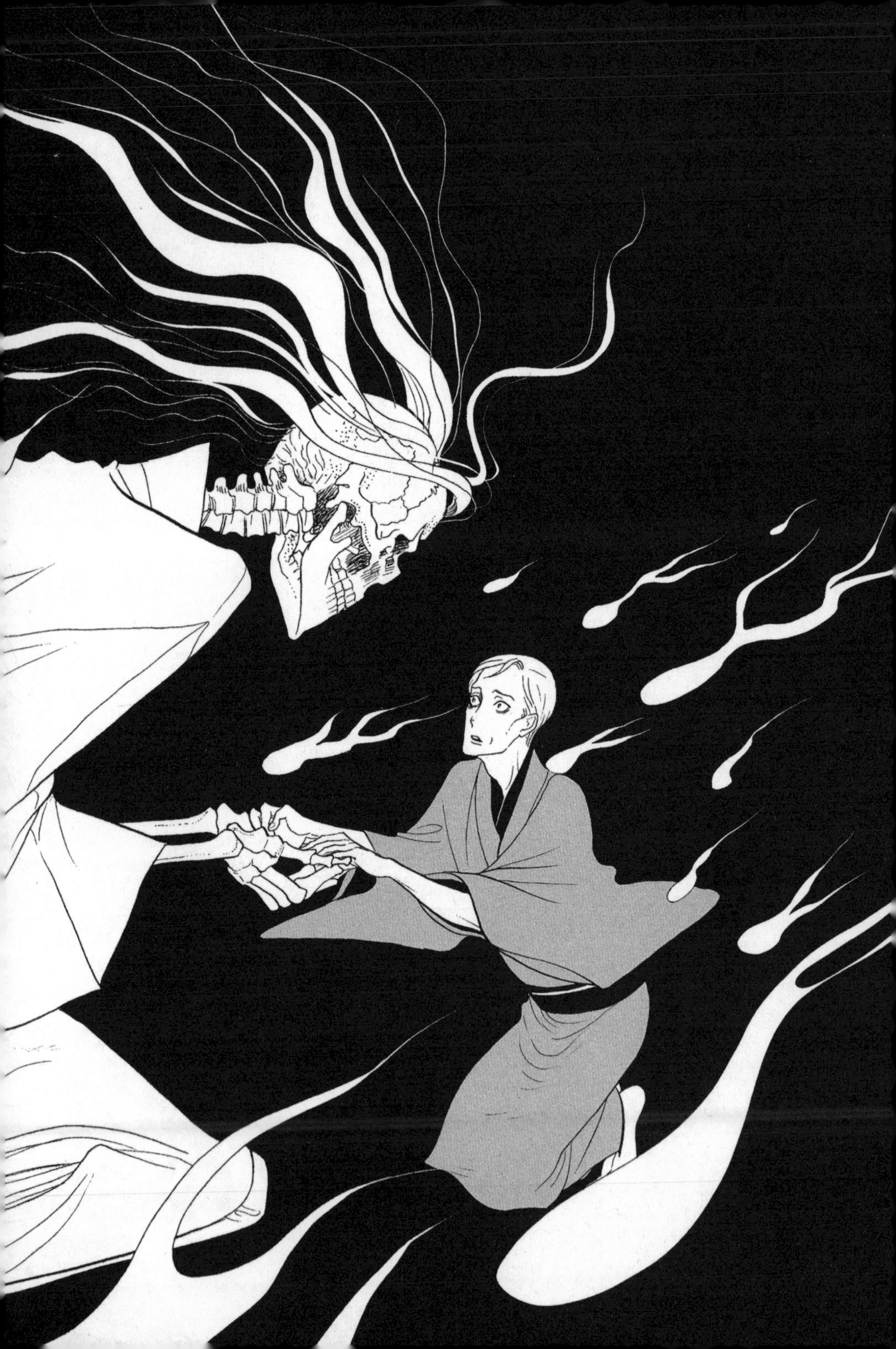

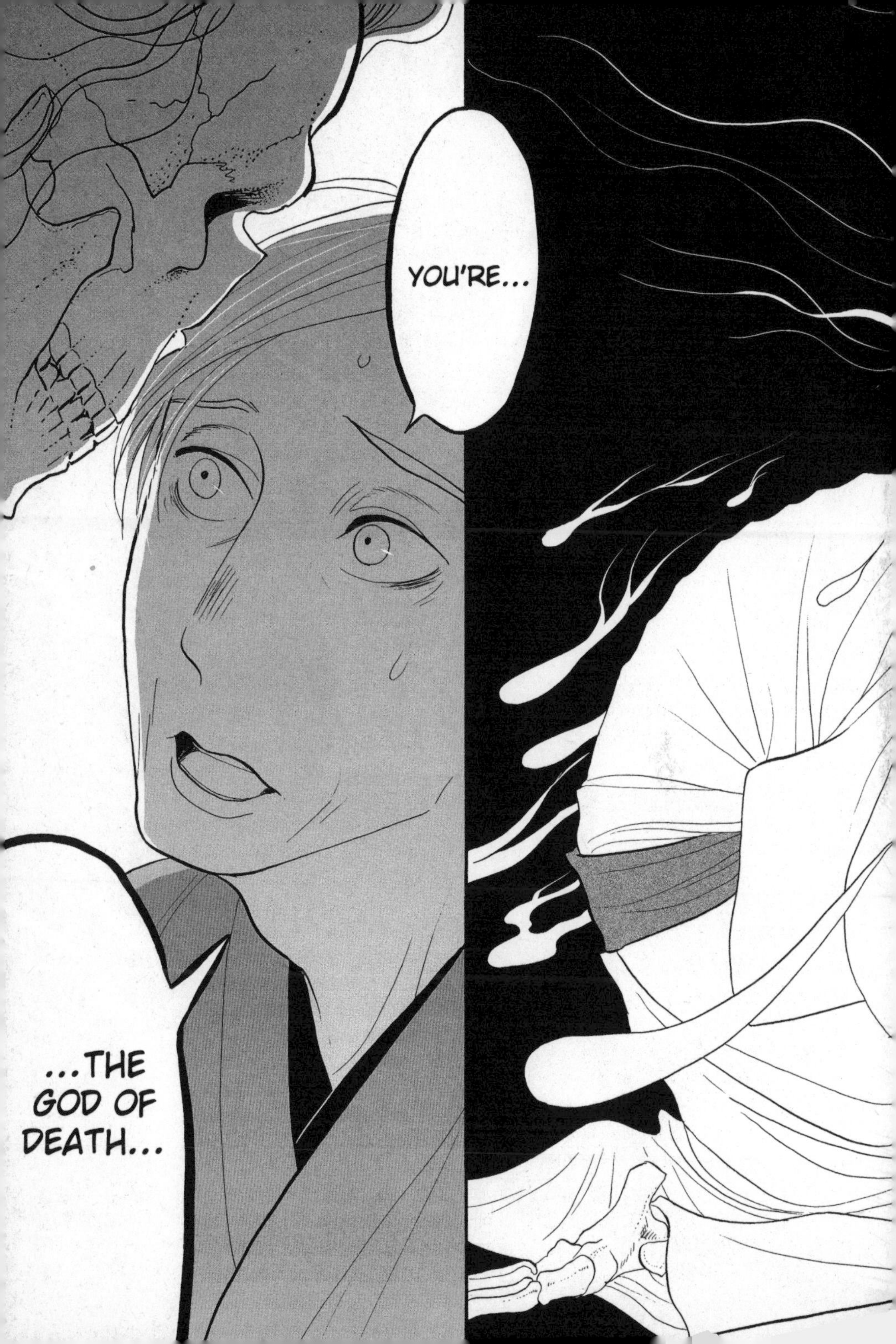
YOU'RE...
...THE GOD OF DEATH...

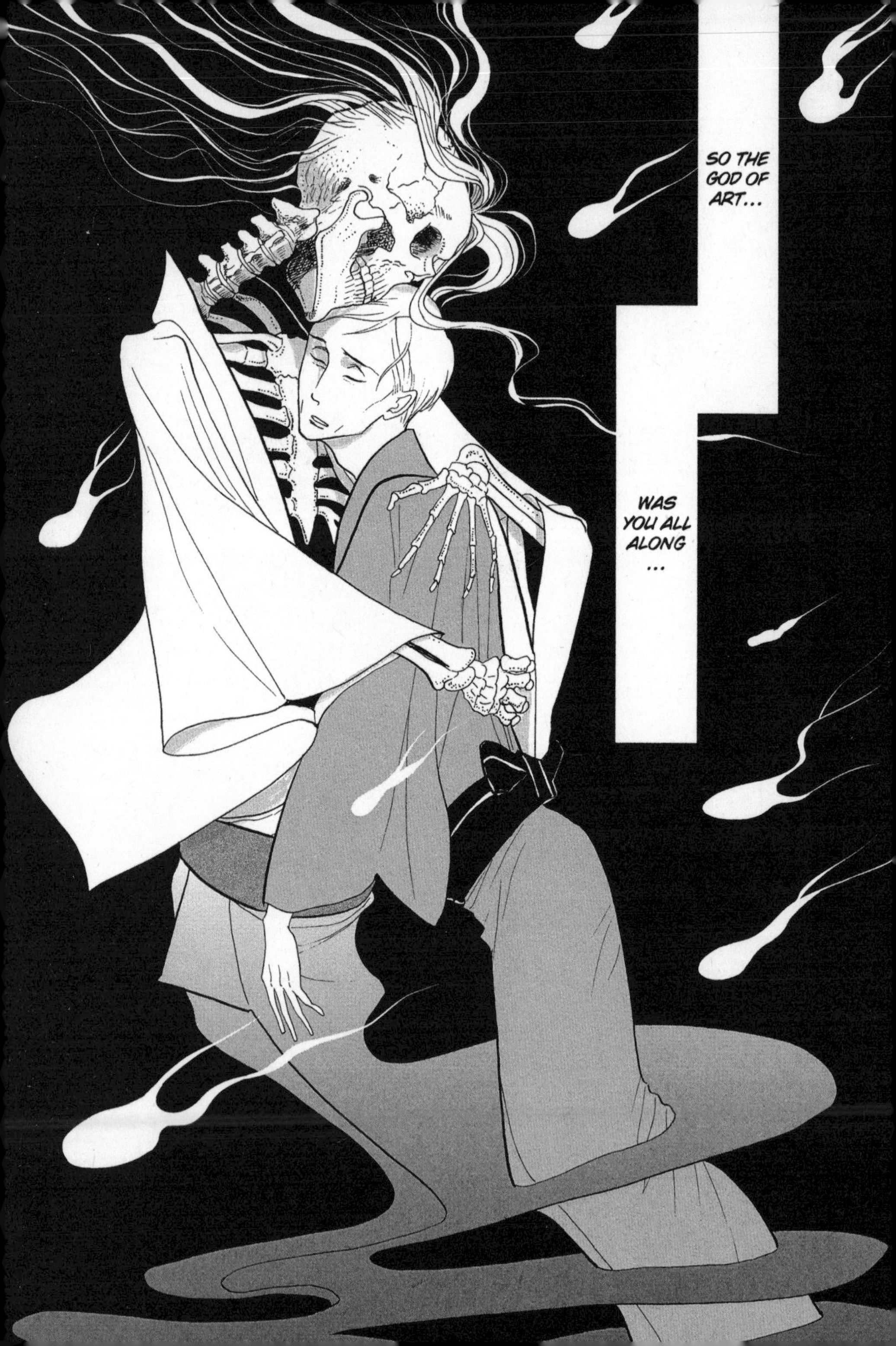
SO THE GOD OF ART...
WAS YOU ALL ALONG ...

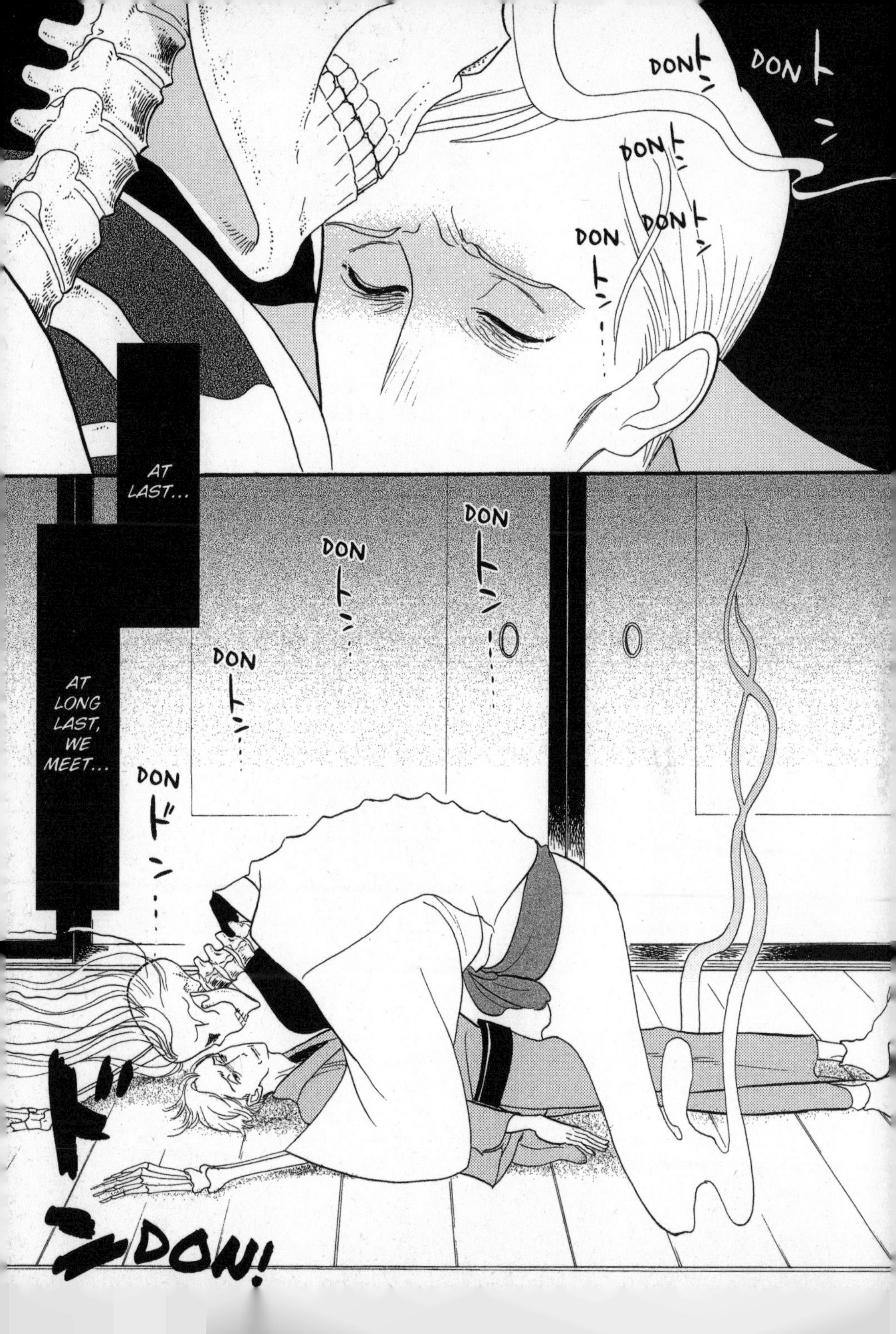
DON ト
DON ト
DON ト
DON ト
DON ト
AT LAST...
AT LONG LAST, WE MEET...
DON ト
DON ト
DON ト
DON ド
ドDON!

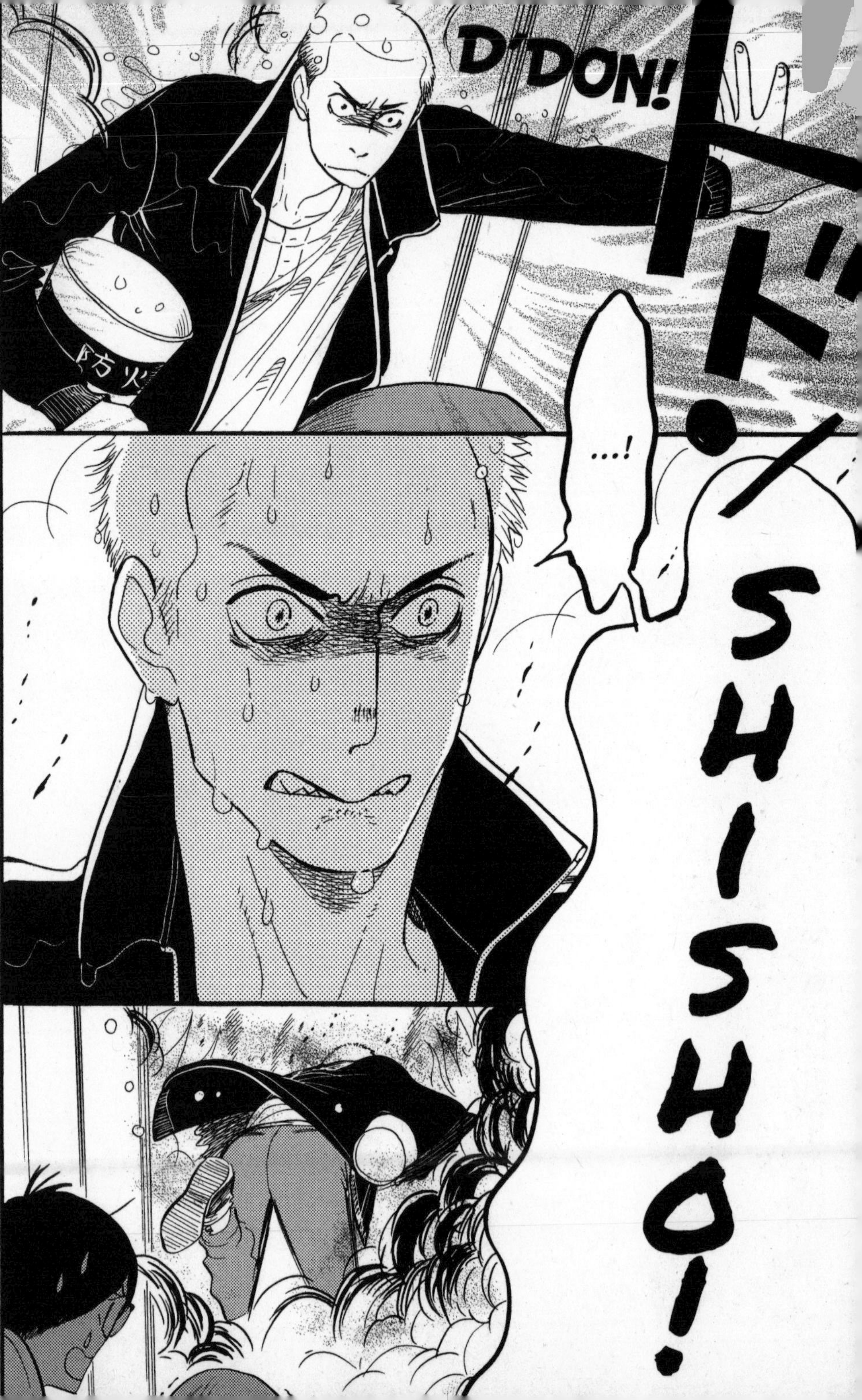
D'DON!
ド
...!
SHISHO!

Bucket: Fire

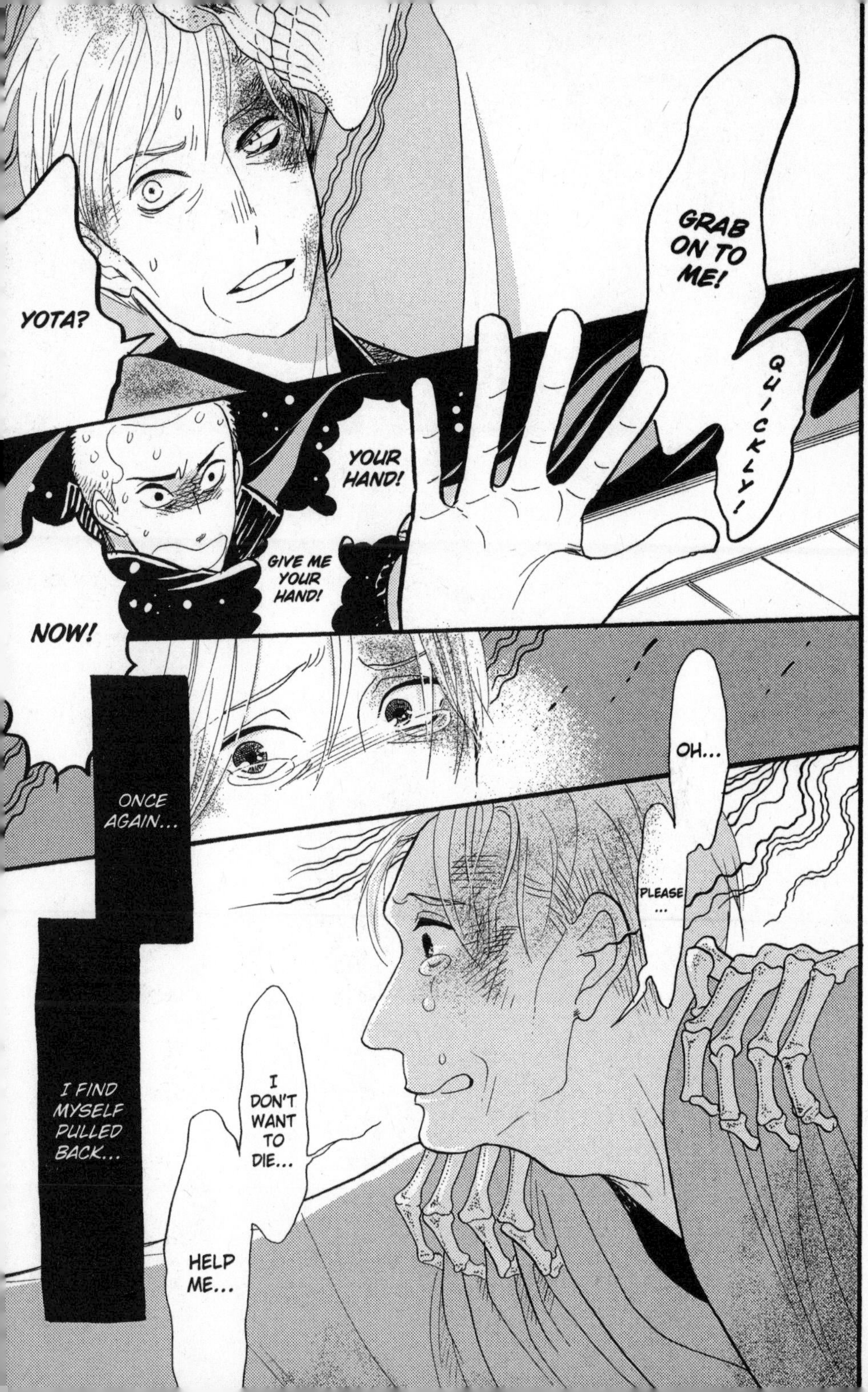
GRAB ON TO ME!
QUICKLY!
YOTA?
YOUR HAND!
GIVE ME YOUR HAND!
NOW!
OH...
ONCE AGAIN...
PLEASE...
I FIND MYSELF PULLED BACK...
I DON'T WANT TO DIE...
HELP ME...

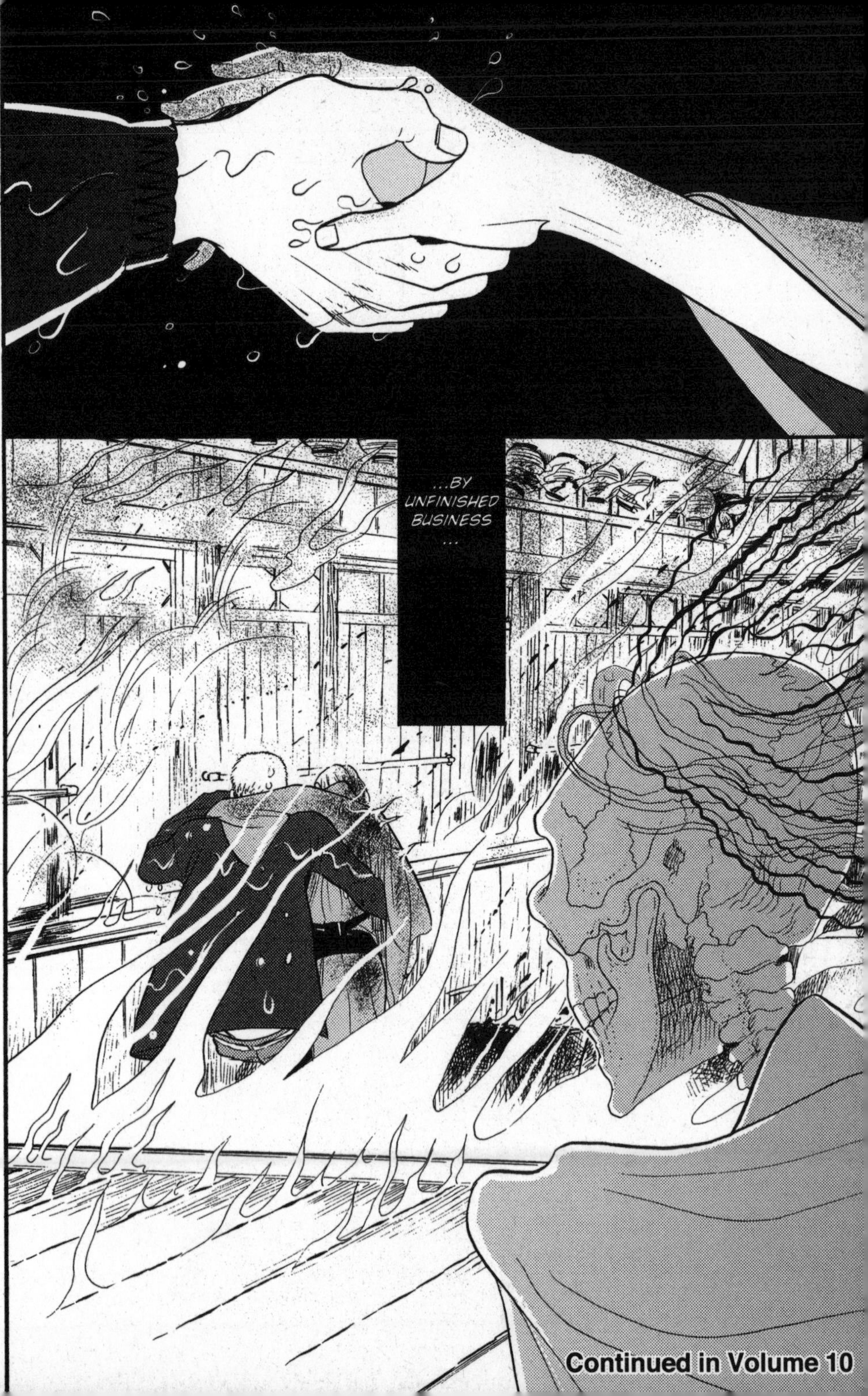
...BY UNFINISHED BUSINESS ...

Continued in Volume 10

Sources

Rakugo Hyakusen: Fuyu (100 Rakugo Stories: Winter)/Chikuma Shobo

DESCENDING STORIES: SHOWA GENROKU RAKUGO SHINJU: BONUS CHAPTER 8

RAKUGO SHINJU FUNNIES

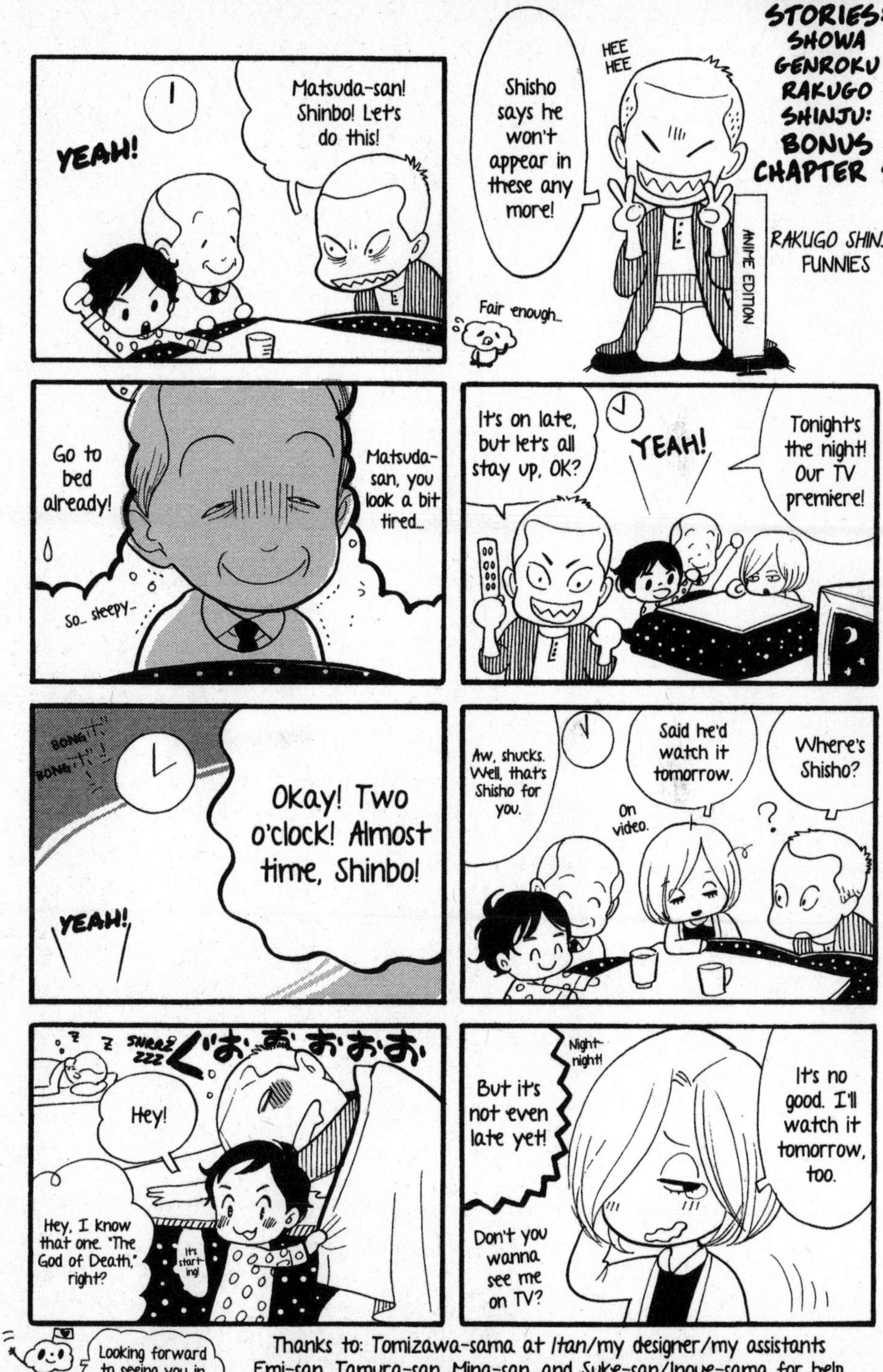
HEE HEE
Shisho says he won't appear in these any more!
ANIME EDITION
Fair enough...
Tonight's the night! Our TV premiere!
YEAH!
It's on late, but let's all stay up, OK?
Where's Shisho?
Said he'd watch it tomorrow.
On video.
Aw, shucks. Well, that's Shisho for you.
It's no good. I'll watch it tomorrow, too.
Night-night!
But it's not even late yet!
Don't you wanna see me on TV?
Matsuda-san! Shinbo! Let's do this!
YEAH!
Matsuda-san, you look a bit tired...
Go to bed already!
So... sleepy...
Okay! Two o'clock! Almost time, Shinbo!
BONG BONG
YEAH!
SNRRZ ZZZ
Hey!
It's starting!
Hey, I know that one. "The God of Death," right?
Looking forward to seeing you in Volume 10!

Thanks to: Tomizawa-sama at Itan/my designer/my assistants Emi-san, Tamura-san, Mina-san, and Suke-san/Inoue-sama for help with Kyoto dialect/the anime staff and cast/Ringo Sheena-sama

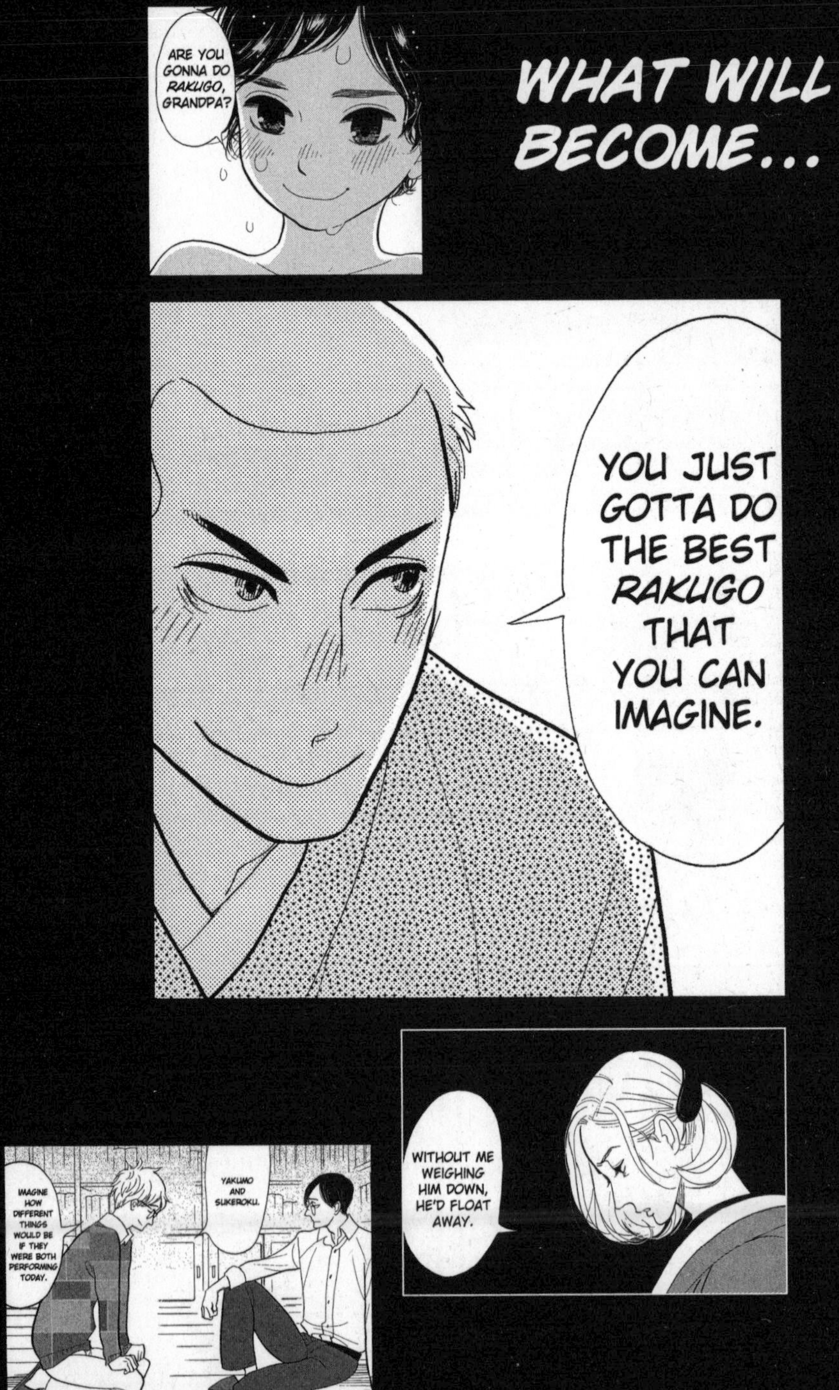
WHAT WILL BECOME...
ARE YOU GONNA DO *RAKUGO*, GRANDPA?
YOU JUST GOTTA DO THE BEST *RAKUGO* THAT YOU CAN IMAGINE.
WITHOUT ME WEIGHING HIM DOWN, HE'D FLOAT AWAY.
YAKUMO AND SUKEROKU.
IMAGINE HOW DIFFERENT THINGS WOULD BE IF THEY WERE BOTH PERFORMING TODAY.

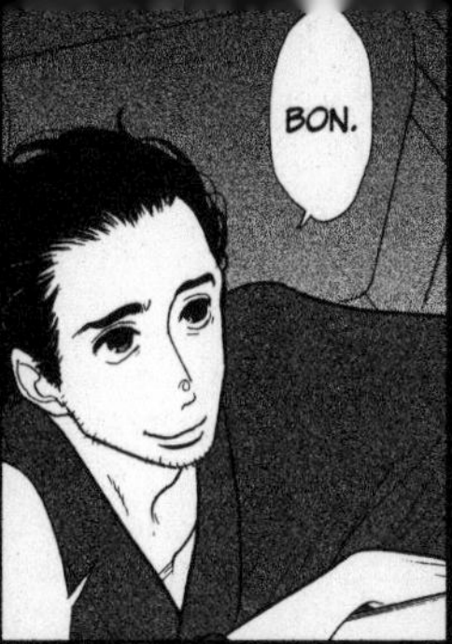
BON.

...OF SUKEROKU AND YAKUMO'S BELOVED RAKUGO?

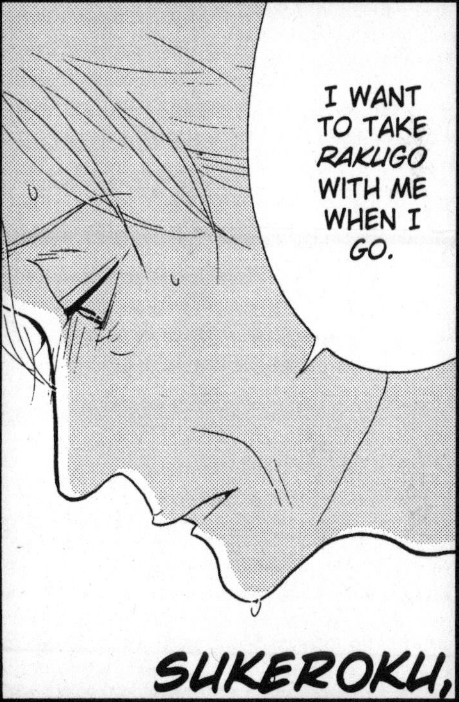
I WANT TO TAKE *RAKUGO* WITH ME WHEN I GO.

SUKEROKU, AGAIN

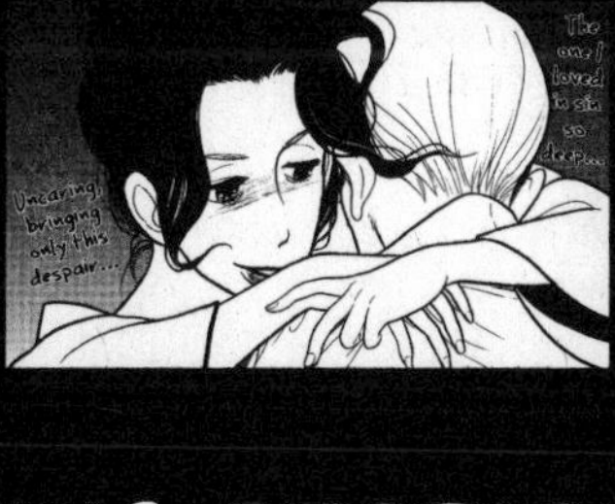
The one I loved in sin so deep...
Uncaring, bringing only this despair...

DESCENDING STORIES: SHOWA GENROKU RAKUGO SHINJU 10: THE FINAL VOLUME

Translation Notes

The end for our *kumi*, page 10
Yakuza gangs are known as *kumi* (or *gumi* in combination with the name of the group).

That *shika-shibai* the two of them put on, page 18
A *shika-shibai* is a *shibai*, or play, put on by *hanashika*, which is a term for *rakugo* performers.
See Volume 3 for the play itself.

Why are you wearing your *montsuki*?, page 26
A *montsuki* kimono is formalwear. Its name literally means "with family crest," a reference to the
crests emblazoned on it in anywhere from one to five locations.

Some guests from the Flower-and-Willow world, page 30
The Japanese here is *okii onesan*, literally "big (older) sisters," the standard way to refer to
senior geisha.

There's 48 *ryo* in here, page 37
The *ryo* was a unit of currency in the Edo period. One *ryo* was supposed to be enough to buy
a year's supply of rice.

Hachiman, page 54
A syncretistic (Shinto and Buddhist) deity of archery, war, and agriculture.

Shiro-ko, page 54
Shiro means "white" in Japanese, and is a common name for white dogs. *Ko* is an affectionate
ending.

Hobby/Marunama, page 56
These are references to two real brands in Japan: "Hoppy," a beer-flavored low-alcohol drink often
mixed with the spirit *shochu*, and "Tarunama," a beer from Asahi. (The "Tarunama" reference
is actually a visual change, with the kanji going from 樽生 to 撙生, but the latter has no good
pronunciation, so "Marunama" was chosen to retain some of the sound.)

Bansai Tsuburaya/Kimio Yodogawa, Mangetsu Tsuburaya/(Kimi–) Yodogawa, page 61
"Bansai Tsuburaya" and "Mangetsu Tsuburaya" are both performing names. Their real names
are on this sign: Bansai's real name was "Kimio Yodogawa," and he apparently gave his son a
name beginning with "Kimi," too (this is not unusual in Japan). Unfortunately, the second half of
Mangetsu's given name is obscured! (Other readings of these characters are possible, but these
are most likely.) Note that "Yodogawa" is also the name of a ward in Osaka.

Kamigata, page 64
An older name for the Kyoto–Osaka region, often viewed in opposition to "Edo" (modern Tokyo).

"The Okyo Ghost," page 68
A story about a female specter that emerges from a painting by Okyo, famous for his ghost
pictures. Performed by Yakumo in Volume 1.

Tachikiri, page 87
From the verb *tachikiru*, literally meaning "run out, end," this term could be translated "timer."

Tamagushi, page 87
Literally meaning something like "jeweled wand," this term originally referred to a small *sakaki* branch ritually decorated with strips of paper to give as an offering at a shrine.

Waka-danna, page 88
Literally "young master," this phrase can refer to a young man in general or the relatively young heir to a family business.

Kuragomori, page 89
Literally, being "enclosed" (*-gomori*) in a storehouse (*kura*), although in this case it's a non-voluntary sequestering.

The 21st day since her death, page 93
One of the points after death when Buddhist observances are traditionally held in Japan.

That *jiuta* you like... "Snow," page 93
Jiuta is an old genre of shamisen music from the Kamigata region characterized by often melancholy or introspective lyrics. "Snow" (*Yuki*) is one of the most famous pieces in the repertoire.

Namu Amida-bu..., page 94
A mantra to Amida Buddha recited by believers.

Habutae, page 102
The formal black silk kimono and *haori* coat that Yotaro is wearing.

We were too busy for this in April, page 103
April is when the school year starts in Japan.

Shiromuku, page 104
A pure white kimono ensemble worn for weddings.

Kobunacho, page 111
This lantern hangs at the Hozomon Gate of Sensoji Temple in Asakusa as a gift from the fishmongers of Kobunacho in Nihonbashi.

Dan-san, page 118
"Dan-san" is short for "Danna-san," a term of respect for a master or patron. Yakumo uses the term for Higuchi because of the events of Volume 6.

Nakamise, page 124
Nakamise is a famous shopping street that is also one approach to Sensoji Temple.

Yotaro-han, page 125
Mangetsu speaks Kansai-ben, a family of dialects spoken in the Kansai region that includes his native Kyoto. Using *han* after names instead of *san* is standard for this dialect group.

Ringo Sheena, page 151
Ringo Sheena (also Ringo Shiina/Shena) is a Japanese singer/songwriter, who collaborated with Megumi Hayashibara on the two opening songs for the *Descending Stories* anime.

RAKUGO STORIES IN THIS VOLUME:

Yumekin (夢金) - The Dream Reward (page 33)
Shinigami (死神) - The God of Death (page 75, 130)
Inokori Saheiji (居残り佐平次) - Saheiji is Kept Behind (page 116)

SHOWA GENROKU RAKUGO SHINJU

DESCENDING STORIES

Haruko Kumota

It is said that the roots of the current *Rakugo Kyokai* Association can be traced to the Tokyo *Rakugo Kyokai* formed thanks to the efforts of Ryutei Saraku V following the 1923 Great Kanto Earthquake. Yanagiya Kosan IV was later appointed its chairman and established it anew as the *Rakugo Kyokai* Association. It received permission to become an incorporated association with the Agency for Cultural Affairs acting as its competent authority in 1977, and its stated goal was to "advance the spread of popular performing arts with a focus on classical *rakugo*, contributing to the cultural development of our country in the process." It later became the general incorporated association it is today in 2012. It conducts performances in four theatres (*yose*) in Tokyo, as well as in halls, assembly spaces, schools, and more around the country.

For an overview of the *Rakugo Kyokai* Association, please visit: http://rakugo-kyokai.jp/summary/

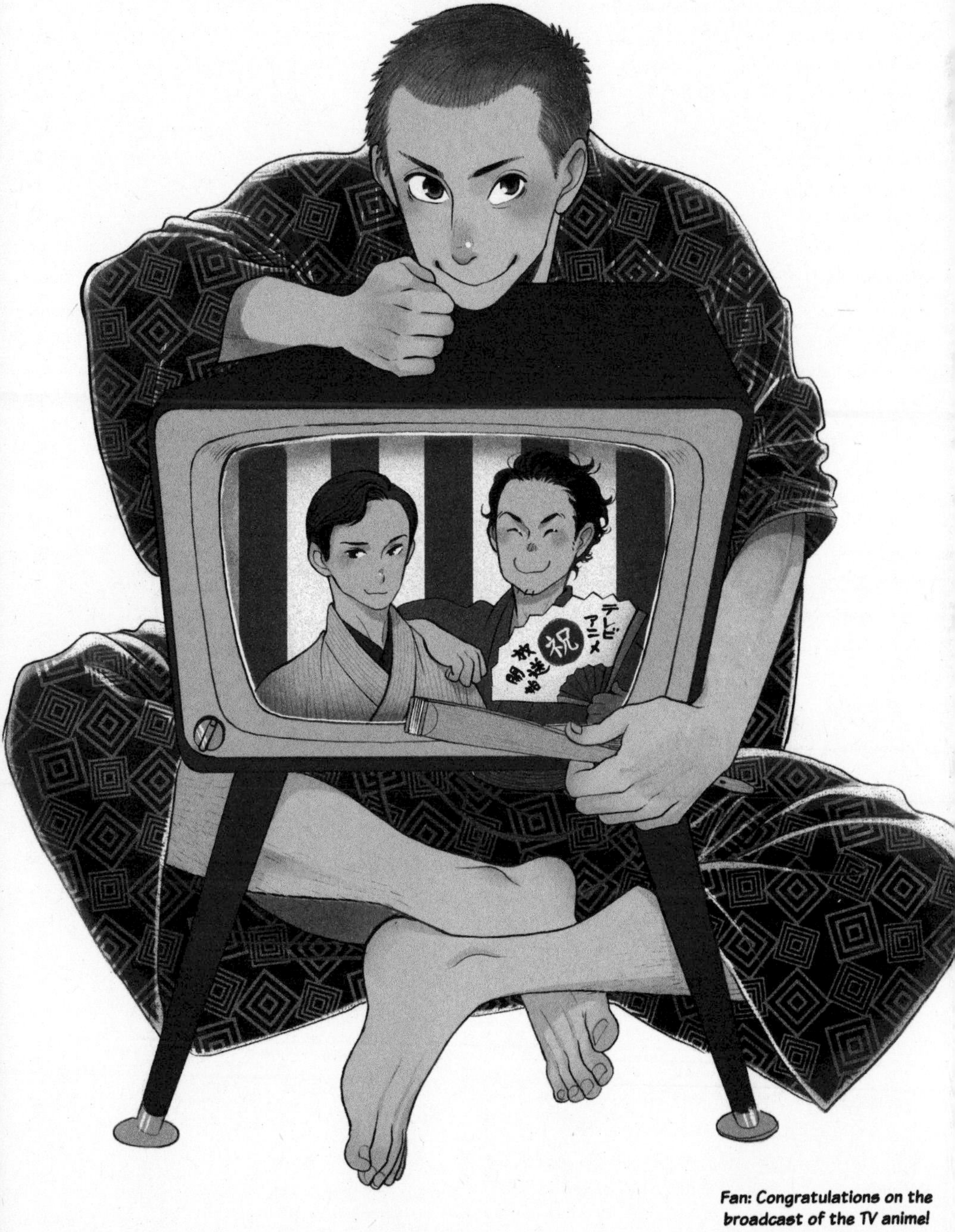
テレビアニメ
祝
放送開始

Fan: Congratulations on the broadcast of the TV anime!

A Kodansha Comics Trade Paperback Original.

Published in the United States by Kodansha Comics, an imprint of Kodansha USA Publishing, LLC, New York.

Publication rights for this English edition arranged through Kodansha Ltd., Tokyo.

First published in Japan in 2016 by Kodansha Ltd., Tokyo.

ISBN 978-1-63236-661-0

Printed in the United States of America.

www.kodanshacomics.com

9 8 7 6 5 4 3 2 1

Translation: AltJapan Co., Ltd. (Matt Treyvaud, Hiroko Yoda, Matt Alt)
Lettering: Andrew Copeland
Editing: Lauren Scanlan
Rakugo term supervision: Rakugo Kyokai Association
Kodansha Comics edition cover design: Phil Balsman